བོད་དབྱིན་ཤན་སྦྱར་གྱི་ཚིག་ཚོགས་དང་གཏམ་དཔེ།

Tibetan Quadrisyllabics, Phrases and Idioms

ཚིག་བཞི་པ་ཕྱུག་ལོ་གེ་ཙོག་ཁ་ཚིག་རྩོམ་ཉུང་རྒྱུ།

Tibetan Quadrisyllabics, Phrases and Idioms

བོད་དབྱིན་ཤན་སྦྱར་གྱི་ཚིག་ཚོགས་དང་གཏམ་དཔེ།

Tibetan Quadrisyllabics, Phrases and Idioms

Acharya Sangye T. Naga
and
Tsepak Rigzin

LIBRARY OF TIBETAN WORKS AND ARCHIVES

ISBN: 81-85102-90-2

Published by the Library of Tibetan Works and Archives (LTWA),
Dharamsala, (H.P.) 176215, India, and printed at Indraprastha
Press (CBT) 4, Bahadur Shah Zafar Marg, New Delhi-110002.

Publisher's Note

A very important element of Tibetan language which has provided life and beauty in the evolution of human thought communication is its rich repository of Idioms and Phrases. It makes for conveying a point or idea just in one single idiom what could not be expressed in so many prosaic sentences. Efficiently effective and melodious, it is very commonly used among the older generation Tibetans. New generation of Tibetans are not very aware of the importance of this aspect of the language. It is feared that if our generation can not preserve this rich aspect of the language, there may be a danger of losing this richly melodious aspect of the language.

Therefore I impressed upon its importance to Mr. Tsepak Rigzin and Mr. Sangye T. Naga to bring this work to light. I am thankful for their response and labour of love. It is hoped that this small effort will contribute in some way towards the enrichment and preservation of the Tibetan language.

Gyatsho Tshering
Director.

January 1994

Publisher's Note

A very important element of Tibetan language which has provided life and beauty in the evolution of human thought communication is its rich repository of Idioms and Phrases. It makes for conveying a point or idea just in one single idiom what could not be expressed in so many prosaic sentences. Efficiently effective and melodious, it is very commonly used among the older generation Tibetans. New generation of Tibetans are not very aware of the importance of this aspect of the language. It is feared that if our generation can not preserve this rich aspect of the language, there may be a danger of losing this richly melodious aspect of the language.

Therefore I impressed upon its importance to Mr. Tsepak Rigzin and Mr. Sangye T. Naga to bring this work to light. I am thankful for their response and labour of love. It is hoped that this small effort will contribute in some way towards the enrichment and preservation of the Tibetan language.

Gyatsho Tshering
Director.

January 1994

ཚིག་གཉིས།

༄༅། །བོད་ཀྱི་གཏམ་དཔེ་དང་ཚིག་ཚོགས་ཀྱི་འཛུག་པ་རྣམས་ནི་བོད་སྐད་ལ་ཉེ་བར་མཁོ་བ་ཙམ་དུ་མ་ཟད་སྐད་ཡིག་འདི་ཉིད་སླན་ཞིང་འཛིན་བས་ལ། གོ་བ་གཏིང་ཟབ་མོ་ཚིག་འབྲུ་རེ་ཟུང་བརྒྱུད་ནས་རྗོད་པར་བྱེད་པ་ལ་མེད་དུ་མི་རུང་བའི་ཁྱད་ཆོས་གལ་ཆེན་ཞིག་ཏུ་མངོན། བོད་མི་ཀུན་རབས་རྣམས་ཀྱིས་རྣམ་ཀུན་གླིང་མོལ་གནང་བའི་སྐབས་དེ་དག་ཉིན་རེའི་འཚོ་བའི་ནང་རྒྱུན་དུ་བེད་སྤྱོད་བཀོལ་བཞིན་པ་ཡིན་ནའང་། བོད་མི་གཞོན་གྲས་སྤྱི་དང་། ལྷག་པར་སྐད་ཡིག་གཞན་ཞིག་ནང་འཆར་ལོངས་བྱུང་བ་རྣམས་ཀྱིས་རང་གི་སྐད་ཡིག་རིག་གཞུང་གི་བང་མཛོད་དེ་ཉིད་འཚོ་བའི་ནང་དུ་བེད་སྤྱོད་བཀོལ་ནུས་ལྟ་ཅི། གཞན་གྱིས་བེད་སྤྱོད་བཀོལ་བ་ན། དེའི་གོ་དོན་འཁྲུལ་མེད་ཅིག་རྟོགས་མི་ནུས་པའི་དཀའ་ངལ་ཞིག་བོད་ཕྱི་ནང་ཀུན་ཏུ་འཕྲད་བཞིན་ཡོད་པ་ནི་མངོན་སུམ་ཚད་གྲུབ་ཀྱི་གཏམ་ཞིག་ཏུ་ཟད། ལྷག་པར་ཕྱི་རྒྱལ་བ་བོད་ཀྱི་སྐད་ཡིག་ལ་དོ་སྣང་ཅན་མང་པོར་ཆོས་སྐད་ནས་གསུངས་པའི་ཐ་སྙད་དང་རྣམ་གཞག་ཐད་དཀའ་ངལ་དེ་ཙམ་མི་འཕྲད་པའི་དབང་དུ་བཏང་ནའང་། གཏམ་དཔེ་དང་ཚིག་ཚོགས་ཀྱི་འཛུག་པའི་ཐད། དཀའ་ངལ་མང་པོ་ཞིག་འཕྲད་ཀྱི་ཡོད་པ་དེ་ཡང་དངོས་འབྲེལ་གྱི་གཏམ་ཞིག་ཏུ་མངོན། ཨིན་ཇི་སོགས་ཕྱི་རྒྱལ་གྱི་སྐད་ཡིག་ནང་བོད་སྐད་དང་བོད་ཡིག་སློབ་འཁྲིད་ཀྱི་སློབ་དེབ་མང་པོ་ཡོད་པ་དེ་ཚོའི་ནང་བོད་ཀྱི་གཏམ་དཔེ་དང་དེ་དག་གི་འཛུག་པ་བཤད་ཡོད་ནའང་ཏ་ཅང་ཉུང་བས་ཐུགས་ཕན་གསོས་པ་དེ་འདྲ་ད་ཕན་མིག་ལམ་དུ་མ་གྱུར་པ་དང་། རང་རེ་བོད་ཀྱི་སྐད་ཡིག་ནང་དུའང་གཞིས་བྱེས་

གཉིས་ཀ་ནས་གཏམ་དཔེ་མཁོ་སྒྲུབ་ཀྱིས་དཔར་དུ་བསྒྲུན་པ་མི་ཉུང་བ་ཞིག
འདུག་ནའང་དེ་དག་ཏུ་གཏམ་དཔེ་དང་ཚིག་ཚོགས་ཀྱི་འཐུག་པ་རྟོད་བྱེད་ཀྱི
ལམ་ནས་མ་བཏད་པར་བཏེན་བློ་གསར་རྣམས་ལ་འདི་ཐད་དོན་གྱིས་དཀའ
ངལ་མི་ཉུང་བ་ཞིག་འཕྱད་ཀྱི་ཡོད། དེར་བརྟེན་སྐྱར་ཡིག་ལ་སྐྱན་འཛིནས
དང་ཉམས་བཟོད་སྟེར་བའི་ཁྱད་ཚོས་དེ་རིགས་མི་ཉམས་གོང་འཕེལ་དང་
ཉམས་པ་སྐྱར་གསོའི་ཆེད་དུ་བོད་དབྱིན་ཡན་སྐྱར་གྱི་ཚིག་ཚོགས་དང་གཏམ
དཔེ་ འདི་བཞིན་རྒྱ་གར་དྲ་མ་ཧཱ་ལཱ་བླུགས་སྐྱར་བོད་ཀྱི་དཔེ་མཛོད་ཁང་གི
ཉམས་ཞིབ་དང་ཚོམ་བསྒྱུར་སྟེ་ཚན་ནས་ཕྱོགས་བསྒྲིགས་བགྱིས་པ་ཡིན་ལ།
འདིས་ཀྱང་བོད་ཀྱི་རྒྱ་མཚོ་ལྟ་བུའི་རིག་གནས་ཕྱོགས་དུས་ཀུན་ཏུ་ཁྱབ་པའི
རྒྱུར་གྱུར་ཅིག་གུ   །ཞེས་སློན་ལམ་དང་བཅས་བོད་ཀྱི་དཔེ་མཛོད་ཁང་གི
ལས་དུ་ཨཱུ་ཀུ་ནཱ་ག་སངས་རྒྱས་བསྟན་དར་དང་ཚེ་དཔག་རིག་འཛིན་ཕྱུན
མོང་ནས་བོད་རྒྱལ་ལོ་ ༢༠༢༠ ཅུ༡། ཕྱི་ལོ་ ༡༩༩༩ རྣབ་དང་པོར
སྦྱལ་བའོ།།

Compiler's Note

I joined the Library of Tibetan Works and Archives on August 1st 1991, as a member of its Research and Translation Bureau. One of the first project that was assigned to me by both Mr. Gyatsho Tshering, Director and Mr. Tsepak Rigzin, the then head of the bureau, was this small collection of quadrisyllabics, and idioms. The Library felt that this type of book was needed for its language students, therefore in 1980 LTWA obtained Mr. Jampa Choedak's initial collection of idioms from Mr.Pema Gyalpo. These idioms and phrases were added to the collection being prepared by Mr.Rigzin, whose' sources were derived from various Tibetan articles, books, most notably from His Holiness the Dalai Lama's public speeches. Having entrusted this project to me, I worked in the sincerity of being able to motivate and aiding individuals, who show a keen interest in the Tibetan Language, be they Tibetans or Westerners.

For further information, one interesting article on quadrisyllabic phrases, entitled: "The Phonetic Structure of ABCD Type Words in Modern Lhasa"[1] and one chapter on "Phrases" in *The Classical Tibetan Language*[2] are suggested. In addition, the following Tibetan language books are also recommended: *Modern Tibetan Language Vol.I & II*[3], *A Basic Grammar of Modern Spoken Tibetan*[4], *Essentials of Modern Literary Tibetan*[5], *Modern Spoken Tibetan: Lhasa Dialect*[6], *Textbook of Colloquial Tibetan*[7] and *New Plan Tibetan Grammar and Translation*[8].

This book is aimed to act as a bridge between the so called literary and colloquial language. Therefore, it is sincerely hoped that this book may be prove to be a source of guidance. Lastly I wish to thank Mr. Tenzin Dorjee, the senior most translator at LTWA, for his assistance in editing this book. May this book help the reader to skillfully master the Tibetan language, whereby one can read both the classical as well as the modern Tibetan literatures!

Acharya Sangye T. Naga
Library of Tibetan Works and Archives,
Dharamshala, H.P. INDIA.

ཁ

ཀ་དག་ལྷུན་གྲུབ། primordial purity with spontaneity/primordial purity with self-perfection ཀ་དག་ལྷུན་གྲུབ་ནི་རྙིང་མའི་གཞུང་ནས་གསུངས་པའི་ལྟ་བ་ཞིག་རེད། The 'primordial purity with spontaneity' is a philosophical view in the Nyingma tradition (of Tibetan Buddhism).

ཀ་བར་འཇོག་མའི་ལྷན་པ། Lit.: decorating pillars with pine branches/ Sense implied: unnecessary aids ཀ་བར་འཇོག་མའི་ལྷན་པ་བརྒྱབ་པ་ནི་སྒོར་མོ་ཁྲི་འབུམ་ཡོད་མཁན་ལ་སྒོར་མོ་བརྒྱ་ཙམ་སྤྲད་པ་ལྟ་བུ། Decorating pillars with pine branches is such as giving one hundred rupees to someone who has thousands of rupees.

ཀ་ཀོར་སྐྱིང་རྐོག complication/controversial issue ལས་ཀ་འདི་འགྲུབ་པ་ལ་ཀ་ཀོར་སྐྱིང་རྐོག་མང་པོ་ཡོད་རེད། There are many complications in accomplishing this task.

ཀ་རེ་ཀོ་རེ། ཀ་རེ་ཀོ་རེ་བྱེད་པ། ཀ་རེ་ཀོ་རེ་བཏང་པ། dilly-dallying/ to complain or make some excuses སློབ་སྦྱོང་བྱེད་དུས་ཀ་རེ་ཀོ་རེ་མ་བྱེད། Do not dilly-dally while studying.

ཀང་རེ་ཀོང་རེ། concave/ uneven/ a land with many holes ས་མཐོ་པོའི་རི་ལམ་ཀང་རེ་ཀོང་རེ་ཐོག་འགྲོ་ཁག་པོ་ཡོད། It is difficult to go through the uneven mountain passses of high lands.

ཀུན་མཁྱེན་ཡེ་ཤེས། omniscient wisdom/all knowing wisdom སངས་རྒྱས་ཤཱཀྱ་ཐུབ་པས་ཀུན་མཁྱེན་ཡེ་ཤེས་ལ་བརྟེན་ནས་སྣར་རྣམ་ལ་ཆོས་ཀྱི་འཁོར་ལོ

དང་པོ་བསྐོར། Buddha Shakyamuni turned the first wheel of Dharma at Sarnath through His omniscient wisdom.

ཀུན་དད་ཀུན་མོས། someone who commands universal faith and respect/admired and respected by all པགོང་ས་པསྐྱབས་མགོན་ཆེན་ པོ་མཆོག་ནི་འཛམ་གླིང་ནང་པ་ཡོངས་ཀྱི་ཀུན་དད་ཀུན་མོས་ཀྱི་དབུ་འཁྲིད་ཡང་དག་པ་ཞིག་ རེད། His Holiness the Dalai Lama is an able and honest leader who commands universal faith and admiration from all Buddhists throughout the world.

ཀུན་སྤྱོད་དག་ཐེར། moral improvement/ethical reconstruction གཞན་གྱི་ཀུན་སྤྱོད་དག་ཐེར་བྱེད་པ་ལ་ཐོག་མར་རང་གི་ཀུན་སྤྱོད་དག་ཐེར་བྱེད་དགོས། One needs to improve one's own moral conduct before improving other's morality.

ཀུན་སྤྱོད་སློབ་གསོ། giving moral guidance or training ཆུང་བྱིས་པའི་ དུས་ནས་ཀུན་སྤྱོད་ཆོག་སློབ་གསོ་གཏོང་དགོས། Moral guidance should be given from childhood onwards.

ཀུན་ཕན་རིང་ལུགས། tradition of universal welfare ཆོས་རྒྱལ་སྲོང་ བཙན་སྒམ་པོའི་སྐབས་སུ་བོད་ཀྱི་རྒྱལ་སྲིད་ཀུན་ཕན་རིང་ལུགས་ཀྱི་སྲོ་ནས་བསྐྱངས། King Songtsen Gampo ruled his empire through the tradition of universal welfare.

ཀུན་ཤེས་གཅིག་དྲགས། jack of all trades and master of none/ སློབ་ སྦྱོང་བྱེད་པ་དེ་ཉིད་གནད་ལ་མ་འཁེལ་ན་ཀུན་ཤེས་གཅིག་དྲགས་ཆག་གི་རེད། If someone does not focus on the point of one's studies, one will become a jack of all trades and master of none.

2

གོ་གྲུ་གར་གཏོང་གཉན་པ། Lit.: The boatman decides where the boat goes./ Sense implied: the one in power makes the decisions གོ་གྲུ་གར་གཏོང་གཉན་པའི་ལག་ཏུ་ཡོད། The boat is in boat man's hand where to lead.

གོ་ཐག་སློད་པ། to let down/to betray some one's trust/to disgrace ཁོང་གིས་དེ་རིང་ཆེད་སྤ་འགྲན་བསྒྱུར་བྱེད་སྐབས་རྒྱལ་ཁ་ཐོབ་ཁར་གོ་ཐག་སློད་སོང་། Today he let the team down in the match at the last minute.

གོ་ཐག་འཆུས་ཤོར། Lit.: to drop the end of a rope/ Sense implied: letting down a cause ལས་དོན་ལ་རོ་སྐྱོག་དང་ཕྱི་ནང་བྱེད་མཁན་དེ་ཚོས་ལས་དོན་ལ་གོ་ཐག་འཆུས་ཤོར་གཏོང་གི་རེད། People who play double deal will drop their end and fail in their work.

གོ་བ་གཅིག་ནས་དྲས་པའི་རྒྱུན་བུ། Lit.: cut from the same cloth (leather); a chip off the old block/ from the same mould རྒྱ་དག་གི་འགོ་འཁྲིད་གསར་པ་ཚོ་ལ་ཡང་བོད་མི་ཚོས་ཡིད་ཆེས་བྱེད་ཀྱི་མ་རེད། གང་ལགས་ཟེར་ན། དེ་ཚོ་ནི་གོ་བ་གཅིག་ནས་དྲས་པའི་རྒྱུན་བུ་ཡ་སྤྲག་རེད། Tibetans do not trust even the new Chinese leaders because they are just a cut from the same cloth.

གུ་གི་གྱུག་གི། curved/zigzag/winding/oblique ས་མཐོས་ལ་རི་ལམ་གུ་གི་གྱུག་གི་མང་པོ་ཡོང་། There are many winding paths on highlands.

གྱག་བའད་གྱག་བའད། beating around the bush མི་གཡོ་སྒྱུ་ཅན་དེས་གནས་ཚུལ་གསལ་པོར་མ་བཤད་པར་གྱག་བའད་གྱག་བའད་བྱེད་ཀྱི་འདུག Those deceitful persons were beating around the bush without giving the information clearly.

ཀྱང་དེ་ཀྱོང་དེ། furrowed/ridged སྤྲང་མཁན་དེ་ལ་རུ་ཡང་རྙིང་པ་ཀྱང་དེ་ཀྱོང་དེ་ ཞིག་འདུག The beggar has an old ridged pot.

ཀྱང་དེ་ཀྱོང་དེ། erect or standing/ upright/ towering/ tall and thin ཁྱིམ་མཚེས་ཀྱི་ཞི་མི་དེས་ཨ་མཆོག་ཀྱང་དེ་ཀྱོང་དེ་བྱས་ཏེ་བལྟ་གི་འདུག The neighbours cat looks with erect ears.

རྒྱུག་ཅར་བྱེད་སྟོ daily duties/customary duties/regular routine ཉིན་རེའི་རྒྱུག་ཅར་བྱེད་སྟོ་ལ་འཁྲུས་ཕོར་མ་བཏང་ན་ལོ་འཁོར་མའི་ལས་དོན་ལྷུན་གྱིས་ འགྲུབ་ཀྱི་རེད། If daily routines are performed unfailingly, then the year's work will be accomplished naturally.

ཀྲོག་མཁྲེགས་པོ། སྲུབ་ཆེན་པོ། durable/ lasting ཕྱི་རྒྱལ་གྱི་རས་ཆ་དེ་ཚོ་ཞེ་ དྲག་ཀྲོག་མཁྲེགས་པོ་འདུག Foreign clothes are very durable and lasting.

སྲུད་རྙིང་མཁྲེགས་བཟུང་། hardliners/ stubborn/ orthodox/ conservative རིགས་པ་ཡང་དག་གི་རྗེས་སུ་འབྲང་དགོས། སྲུད་རྙིང་མཁྲེགས་ བཟུང་གི་རྗེས་སུ་འབྲང་མི་རུང་། One should follow right reasonings but not conservative people/hardliners.

རྒྱན་ཀ་ཡོང་གཞི། the background of the dispute ཁ་མཆུ་འདིའི་རྒྱན་ཀ་ ཡོང་གཞི་ནི་མགོ་མ་ཚོད་པ་འགའ་ཤས་ཀྱིས་དཀྲུག་ཤིང་ལ་བརྟེན་ནས་བྱུང་། The background of the dispute in the case is the divisive act of some foolish people.

དཔའ་ངལ་ཁྱད་བསད། overcoming the difficulties with courage

ཐོན་མི་སམྦྷོཊ་ཆ་གྱང་དཀའ་ངལ་ཁྱད་བསད་ཐོག་རྒྱ་གར་འཐབས་པའི་ཡུལ་དུ་ཕེབས། Thonmi Sambhota visited India by overcoming the difficulties of extreme climate with courage.

དཀའ་ངལ་གདོང་ལེན། facing difficulties/bearing the burden/ willingly accepting the difficulties གཞན་ཕན་གྱི་དོན་དུ་དཀའ་ངལ་ དང་དུ་ལེན་པ་ནི་བྱང་སེམས་ཀྱི་སྤྱོད་པ་ཡིན། It is a Bodhisattva practice to accept difficulties willingly for the welfare of others.

དཀའ་ངལ་འཐབ་འཛིང་། struggling through hardships རོད་རང་ བཙན་ཐོབ་པ་ལ་དཀའ་ངལ་མང་པོར་འཐབ་འཛིང་དགོས་པ་ཡིན། We have to struggle through many problems in order to get independence.

དཀའ་ངལ་བཟབས་གསིག to create troubles and burdens ཕྱུ་གུ་ སྤྱོད་ངན་རེ་ཚོས་རང་གི་ནང་ལ་དཀའ་ངལ་བཟབས་གསིག་བཟོ་བ་རེད། Bad and naughty children create troubles and burdens in their homes.

དཀའ་ངལ་སྣ་མང་། various problems དམིགས་ཡུལ་ཆེན་པོ་ཞིག་འགྲུབ་པ་ལ་ དཀའ་ངལ་སྣ་མང་ཞིག་འཕྲད་འགྱུར་དེ་ལ་གདོང་ལེན་བྱེད་དགོས། One has to counter various problems in order to accomplish a great aim.

དཀའ་ངལ་གཅོད་སེལ། to solve the problems completely ཁྱེད་རང་ གི་དཀའ་ངལ་རྣམས་དཔུ་འཛིན་མཆོག་ནས་གཅོད་སེལ་གནང་ཐུབ་ཀྱི་རེད། All your troubles can be solved by the boss.

དཀའ་རྟོག་ཆེད་བཟོས། intentionally created problems དགྲ་ཕྱོགས་ ནས་དཀའ་རྟོག་ཆེད་བཟོས་བྱས་པ་རྣམས་མ་ཐོང་ཐུབ་པ་དང་མགོ་མ་འཁོར་བ་དགོས།

5

One should not get deceived by problems created intentionally by enemies.

དགའ་སྤྲུད་སྙིང་རུས། courage and diligence/ perseverance to endure དགའ་སྤྲུད་སྙིང་རུས་བསྟེན་ནུས་ན། །བྱ་བ་གང་ཡང་དགའ་བ་མེད། །
No work is difficult provided one has courage and diligence.

དགའ་སྤྲུད་སྡུག་རུས། stoic endurance/ austerity གཞིས་ལུས་བོད་རིགས་རྣམས་བཙོན་ཁང་དུ་དགའ་སྤྲུད་སྡུག་རུས་མང་པོ་བཅུབ་སྟེ་མྱང་ཡོད།
Tibetans in Tibet experienced many painful austerities in prisons.

དགའ་སྤྲུད་བབ་ཆགས། hard working and simple way of life ཁོང་ནི་རང་གི་ལས་དོན་ལ་དགའ་བ་སྤྲུད་བཟོད་པ་ཙམ་མ་ཟད་ཕྱུག་ལས་གནང་སྤྱངས་ཤིན་ ཏུ་བབ་ཆགས་པོ་འདུག He is not only hard working but also maintains a simple way of life.

དགའ་སྤྲུད་འབད་བརྩོན། steadfast perseverance སྒོམ་ལ་དགའ་སྤྲུད་འབད་ བརྩོན་ན། །ཡི་དམ་ཞལ་གཟིགས་མྱུར་པོ་ཡོང་། । One will have a vision of the deity very soon if one perseveres steadfastly in one's meditation.

དགའ་བ་ཕྱིན་སྒྲོད། སྐྱིད་པ་རྗེས་སྒྲོད། work hard now and enjoy the fruit later ཚོ་སྤྲན་དགའ་བ་ཕྱིན་དུ་སྒྲོད། །དེ་འབྲས་སྐྱིད་པ་རྗེས་སུ་སྒྲོད།། A wiseman works hard first and then enjoys happiness consequentially.

དགར་ནག་གོ་ལྡོག Lit.: to confuse white from black/ Sense implied: to confuse right from wrong/ misunderstanding

6

བསླབ་བྱ་གཟབ་གཟབ་མ་བསྒྲོན་ན། དོན་ལ་དཀར་ནག་གོ་ལོག་ཡོང་། One would confuse right from wrong if the instructions were not given clearly.

དཀར་ནག་འདྲེས་མ། Lit.: a mixture of white and black/ Sense implied: to have both good and bad qualities/ ཚེ་འདི་ནང་གི་སྐྱིད་སྡུག་རྣམས། ལས་དཀར་ནག་འདྲེས་མའི་འབྲས་བུ་ཡིན། The happiness and suffering of this life are the results of good and bad actions.

དཀར་ནག་བདེན་རྫུན། right and wrong/ true and false ལུགས་ཟུང་ཁྲིམས་བདག་རིན་པོ་ཆེ། །དཀར་ནག་བདེན་རྫུན་འབྱེད་དུ་གསོལ། O! magistrate the holder of the law; kindly discriminate between the true and the false.

དཀར་ནག་ཤན་འབྱེད། Lit.: distinguishing white and the black/ Sense implied: to distinguish right from wrong དྲང་པོའི་མིག་གིས་དཀར་ནག་ཤན་འབྱེད་ནུས། An honest eye can distinguish what is right and wrong.

དཀར་པོ་དཀར་ཀྱང་། pure white/ complete white སྐུ་ངོ་མཆོག་ནས་ཕྱུ་པ་དཀར་པོ་དཀར་ཀྱང་གཅིག་གཟིགས་སོང་། The lord bought a pure white chupa (Tibetan traditional dress).

དཀར་པོ་གྱེན་དེད་དང་ནག་པོ་ཐུར་དེད། promoting the white (right) and putting down the black (wrong) ཁྲིམས་དཔོན་ནས་དཀར་པོ་གྱེན་དེད་དང་ནག་པོ་ཐུར་དེད་ཀྱི་དབྱད་ཁྲ་གཏོང་ཐུབ་ཀྱི་རེད། The judge can issue decrees to promote the white (right) and put down the black (wrong).

དཀར་སེམས་ནག་སྒྲིབ། Lit.: white mind is veiled by black/ Sense implied: a virtuous mind is obscured by a negative appearance དུས་ངན་སྙིགས་མའི་དུས་འདིར། དཀར་པོ་དགེ་བའི་སེམས་རྣམས། ནག་པོ་མི་དགེས་བསྒྲིབ་ཡོང་། In this period of (five) degenerations white virtuous thoughts are veiled by black nonvirtues.

དགོན་གཉེར་ཕྱིས་བདར་མཁས་དྲག་ན། གསེར་སྐུ་རག་ལ་བཏང་ཡོང་དོ། The over industrious monastic caretaker may turn the golden statue into brass. ལས་དོན་གང་ལ་ཡང་ནུས་ཤུགས་ཆེ་དྲག་ན་དགོན་ གཉེར་ཕྱི་བདར་མཁས་པས་གསེར་སྐུ་རག་ལ་བཏང་བའི་དཔེ་བཞིན་ཡོང་། If someone is over-industrious in one's work then it will resemble the over-industrious caretaker who turned the gold into brass by rubbing so much that gilding worn away.

དཀྱིལ་འཁོར་བཞེངས་པ། construction of a mandala བོད་ཀྱི་དཔེ་ མཛོད་ཁང་དུ་སྤྱན་རས་གཟིགས་ཀྱི་དཀྱིལ་འཁོར་གཅིག་བཞེངས་ཡོད། A mandala of Avalokiteshvra is constructed at the Tibetan Library.

དཀྲུག་ཤིང་དབྱེན་སྦྱོར། to incite/provoke dispute/to create dissenstion བོད་མི་རྣམས་རྒྱ་མིའི་དཀྲུག་ཤིང་དབྱེན་སྦྱོར་གྱི་གཞན་དབང་དུ་ནམ་ ཡང་མ་སོང་བ་དགོས། Tibetans should never be overcome by the divisive provocations of the Chinese.

དགོག་གཏམ་དཀྲུག་ཤིང་། to provoke through rumours/ to stir up trouble through divisive talk གཞན་གྱི་དགོག་གཏམ་དཀྲུག་ཤིང་ གི་རྗེས་སུ་འབྲང་ན་ཆིག་བསྒྲིལ་ལ་གནོད་ཀྱི་རེད། It would be detrimental to the unity if someone follows others' provocative rumours.

8

དགྲོག་གཏམ་གོ་ཐོས། rumours spreading about/ to spread rumours ཁྱེད་ཚོ་མཐུན་པོ་མེད་པའི་དགྲོག་གཏམ་གོ་ཐོས་འདུག །བདེན་པ་རེད་ པས། I heard a rumour that you are not getting on well with one another. Is it true?

བཀག་བསྐྱིལ་ཁེ་སྒྲུག hoarding for gain ན་ལོ་མཉམ་སྦྲེལ་ལས་ཁུངས་ནས་ ཀྲ་ཀན་དུས་ཐོག་མ་བཙོང་པར་བཀག་བསྐྱིལ་ཁེ་སྒྲུག་བྱས་ཀྱང་ཕན་འབྲས་མ་བྱུང་། Last year, although the co-operative society kept the maize crop corn for profit by not selling it on time, but it was not beneficial.

བཀག་ཁྱིའི་དངོས་རྫས། contraband goods/ prohibited goods/ illegal goods རྒྱ་བོད་ས་མཚམས་ཁྱལ་ས་ལ་ཁོས་བཀག་ཁྱིའི་དངོས་རྫས་རྣམས་ བསྟན་མི་འདུག He did not show his contraband goods at the Sino-Tibetan border check-post.

བཀག་བཞེར་དམ་བསྒྲགས། restriction by stopping & inspecting/ stop and check control དེང་སང་ས་མཚམས་ཁག་ལ་བཀག་བཞེར་དམ་ བསྒྲགས་ནན་པོ་བྱེད་ཀྱི་འདུག They are imposing strict restriction by stopping and checking at the border areas these days.

བཀབ་བཀབ་བསུབ་བསུབ། to conceal or obliterate རང་གི་ཉེས་སྐྱོན་ བཀབ་བཀབ་བསུབ་བསུབ་བྱས་ཀྱང་ནམ་ཞིག་གཞན་གྱིས་ཤེས་ཀྱི་རེད། Even if one conceals a fault, others will know it someday.

བཀའ་བཀྱོན་སྤྲིགས་མོ། to reprimand or warn/ to upbraid/ to come down on someone ངའི་གྲོགས་པོས་ཐ་མག་འཐེན་ཙང་ཉུན་ལགས་

ཀྱིས་བཀའ་བཀྱོན་གནང་སོང་། The teacher reprimanded my friend for having smoked.

བཀའ་གྲོས་གསུང་གླིང་། to discuss/ to confer གཙུག་ལག་སློབ་གྲྭའི་དགེ་རྒན་ཆེན་མོ་གཉིས་བཀའ་གྲོས་གསུང་གླིང་གནང་གི་འདུག The teacher and the head-master are conferring.

བཀའ་འགྱུར་ལ་ཕོག་ལྷན། Lit.: to put a patch on the Kangyur/ Sense implied: to make an unnecessary contribution or correction བཀའ་འགྱུར་ལ་ཕོག་ལྷན་བརྒྱབ་པ་ནི་དགོས་མེད་ཀྱི་བྱ་བ་ཞིག་རེད། It is an unnecessary task to put a patch on the Kangyur (the collection of the Buddha's teachings).

བཀའ་བསྟན་ལྷ་ཁང་། temple of Kagyur and Tangyur བཀའ་བསྟན་ལྷ་ཁང་ནང་དུ་ཕྱག་དཔེ་བརྒྱ་ཕྲག་མང་པོ་བཞུགས་ཡོད། Hundreds of scriptural texts are found in the temple of Kangyur and Tangyur.

བཀའ་དྲིན་སྙིང་བཅངས། remembering one's kindness ཕ་མའི་བཀའ་དྲིན་རྟག་ཏུ་སྙིང་གི་དབུས་སུ་བཅངས་དགོས། One should always feel parents' kindness in the heart.

བཀའ་དྲིན་བསམ་ཤེས། to acknowledge kindness/ one who knows how to repay the kindness གཞན་ལ་ཕན་གྲོགས་བྱེད་ཐུབ་ན།། བཀའ་དྲིན་བསམ་ཤེས་ལས་ཀྱིས་ཡོང་།། There will be acknowledgement of one's kindness if one can help others.

བཀའ་འབངས་མི་སེར། the subjects of a ruler དཔོན་བཟང་ཁྲི་ཏུ་འཕོད་ན།

བཀའ་འབངས་མི་སེར་ལ་བདེ་སྐྱིད་ཡོང་། The subjects will have
happiness when a good chief is enthroned.

བཀའ་རྩོམ་གཅེས་བཏུས། an anthology/ selected writings པགོང་ས་
མཆོག་གི་གསུང་རྩོམ་གཅེས་བཏུས་དེ་ཞེ་དྲག་གོ་བདེ་པོ་འདུག The anthology
of His Holiness the Dalai Lama's speeches and writings is
very easy to understand.

བཀའ་བརྟེ་ཁྲིམས་ཁུར། to keep or abide by the law and order
མི་ངན་རེ་ཟུང་གིས་བཀའ་བརྟེ་ཁྲིམས་ཁུར་མ་བྱས་པ་སོང་ཙང་ང་ཚོ་ཚང་མ་ཕུང་ལ་འབྱར་
སོང་། Some bad people did not abide by the law and that's
why all of us are ruined.

བཀའ་ལན་སྔོན་པོ་ལ་ལུ་ལན་ལྗང་ཁུ། lit. to give a green rejoinder
to a blue response/ Sense implied: to give a rude
rejoinder to one's polite response བོད་གཞུང་གི་བཀའ་ལན་སྔོན་པོ་
ལ་རྒྱ་ནག་གཞུང་གིས་ལུ་ལན་ལྗང་ཁུ་ཕུལ་བ་རེད། The Chinese government
gave a rude rejoinder to a polite message from the Tibetan
government in exile.

བཀའ་ལན་ལྷུག་རྗེན། immediate oral reply དཔོན་བཟང་ཞལ་གསང་།
རྗེ་བར་བཀའ་ལན་ལྷུག་རྗེན་གནང་། Good leaders are open by nature.
They give an immediate reply to one's questions.

བཀའ་སློབ་བསྒྱུར་བསྒྲིགས། revised talk/ edited speech པགོང་ས་
མཆོག་གི་བཀའ་སློབ་བསྒྱུར་བསྒྲིགས་གནང་བ་དེ་བོད་གཞུང་ཕྱི་དྲིལ་ལས་ཁུངས་ནས་སྤར་
བསྐྲུན་ཞུས། The Department of International and Information
relations of the Tibetan-government-exile published the
edited speeches of His Holiness the Dalai Lama.

11

བཀའ་སློབ་ཟབ་མོ། profound advice བོད་མི་ཚང་མས་པ་གོང་ས་མ་ཚོག་གི་

བཀའ་སློབ་ཟབ་མོ་རྣམས་ལ་སློབ་སྦྱོང་ཡག་པོ་གནང་དགོས། All Tibetans
should study well the profound advices of H. H. the Dalai
Lama.

བཀའ་གསུང་དང་ལེན། to comply faithfully with an order དྲང་པོ་

དྲང་འཁ་གནང་དང་། བཀའ་གསུང་དང་ལེན་ཞུས་ཆོག Be honest; we will
comply with your orders faithfully.

བཀའ་གསུང་ཅི་སྒྲུབ། to do whatever one says/ to do as
advised/ to act upon their orders/ to be very obedient
མི་ངན་དཔོན་དུ་བསྐོས་གྱུར་ན། བཀའ་གསུང་ཅི་སྒྲུབ་ལུ་མི་ཐུབ། If bad leaders
are appointed we cannot act upon their orders

བཀུར་སྟི་ཞི་ཞུ། to respect and honour/ to offer service རྒྱ་མ་ལ་

བཀུར་སྟི་དང་རྒྱལ་ཁབ་ལ་ཞི་ཞུ་དགོས། One should honour the
teachers and serve the nation.

བཀོད་སློན་གནད་ཐུབ། a competent instructor དེང་སང་བཀའ་སློན་དེང་

ཐུབ་གནང་ཐུབ་མཁན་དགི་ཉན་དགོན་པོ་འདུག It is rare to find a
competent instructor these days.

བཀོད་པ་དོད་པོ། well made/ well arranged (e.g. a building, a
craft work) well set བཀོད་པ་དོད་པོའི་རྒྱལ་ཁང་འདི། །སྤྲ་ན་སྤྲུག་པའི་ཕོ་

བྲང་འདྲ། This well set castle looks like a magnificent mansion.
བཀོད་པ་དོད་པོའི་མཆོད་པ་འདིས། རང་དབང་མེད་པར་ཡིད་དབང་འཕྲོག This
well arranged offering irresistibly attracts every mind.

12

བཀྲ་ཤིས་ཕེམ་པ་ཡར་འཛེགས། to make excellent progess/ success after success མཐུན་ལམ་རོག་རྩ་ཆིག་བསྐྱིལ་ཡོད་ན། ལས་དོན་བཀྲ་ཤིས་ཕེམ་པ་ཡར་འཛེགས་ཡོང་། There will be excellent progress when there is unity and friendship.

བཀྲ་ཤིས་བདེ་ལེགས། good-luck/ hello/ congratulations གནམ་ལོ་གསར་ཚེས་ལ་བཀྲ་ཤིས་བདེ་ལེགས་ཞུ། Greetings for the New Year. བཀྲ་ཤིས་བདེ་ལེགས། ག་བ་ཕེབས་ཀ Hello, where are you going ? ཡིག་ཚད་ཨང་ཀི་དང་པོ་ལོན་པར་བཀྲ་ཤིས་བདེ་ལེགས་ཡོད། Congratulations for obtaining the first position in the examination. བཀྱེས་བདེ་ ལེགས། ཡང་བསྐྱར་མཇལ་ཡོང་། Good-bye, see you again.

བཀྱེས་ལོ་ལེགས། Lit.: excellent crops or year/ Sense implied: happily and successfully འཁྲུངས་སྐར་གྱི་མཛད་སྒོ་བཀྱེས་ལོ་ལེགས་དང་ ནས་གྲོལ་སོང་། The birthday celebrations of His Holiness the Dalai Lama have been concluded happily and successfully.

བཀྲག་མདངས་གཟི་བརྗིད། impressive/ dazzling/ splendid/ glorious གེ་སར་རྒྱལ་པོའི་དམག་ཆས་ནི། བཀྲག་མདངས་ལྷུན་ལ་གཟི་བརྗིད་ཆེ་ བ་འདུག The war-robe of king Geser is very impressive and glorious.

བཀྱེས་སྐོམ་ལྟོགས་ཤི། death by starvation/ to die of thirst and hunger རྒྱ་མིའི་བཙོན་ཁང་ནང་དུ། བོད་མི་ས་ཡ་བཅལ་བ། བཀྱེས་སྐོམ་ལྟོགས་ ཤིར་བཏང་ཡོད། More than one million Tibetans died of thirst and starvation in the Chinese prisons.

ཀང་འཁྱམས་ལག་འཁྱམས། to be afraid of/ cowardly over cautious སྤྱར་མ་དགུ་ཨི་མ་དུན་མར། ཀང་འཁྱམས་ལག་འཁྱམས་ཆག་ཡོང་། Cowardly people get frightened at the sight of an enemy.

ཀང་འཁོབ་ལག་འཁོབ། clumsy hands and feet/ stiff hands and feet/ to become awkward དགུན་ཁ་ཀང་ཕྱབ་དང་ལག་ཕྱབ་ལག་པོ་མ་གྱོན་ན་ཀང་འཁོབ་ལག་འཁོབ་ཆགས་ཏེ་ཕར་ཚུར་འགྲོ་བསྐྱོད་དང་ལས་ཀ་བྱེད་རྒྱ་ལག་ཞི་དག་ཡོང་། If socks and gloves are not worn properly in winter, one's hands and feet will become stiff and awkward, making it very difficult to work and go here and there.

ཀང་འཁྲབ་ལག་འཁྲབ། lit. dancing hands and feet/ Sense implied: dancing with joy/ to dance with abandon ཕྲུ་གུ་ཆུང་ངུ་དགའ་བའི་ནམ་འགྱུར་སྟོན་དུས། ཀང་འཁྲབ་ལག་འཁྲབ་བྱས་ཡོང་། Small children will dance with joy swinging their hands and feet when they are happy.

ཀང་སྒྲོག་ལག་ལྕགས། fetters and hand cuffs བསྐོར་བསྲུང་བས་ཀུན་མ་གཟུང་དུས་ཀང་ལྕགས་ལག་ལྕགས་བརྒྱབ་ཡོང་། The police when they catch a thief, would chain them with fetters and hand cuffs.

ཀང་སྒྲོག་ལག་བསྡམས། fettered hand and foot བོད་ཀྱི་ཆབ་སྲིད་བཙོན་པ་མང་པོ་ཅུ་དམག་གིས་ཀང་སྒྲོག་ལག་བསྡམས་བྱས་པ་རེད། Many Tibetan political prisoners were chained hand and foot by the Chinese army.

ཀང་གཅིག་རང་གཅིག only one single piece ཐ་མག་ཀང་གཅིག་རང་གཅིག་ལས་མེད། དེ་འདུ་སོང་ཙང་ཁྱེད་རང་ལ་ཕུལ་ཐུབ་ས་མ་རེད། I have only one cigarette and therefore I cannot offer to you.

རྐང་ཆག་ལག་གྲུམ། crippled legs and broken arms གནས་ས་ལ་སྐྱོང་
མཁན་རྐང་ཆག་ལག་གྲུམ་མང་པོ་མཐོང་རྒྱུ་འདུག Many crippled beggars
with broken arms are seen at holy places.

རྐང་རྗེས་ལག་བསུབ། lit. erasing foot print with one's hand/
Sense implied: wiping away previous reputation ཁོང་གིས་
དེང་སང་ཕྱག་ལས་གནང་སྟངས་འདི་ལ་བལྟས་ན་ཏན་ཏན་རྐང་རྗེས་ལག་བསུབ་གཏོང་ཉེན་
འདུག Looking at how he works at present, there is a definite
danger that he might wipe away his past deeds.

རྐང་སྟེང་ལུས་བརྟེགས། lit. body supported by legs/ Sense
implied: self-supporting སློབ་སྦྱོང་ཡག་པོ་གནང་ན། མི་ཚེ་སྐྱིད་པོའི་ཐོག་
ནས། རྐང་སྟེང་ལུས་བརྟེགས་བྱེད་ཐུབ། If one studies properly, one can
support one's life comfortably.

རྐང་མཐིལ་ལ་ཉི་མ་མ་འཁར་བར་དུ། lit. until the sun strikes the
soles/ Sense implied: something that will never happen
ནང་ལས་ག་ཚོད་བྱས་ཀྱང་རྐང་མཐིལ་ལ་ཉི་མ་མི་འཁར་བའི་དཔེ་བཞིན་ཚར་དུས་མེད།
However hard one might do house work, there will never be
an end, just as the sun will never strike the soles of one's
feet.

རྐང་བརྡ་ལག་བརྡ། gesturing with hands and feet/the gesture
of a mute/body language གཏམ་བརྗོད་དེའི་ནང་དུ་ལྐུགས་པ་གཉིས་ཐན་
ཚུན་རྐང་བརྡ་ལག་བརྡ་བྱས་ཏེ་བགྲོ་གླེང་བྱེད་ཀྱི་འདུག Two mutes in a drama
have a discussion with gestures of their hands and feet.

རྐང་བརྡབ་ལག་བརྡབ། lit. banging hands and feet (e.g. when

angry) in full swing ཐག་དཔོན་དེ་ཁོང་ཁྲོ་ལངས་ཏེ་ཀུང་བཏབ་ལག་ བཟེབ་དང་བཅས་ཆོགས་གཏུམ་བཏུང་སོང་། The ring leader of the bandits was very angry and berated the group, banging his hands and legs in full anger.

ཀུང་བཟེབ་ལག་ཕུར། Lit.: rubbing hands and banging feet/ Sense implied: intimidation མི་ཁོང་ཁྲོ་ཚ་པོ་དེས་ཐོག་མར་ཀུང་བཟེབ་ལག་ཕུར་ བྱས། དེ་ནས་རང་གི་གཡོག་པོའི་འགྲམ་པར་གཞུས་སོང་། The angry man first rubbed his hands and banged his feet at his servant and then he whacked him on the cheek.

ཀུང་དུམ་ལག་དུམ། maimed hands and legs མི་འདི་ཚོ་དམག་ཆེན་གཉིས་ པའི་སྐབས་ཀུང་དུམ་ལག་དུམ་ཆགས་པ་རེད། The hands and legs of these men were maimed during II World War.

ཀུང་ནད་ལ་མགོ་སྨན་སྤྲད་པ། Lit.: giving medicines of headache to someone with leg problem/ Sense implied: inappropriate treatment དཔོན་ངན་དེ་ཚོས་མི་མང་ལ་དུས་རྟག་ཏུ་ཀུང་ནད་ལ་ མགོ་སྨན་ལྟ་བུ་སྤྲད་པ་རེད། These bad officials have always given inappropriate treatement to the public.

ཀུང་པ་གཅིག་ལ་ཚེར་མ་བརྒྱ་ཟུག lit. to have one foot pricked by a hundred thorns/ Sense implied: to have too many problems མི་ཚང་ནམ་ཐག་ལ་ཕྲུ་གུ་མང་པོ་བྱུང་ན་ཀུང་པ་གཅིག་ལ་ཚེར་མ་བརྒྱ་ ཟུག་པ་ལྟར་དཀའ་ངལ་འབར་མ་ཆད་པ་ཡོང་གི་རེད། There will be unending problems if a poor family has many children.

ཀུང་ཞ་ལག་འཐེང་། lit. to have crippled hands and legs/ Sense

16

implied: to utter excuses for not fulfilling one's duty རང་
གི་ལས་འགན་ལ་ཁད་ཞ་ལག་འཐེན་ནམ་ཡང་བྱེད་མི་རུང་། One should never make excuses for not fulfilling one's duty.

ཀང་འོག་གི་རྡེའུ་དཔུལ་བར་འཕར་བ། lit. pebbles beneath one's foot, striking at one's forehead / Sense implied: to be abused, even by those subservient to you སོ་སོ་འབྲིར་དམན་ གྱི་གནས་སྐབས་སུ་གྱུར་ཚེ། ཀང་འོག་གི་རྡེའུ་རྣམས་ཀྱང་དཔུལ་བར་འཕར་ཡོང་། When one is in a miserable condition even those subservient to you, will abuse and insult you.

ཀུ་མ་ཚ་པོ། a terrible thief རམ་པ་ཀུ་མ་ཚ་པོ་ཞིག་དུག་ཡོད་རེད། Rampa is a terrible thief.

ཀུ་སེམས་ལ་ཉེ་རིང་མེད། Lit.: a thief's mind knows no distance/ Sense implied: A thief can even steal his relatives'.. ཀུ་ སེམས་ལ་ཉེ་རིང་མེད་པས་དྭག་ཏུ་བག་གཟོན་གནང་དགོས། Always be cautious with a thief, since he knows no distance of relationship.

ཀུན་ཁག་གཞན་གཡོགས། to accuse others for one's theft མི་ངན་དེ་ ཚོས་ཀུ་མ་རང་གིས་བཀུས་པའི་ཀུན་ཁག་གཞན་ལ་གཡོགས་སོང་། Bad people not only steal but blame others of their theft.

ཀུན་རྒྱབ་རྫུན་བསྐྱོན། a thief supported by lie ཀུན་མས་རང་ཉིད་ཀུན་མ་ མིན་པའི་ཁུངས་སྐྱེལ་དུ་རྫུན་བསྐྱོན་ཁོད་དགོས་ཐུག The thief relies on the support of a lie to prove his innocence.

རྐུན་ཇག་འཛིན་ན་གཏི་པོ་གཟུང་། Catch the ring leaders if one needs to catch thieves and robbers. རྐུན་ཇག་གཏི་པོ་མ་བཟུང་ན། གཞན་རྣམས་གཟུང་ཡང་དགོས་པ་ཆུང་། If the ring leader is not caught, it would be no significant even if othere are caught.

རྐུན་པོ་གསོས་ན་ཚོང་པ་བསད་པ་འདྲ། Lit.: If a merchant rears a thief, it would be as though he were killing himself/ Sense implied: having a servant who steals ལག་པ་གཙང་མ་མེད་པའི་གཡོག་པོ་ཉར་བ་ནི། ཚོང་པས་རྐུན་པོ་གསོས་ནས་རང་ཉིད་བསད་པ་དང་འདྲ། Keeping a thief servant resembles a merchant rearing a thief who kills him in return.

རྐུ་མ་གཅིག་ལ་ཉེས་པ་བརྒྱ། lit. a hundred blames for one theft/ Sense implied: to have something stolen and to suspect everyone of the crime. This suspicion is deemed as a sin. རྐུ་མ་གཅིག་གིས་བཀུས་ཀྱང་། དོགས་པ་བརྒྱ་ལ་ཟ་བས། རྐུ་མ་གཅིག་ལ་ཉེས་པ་བརྒྱ་ཡོད། Though the theft was done by only one, the owner suspected one hundred different people, it is said that he committed one hundred sins.

རྐུན་མ་ནང་ལ་བཞག་ནས་སྒོ་ལྱགས་ཕྱི་ནས་བརྒྱབ་པ། Lit.: to lock the door from outside keeping the thief inside/ Sense implied: the enemy is within or inside ནང་གི་དགྲ་པོ་མ་བཏུལ་བར། ཕྱི་ཡི་དགྲ་པོ་གང་ནས་ཐུལ། རྐུན་མ་ནང་དུ་བཞག་པ་ལ། ཕྱི་ནས་སྒོ་ལྱགས་བརྒྱབ་དོན་མེད། If the enemy within is not subdued, how can one conquer the enemy outside, as there is no point in locking the door from the outside keeping the thief inside.

རྐུ་མ་བརྐུ་བར་རོ་ཚ་ཡོད། ཁ་ཆད་བྱེད་པར་རོ་ཚ་མེད། Stealing is shameful but to bargain is not a shame.

རྐུན་མ་ལ་ཇག་པ་ཤོར། a bandit robbing a thief དཔོན་ངན་རེས་སྲོན་ངན་དེ་གནས་དབྱུང་བཏང་སོང་། འདི་ནི་རྐུན་མ་ལ་ཇག་པ་ཤོར་བ་དང་མ་ཚུངས། The evil minister was dismissed by the evil chief. It was like a bandit robbing a thief.

རྐུན་མ་ལ་དཔའ་དར་དང་སྤྱང་ཀི་ལ་ཚེ་ཐར། lit. rewarding a thief and saving a wolf/ sense implied: to act unjustly དྲང་མིན་གྱི་ལས་ལ་དམིགས་བསལ་གཏོང་བ་ནི་རྐུན་མ་ལ་དཔའ་དར་དང་དང་སྤྱང་ཀི་ལ་ཚེ་ཐར་གཏོང་བ་ {འདུ་མཚུངས་ཆགས་པ་རེད།} རེད། Excusing unjust deeds is rewarding a thief and saving the life of a wolf.

རྐུབ་སྲ་པོ། a woman with loose character བུད་མེད་རྐུབ་སྲ་པོ་རྣམས་ནི་མི་རིགས་དང་སྤྱི་ཚོགས་ཀྱི་ཁུང་འཛིན་རེད། A woman with loose character is a disgrace to the society.

རྐྱལ་གོག་མ་ཐིལ་རྡོལ། Lit.: a leather bag with holes at the bottom/ Sense implied: to have nothing left ཐག་རིང་གི་འགྲུལ་པ། རྐྱལ་གོག་གི་མ་ཐིལ་རྡོལ། རྩམ་པ་རེ་དགོས་ན། ང་རང་གིས་ཕུལ་ཆོག Oh! long distance traveller whose bottom of the leather bag is torn: if you need tsampa, I shall offer you some.

ཀྱེན་གང་ལ་ཐུག་རུང་། whatever the circumstances may be མི་ཚེ་ཡི་རིང་ལ། ཀྱེན་གང་ལ་ཐུག་རུང་། རང་བཙན་གྱི་བསམ་བློ། ནམ་ཡང་དོར་མི་རུང་། Throughout one's life whatever the circumstances one may face, one should never abandon the thought of Independence

ཀྱེན་ངན་གྲོགས་འར། misfortune brings a good opportunity/ a blessing in disguise དཀའ་ངལ་མང་པོ་འཕྲད་པའི་མི་ཉམས། མཐར་ཕྱུག་ ཆོས་ལ་ཁློ་ཁ་ཕྱུག་ན། ཀྱེན་ངན་གྲོགས་སུ་འར་བ་ཡིན། If a person faces many problems, and becomes religious-minded in the end, then those misfortunes have been a blessing in disguise.

ཀྱེན་ངན་ཐོག་བབས། misfortune falling like a thunderbolt བྱིས་པ་ རང་ལོ་བཅུ་གསུམ་ལོན་དུས་སྐུ་རིམས་ལག་པོ་མ་གནང་ན་ཀྱེན་ངན་ཐོག་ཏུ་བབས་པའི་ཉེན་ ཁ་ཡོད། When a child is thirteen years old, a certain misfortune may befall him like a thunderbolt if the ritual prayers are not done for him.

ཀྱེན་ངན་སྲུག་ཁུར། bearing hardships in difficult circumstances གཞིས་ལུས་བོད་མི་ཉམས་ཀྱིས་མི་ལོ་སུམ་ཅུའི་རིང་རྒྱ་མིའི་གདུག་རྩུབ་འོག་ཏུ་ཀྱེན་ངན་ སྲུག་ཁུར་ཀྱེན་བསྲིང་མྱང་ཡོད། Tibetans in Tibet had to bear the Chinese atrocities for thirty years.

ཀྱེན་ངན་བར་ཆད། misfortunes and hindrances/ discordant factor མཐུན་པའི་ཆ་ཀྱེན་གྱི་ཕློག་ཕྱོགས་ལ་ཀྱེན་ངན་བར་ཆད་ཟེར། The opposite of concordant factors are called misfortunes, hindrances, and discordant factors.

ཀྱེན་ངན་ཡོ་ལང་ས། unfavorable events/ calamity དམག་ཆེན་གཉིས་ པའི་ཀྱེན་ངན་ཡོ་ལང་ས་ལ་བརྟེན་ནས་བགྲང་བ་ལས་འདས་པའི་མི་གསོད་ཁྲག་སྦྱོར་བྱུང་བ་ རེད། Due to the calamity of the II World War, innumerable people were killed and much blood shed.

ཀྱེན་ངན་དུ་འཛིང་ས། entangled misfortunes ཕྱིན་གྱི་ལས་ངན་གྱི་ནམ་སྨིན་

ལ་བརྟེན་ནས་ཉམ་ཐག་པའི་སྐབས་སུ་ཉིན་ངན་དུ་འཛིངས་ཐམ་མ་ཆད་པ་བྱུང་རབས་འདུག
I had misfortunes entangled in a miserable condition due to the previous bad actions.

རྒྱན་ཆག་སྙེ་འདོམས། convergence of misfortunes བསོད་ནམས་ཉམས་
པའི་སྐབས་སུ་རྒྱེན་དང་ཆག་སྙོ་སྙེ་འདོམས་ཏེ་འཛོམས་ཡོང་། When one's merits diminish, all misfortunes converge.

ཀླུགས་པ་གླད་སྟོང་། a brainless fool/dull and empty headed རྒྱ་
མིས་བོད་ཕྲུག་རྣམས་ལ་སློབ་སྦྱོང་གི་གོ་སྐབས་མ་སྤྲད་པར་ཀླུགས་པ་གླད་སྟོང་ཁྱུ་གཅིག་
བཟོ་བརྩིས་བྱས་པ་རེད། The Chinese tried to make a number of Tibetan children empty-headed by depriving them of their educational opportunity.

ཀླུགས་པ་ཀླུགས་རྒྱང་། real idiot/fool/stupid སྙིང་རྗེ། ངའི་གྲོགས་པོ་ད་
ཀླུགས་པ་ཀླུགས་རྒྱང་རེད། I am sorry my friend is a stupid person.

ཀླུགས་པ་ཡུ་ཚུགས། foolish persuasion/ obstinate རྒྱུ་མཚན་གྱི་རྗེས་སུ་
འབྲངས་དགོས་པ་ལས་ཀླུགས་པ་ཡུ་ཚུགས་བྱ་མི་རུང་། One should follow reasonings rather than foolish persuastion.

ཀླུགས་པས་སྤྱང་མདོག་ཁ་པོ། a fool trying to be smart གསང་བར་རང་
མཁས་ཀྱང་། གོད་མི་མཁས། རང་སྐྱོན་སྦས་གསང་བྱེད་པ་ནི་ཀླུགས་པས་པས་སྤྱང་མདོག་
བྱེད་པ་དང་ཁྱད་པར་མེད། One may be expert in keeping the secret while others are expert in disclosing them. Therefore it is just like a fool trying to be smart if one hides one's faults.

སྐོག་སྐོག་སུད་སུད། secretly and stealthily དམ་ཚིག་མེད་པའི་ནང་མི་བས།
ནང་གི་དཔལ་འབྱོར་གཞན་ལ། སྐོག་སྐོག་སུད་སུད་སྤྲེར་ཡོང་། Disloyal

members of a family secretly give away their household's property to other people.

སློག་ནར་ཉམ་ཚོང་། to speculate in goods and sell them སུ་གི་ དང་དམག་གི་དུས་སུ་ཚོང་པ་ཚོས་འབྲུ་སློག་ནར་ཉམ་ཚོང་བྱེད་པ་རེད། Traders speculate in grains and sell them indiscreetly during war and famine.

སློག་མཚང་རྗེན་འབྱིན། revealing someone's secret bad habit/ making an open declaration of someone's secret faults གཞུང་དངུལ་བར་བཙོས་བྱས་ན། སྐྱེན་དང་འཕྲད་པའི་དུས་སུ། སློག་མཚང་རྗེན་འབྱིན་ བདེན་ཡོང་། If someone embezzles government money, their secret would be disclosed when the circumstances were not favorable.

སློག་འཇུལ་འཁྲུག་སློང་། infiltrate and create trouble རྒྱ་མཚམས་ཁབ་ནས་རྒྱ་མིས་སློག་འཇུལ་བྱས་ཏེ་རྒྱ་གར་ནང་འཁྲུག་པ་མང་པོ་སྐྲུངས་ཡོད། The Chinese secretly infiltrated across the Indian border and incited many troubles in India.

སློག་ཟ་ཁོག་རུལ། Lit.: eating secretly and spoiling the stomach/ Sense implied: engaging in corruption and spoiling one's image བོད་མི་མང་གི་འཐུས་མི་རྣམས་ནི་སློག་ཟ་ཁོག་རུལ་ཅན་ མིན་པ་ཞིག་དགོས། Representatives of Tibetan people should not be involved in corruption and spoil their image.

སློག་གཡོའི་དན་བུས། underground conspiracy གཞན་གྱི་སློག་གཡོའི་ དན་བུས་ལ་མགོ་འཁོར་མ་ཐེབས་པ་བྱེད་དགོས། One should not be deceived by others' secret conspiracy.

སློག་གཤོམ་སྲིད་བྱུས། covert policy རྒྱལ་ཁབ་ཕན་ཚུན་གྱི་སློག་གཤོམ་སྲིད་བྱུས་ནི་གཅིག་ལས་གཅིག་བརྟག་པ་ཡོད། The covert policy of one nation is worse than that of other nation.

སྐད་ཅིག་སྐད་ཅིག Lit.: momentary/ Sense implied: very fast སྐད་ཅིག་སྐད་ཅིག་གི་འགྱུར་བ་དེ་ཞེ་དྲག་ཤེས་ཁག་པོ་རེད། It is very difficult to know the momentary change.

སྐད་ཅིག་ཆ་མེད། Lit.: momentary and partless/ Sense implied: shortest instant སངས་རྒྱས་བཅོམ་ལྡན་འདས་ཀྱིས་སྐད་ཅིག་ཆ་མེད་གཅིག་གི་ནང་ཆོས་ཐམས་ཅད་མངོན་སུམ་དུ་མཁྱེན་ཐུབ། At any instant, Buddha knows all phenomena with direct perception.

སྐད་སྙན་འགྱུར་ཁུག melodious voice དགེ་སློང་སྙན་པ་བཟང་ལྡན་གྱི་སྐད་སྙན་འགྱུར་ཁུག་དང་ལྡན་པ་ནི་ཚེ་སྔོན་མའི་བསོད་ནམས་ཀྱི་འབྲས་བུ་ཡིན། The melodious voice of Bikkhu Nyenpa Zangden was the result of his previous virtues.

སྐད་མེད་སྐད་བཟོས། creating a noise out of nothing/ making a fuss about nothing ལས་ཀ་མ་བྱེད་པར་སྐད་མེད་སྐད་བཟོས་བྱས་ན་ཕན་ཐོགས་གང་ཡོང་། What is the use of making a fuss about nothing without having worked.

སྐབས་བསྟུན་ཁེ་འཚོལ། an opportunist སྐབས་བསྟུན་ཁེ་འཚོལ་བྱེད་མཁན་གྱི་མི་ལ་ཡིད་ཆེས་བྱེད་ཀྱི་མ་རེད། One cannot fully trust an opportunist.

སྐབས་བསྟུན་གང་བདེ། to act in accordance with the time སྐབས་

བསྒུན་གང་བའི་བྱེད་ཤེས་ན། དེ་ལ་ཤེས་རབ་ཅན་ཞེས་བྱ། He who acts in accordance with time is said to be wise.

སྐབས་བསྟུན་བརྫས་བཙོས། to kick someone when they are down/ an insult ཉམ་ཐག་པའི་སྐྱང་ལ་མཐོངས་ཆུང་བྱེད་པ་ནི་སྐབས་བསྟུན་བརྫས་བཙོས་རང་རེད། To kick someone when they are down is the insult of an opportunist.

སྐབས་བསྟུན་འཕོ་འགྱུར། to change in accordance with the situation གཞུང་གི་སྲིད་བྱུས་ནི་སྐབས་བསྟུན་འཕོ་འགྱུར་དང་བསྟུན་ཏེ་ཕྱག་བསྟར་གནང་དགོས། The policy of government should be implemented according to the changing situation.

སྐབས་འཕྲལ་སྲིད་གཞུང་། an interim government སྲིད་དོན་ཚོགས་པ་རྣམས་མཐུན་པོ་མེད་པའི་སྐབས་སུ་སྐབས་འཕྲལ་སྲིད་གཞུང་འཛུགས་དགོས་པ་ཡིན། There has to be an interim government when the political parties are not on good terms.

སྐམ་པོ་སྐམ་རྐྱང་། completely dry ཕྱུ་པ་འདི་སྐམ་པོ་སྐམ་རྐྱང་རེད། This chupa is completely dry. འབྲས་སྐམ་པོ་སྐམ་རྐྱང་གང་འདྲ་སེ་ཟ་དགོས་རེད། How can one eat only dry rice ?

སྐུ་ཚེ་མཛད་འཕྲིན། a life's deeds སྐུ་ཚེ་མཛད་འཕྲིན་དར་རྒྱས་ཡོང་བའི་སྨོན་ལམ་ཞུ། I wish you successful deeds in your life.

སྐུ་ཡོན་གསན་སྦྱོང་། study/ training (e.g. spiritual training) དགེ་བའི་བཤེས་གཉེན་མ་དུན་ནས། སྐུ་ཡོན་གསན་སྦྱོང་གནང་དུས། ཐུགས་རེག་རབ་ཏུ་བསྐྱིལ་

24

དགོས། One should give full attention while studying with one's teacher.

སྐུ་གསུང་ཐུགས་རྟེན། representations of (the Buddha's) body, speech and mind/ sacred objects ལྷ་ས་གཙུག་ལག་ཁང་དུ་སྐུ་གསུང་ ཐུགས་རྟེན་བསམ་གྱིས་མི་ཁྱབ་པ་ཡོད། There are inconceivably sacred objects in Lhasa Cathedral.

སྐུད་པ་མདུད་པ་ཅན་ཁབ་མིག་ཏུ་མི་འགྲོ Lit.: A knotted thread can not pass through the eye of a needle. Sense implied: something that is impossible དམ་ཉམས་ལ་དངོས་གྲུབ་པ་མི་འཕེར། དཔེར་ན་ སྐུད་པ་མདུད་ཅན་ཁབ་མིག་ཏུ་མི་འགྲོ་བ་བཞིན་ནོ།། Spiritual commitment breakers can not achieve realisation, just as a knotted thread can not pass through the eye of a needle.

སྐེ་འཁྱེར་ནས་ཞགས་པ་ཉོ་བ། Lit.: to buy lasso presenting one's neck/ Sense implied: to invite trouble རྒག་ཚོང་བརྒྱབ་པ་ནི་སྐེ་ འཁྱེར་ནས་ཞགས་པ་ཉོ་བ་རང་རེད། Indulging in smuggling is inviting trouble.

སྐེ་བཅད་ནས་ཨོག་མར་བྱིལ་བྱིལ། Lit.: even though the neck has been cut the chin is still shaking/ Sense implied: to be very arrogant despite being defeated རམ་པ་འཛིན་གྲྭ་བཅུ་པར་ ཡིག་ཚད་ལས་སློང་མ་བྱུང་ན་ཡང་དདུང་སློབས་པ་མཐོ་པོ་འདུག འདི་ནི་སྐེ་བཅད་ནས་ ཨོག་མ་བྱིལ་བྱིལ་བྱེད་པ་རང་རེད། Although Rampa has failed in his class X examinations, still he is very proud. This is just like shaking one's chin in spite of one's neck having been cut.

25

སྐེ་བཅད་ན་འོ་མ་མ་གཏོགས་འབབ་རྒྱུ་མེད། Lit.: only milk will flow even if the neck is cut/ Sense implied: innocence/ not guilty གནད་དོན་འདི་ཐོག་ཆ་འདི་བདུང་བ་མ་ཟད་སྐེ་བཅད་ན་ཡང་ངོ་མ་མ་གཏོགས་ ཁག་འབབ་རྒྱུ་མེད། On this issue, on top of police interrogation even if someone cuts my throat only milk will flow.

སྐེ་འདོད་ནས་ལྦ་ལྦ་མི་འདོད། Lit.: wanting the neck but not the goitre/ Sense implied: wanting a rose but not its thorn བུ་མོ་འདོད་ཀྱང་དེའི་ཕ་མར་མི་དགའ་བ་བྱེད་པ་ནི་སྐེ་འདོད་ནས་ལྦ་ལྦ་མི་འདོད་པ་བྱེད་པ་ དང་མཚུངས་སོ།། One wants the girl but not her parents. This is like wanting a neck but not the goitre.

སྐོམ་པ་རྒྱ་འདོད། Lit.: urge for water/ Sense implied: very anxious བོད་རྒྱ་ཁྱབ་ཏུ་རང་བཙན་གྱི་ཉི་མ་དེ་སྐོམ་པ་རྒྱ་འདོད་བཞིན་བསྒུག་སྟེ་ བསྡད་ཡོད། The day of Independence is anxiously awaited throughout Tibet.

སྐྱ་མིན་སེར་མིན། neither a layman nor a monk (sarcastic remark) སྐྱ་མིན་སེར་མིན་དུ་བཞུགས་པ་ལས་འཁྱུངས་ས་བསྐོན་པ་དགའ། It is better to be married than to lead a life of neither as a layman nor a monk.

སྐྱ་ཟད་རྩོ་གཏུགས། Lit.: to resort to grass having run out of grain/ Sense implied: at the brink of starvation སྐྱ་གིའི་ སྐབས་སུ་བཀར་འཇུག་ནས་འབྲུ་མ་བཏོན་ན་མི་མང་སྐྱ་ཟད་རྩོ་གཏུགས་ཀྱི་གནས་སུ་གྱུར་ ཡོང་། If grains are not taken out from the stock during famine, the poor people might reach the brink of starvation.

སྐྱག་པ་ཧོར་ཧོར། Lit.: until the shit comes out/ Sense implied: to work to death སྤྱིན་བདག་མི་ངན་དེ་ཡིས། ལས་ཀ་སྐྱག་པ་ཧོར་ཧོར་བསྒྱལ་ཀྱང་། སྒྱ་ཆ་སྒོར་མོ་གཅིག་ཀྱང་སྤྲད་མ་བྱུང་། The bad master did not pay me even a rupee in spite of working for him to death.

སྐྱག་རྫུན་སྐྱག་ནག a complete lie or liar ཁོང་གིས་གསུངས་པའི་བཀའ་མོལ་དེ་སྐྱག་རྫུན་སྐྱག་ནག་རེད། What he said is a complete lie.

སྐྱག་རྫུན་ཚ་པོ། a great liar or a cheater སྐྱག་རྫུན་ཚ་པོ་བྱེད་ན་གཞན་གྱིས་སླར་ཡིད་ཆེས་བྱེད་ཀྱི་མ་རེད། A terrible liar is not trusted by other people.

སྐྱབས་བཅོལ་རོགས་རམ། refugee aid རྒྱ་གར་གཞུང་ནས་བོད་མི་ཚོར་སྐྱབས་བཅོལ་རོགས་རམ་གནང་བ་རེད། The government of India has given refugee aid to the Tibetans.

སྐྱབས་ཡུལ་མཆོད་གནས། object of worship དཀོན་མཆོག་གསུམ་ནི་ནང་པ་ཚང་མའི་སྐྱབས་ཡུལ་མཆོད་གནས་བསླུ་མེད་གཅིག་རེད། The non-deceptive object of worship of all Buddhists is the three-jewels.

སྐྱབས་གསོལ་སྙན་སྒྲོན། Lit.: bring to notice and attention/ Sense implied: an appeal ཚོགས་མང་ལ་སྐྱབས་གསོལ་སྙན་སྒྲོན་གསལ་བསྒྲགས་མ་གནང་གོང་གྲོས་བསྡུར་ལུགས་པོ་གནང་དགོས། There should be good discussion before an appeal is announced to the public.

སྐྱུར་མོས་ཉ་ལེན། Lit.: a crane's (way of) catching fish/ Sense implied: to be very skillful ལས་དོན་གང་ལ་ཡང་སྐྱུར་མོས་ཉ་ལེན་དང་

མཚོངས་པའི་ཐབས་མཁས་དེ་ཤེས་དགོས། One should be skillful in every action just like a crane catching fish.

སྐྱིད་ཆགས་སྡུག་བྲོལ། Lit.: liberating from the suffering and being attached to happiness གཞུང་གི་ལས་འགན་ནི་ཡུལ་མི་རྣམས་ སྐྱིད་ཆགས་སྡུག་བྲོལ་ལ་འགོད་རྒྱུ་དེ་ཡིན། It is the duty of government to liberate the citizens from suffering and to give them pleasure or happiness.

སྐྱིད་ཉམས་དོད་པོ། cheerful and jolly ངའི་གྲོགས་པོ་དེ་ཉམས་ཐག་ཡིན་ཡང་ སྐྱིད་ཉམས་དོད་པོ་བྱས་ནས་སྡོད་ཀྱི་འདུག Although my friend is poor, he is cheerful and jolly.

སྐྱིད་འདོད་འགུལ་འཚོར། Lit.: wanting happiness but reluctant to work སྐྱིད་འདོད་པ་དང་འགུལ་འཚོར་བ་གཉིས་མཉམ་དུ་ཡོང་ཐབས་མེད། Wanting happiness and being reluctant to work, do not go together.

སྐྱིད་སྡུག་མཉམ་འབྱར། to share the joys and sorrows together བཟའ་ཟླ་གཉིས་ཀས་མི་ཚེ་ཧྲིལ་པོར་སྐྱིད་སྡུག་མཉམ་འབྱར་བྱེད་དགོས། Both spouses should share their joys and sorrows together throughout their lives.

སྐྱིད་སྡུག་ཉམས་མྱོང་། experience of joys and sorrows of life/ སྐྱིད་སྡུག་ཉམས་མྱོང་ཅན་གྱི་རྒན་རབས་ལ་གུས་ཞབས་ཞུ་བ་དང་འཕྲིན་བསླབ་བྱ་ལེན་ དགོས། One should respect and take advice from the experienced seniors or elders who had gone through many expereinces of life.

28

སྐྱིད་སྡུག་དར་རྒུད། ups and downs of a life/ vicissitudes of a life མི་ཚེའི་ནང་ལ་སྐྱིད་སྡུག་དར་རྒུད་སྣ་ཚོགས་ཡོང་གི་རེད། There will be various ups and downs in one's life.

སྐྱིད་སྡུག་གནས་ལུགས། report on the condition of one's welfare ལུང་པ་ལ་རྐྱེན་ངན་བྱུང་དུས་གཞུང་ལ་སྐྱིད་སྡུག་གནས་ལུགས་རྣམས་ཞུ་དགོས། One should report the government on the condition of one's welfare when there is calamity in one's country.

སྐྱིད་སྡུག་མི་དང་འཇེར་པ་ཤིང་། Lit.: ups and downs for men and knots for trees/ Sense implied: One can use this expression to console somebody in misfortunes. དཀའ་ངལ་འཕྲད་པའི་སྐབས་སུ། ཐུགས་སེམས་སྐྱོ་བ་མ་གནང་། མི་ལ་སྐྱིད་སྡུག་སྣ་ཚོགས། ཤིང་ལ་འཇེར་བ་སྣ་ཚོགས། ཟེར་བ་ལྟར་རེད One should not be sad at the time of difficulty. It is natural that joys and sorrows come in life as knots occur in trees.

སྐྱིད་སྡུག་བཟང་ཞན། living standard ཡུལ་མི་རྣམས་སྐྱིད་སྡུག་བཟང་ཞན་ཇི་འདྲ་ཞིག་བྱུང་ན་ཡང་མཉམ་ཟ་མཉམ་སྦྱང་གནང་དགོས། All the countrymen should share their food and drink with one another irresepective of their living standard.

སྐྱིད་ན་སྐྱིད་མཉམ་དང་སྡུག་ན་སྡུག་མཉམ། to share joys and sorrows at all times གྲོགས་པོ་ངོ་མ་ཡིན་ན་སྐྱིད་ན་སྐྱིད་མཉམ་དང་སྡུག་ན་སྡུག་མཉམ་བྱེད་དགོས། Real friends always share their joys and sorrows with one another.

སྐྱིད་པོ་བདེ་མོ། happy and well ཉིང་སང་ང་བོད་ཀྱི་དཔེ་མཛོད་ཁང་དུ་སྐྱིད་པོ་

བདེ་མོ་ཨིན། These days I am happy at the Library of Tibetan Works and Archives.

སྐྱིད་པོ་རང་གིས་མ་བྱས་ན། སྡུག་པོ་གཞན་གྱིས་བཏང་ཡོང་། Make yourself happy lest others may trouble you.

སྐྱིད་ལ་ཁའི་རྩྭ་ལ་མཉམ་ཟ་དང་སྡུག་སྟོན་མོའི་ཆུ་ལ་མཉམ་འཐུང་། Lit.: together we shall eat the grass of the mountain pass and drink the murky water of suffering/ Sense implied: to be together in times of joy and suffering/ This expression is used to indicate friendship and intimacy by sharing all joys and sorrows together.

སྐྱིན་པ་ཆུ་ཡིན་ཡང་སྐྱ་རུ་མ་གཏོང་། Lit.: even if you are repaying water, don't make it thin/ Sense implied: remindful of repaying one's kindness. This expression is used to indicate the best way to respond to kindness.

སྐྱུག་བྲོ་བོ། abominable/ disgusting སྤྱོད་ལམ་སྐྱུག་བྲོ་པོ་དེ་འདྲ་མ་གནང་། Do not behave in such a disgusting manner.

སྐྱུག་མེར་ལངས་པ། vomit or nauseous feeling/ disgusting/ bad taste མོ་ཊའི་ནང་ལ་སྐྱུག་མེར་ལང་གི་རེད། One feels nauseous in the car.

སྐྱེ་རྒ་ན་འཆི། birth, aging, sickness and death, the four basic human sufferings ཐར་པ་ཐོབ་ན་སྐྱེ་རྒ་ན་འཆིའི་སྡུག་བསྔལ་ལས་གྲོལ་བ་རེད། When one achieves liberation, one is released from the sufferings of birth, aging, sickness and death.

སྐྱེ་མས་ཡར་འཐེན། སྤྱོད་པས་མར་འཐེན། exalted by birth and degraded by conduct/ This proverb is used when a noble or high family member indulges in bad habits, such as drinking too much alchohol.

སྐྱེད་ལ་སྐྱེད་རྒྱག Lit.: interest upon interest/ Sense implied: compound interest ཞིང་པ་ནས་ཐག་རྣམས་ལ་ཕྱུག་པོ་ཚོས་དངུལ་གཡར་སྐབས་སྐྱེད་ལ་སྐྱེད་རྒྱག་བྱེད་པ་རེད། The rich men charged compound interest on their loans for the poor farmers.

སྐྱེས་རྡིན་ལས་གསོས་རྡིན་ཆེ། The one who raised you up is more kind than the one who gave you birth. This saying is used to express the kindness of one who brought one up.

སྐྱེས་སྦྱངས་ཀྱི་ཡོན་ཏན། acquired and innate knowledge སྐྱེས་སྦྱངས་ཀྱི་ཡོན་ཏན་གཉིས་དང་ལྡན་པའི་མཁས་པ་དཀོན་པོ་རེད། Scholars with both acquired and innate knowledge are rare.

སྐྱོ་སྡུང་ཡི་ཆད། despair and discourage/ to feel sad and despondent ན་གཞོན་ཚོས་ཕྱག་ལས་ཡག་པོ་མ་གནང་ན་ནན་རབས་ཚོར་སྐྱོ་སྡུང་ཡི་ཆད་ཀྱི་རྒྱགས་པས་ཡོང་གི་རེད། If youths do not work properly the elders will feel sad and despondent.

སྐྱོན་ཀུན་སེལ་ཡོན་ཏན་ཀུན་ལྡན། one who had abandoned all faults and acquired all knowledge སངས་རྒྱས་རྣམས་སྐྱོན་ཀུན་བཏད་དང་ཡོན་ཏན་ཀུན་ལྡན་པ་ཕྱག་རེད། All Buddhas have abandoned all faults and acquired all knowledge.

སྐྱོན་བརྗོད་ཁག་འདོགས། to criticise and blame someone ཉེས་པ་རང་གིས་བྱས་ཏེ་གཞན་ལ་ཁག་འདོགས་སྐྱོན་བརྗོད་བྱེད་ན་འབྲས་བུ་ངན་པ་རང་གི་ཐོག་ཏུ་སྨིན་ཡོང་། Having committed mistakes, if one still criticises and blame others, the bad consequences will ripen upon oneself.

སྐྱོན་སྤོང་དགེ་བསྒྲུབ། to eliminate faults and cultivate virtues སྐྱོན་དང་འདྲ་བའི་སྡིག་པ་སྤོངས། དུས་ཏུ་དགེ་བ་འབའ་ཞིག་སྒྲུབས། Avoid sins like faults and always cultivate only virtues.

སྐྱོན་མེད་སྐྱུས་དག perfect/ not damaged སངས་མ་རྒྱས་བར་ཏུ་སྐྱོན་མེད་སྐྱུས་དག་ཆགས་རྒྱུ་ཁག་པོ་རེད། It is difficult to become perfect until one is enlightened.

སྐྱོན་བསྱང་ལོ་བཙོ། to make corrections to mistakes རྩ་ཁྲིམས་ཁོ་ནས་ལུགས་སྲོལ་ངན་པ་ལ་སྐྱོན་བསྱང་ལོ་བཙོ་བྱེད་ཐུབ། Only the constitution can make correction to the social evils.

བསྐྱར་བཟློས་ཡང་ཟློས། repetition/ overlapping མཁས་པའི་རྩོ་ལ་བསྐྱར་བཟློས་ཡང་བཟློས་མི་ཡོང་། No good scholars will make repetitions in their compositions.

ཁ་དཀར་ཁོག་ནག Lit.: white mouth and black heart/ Sense implied: sweet words with cold heart ཁ་དཀར་ཁོག་ནག་མི་ལ་ ཡིད་ཆེས་མ་བྱེད། Do not trust persons of sweet words with cold heart. ཁ་དཀར་གཏིང་ནག ཁ་དཀར་ཞེ་ནག same as above

ཁ་སྐྱེངས་སྐྱོ་ལང་ས། embarassment/to be speechless with rage སློབ་དཔོན་འཕགས་པ་ལྷས་སློབ་དཔོན་ཏུ་དབྱུག་ས་ཁ་སྐྱེངས་སྐྱོ་ལངས་ཀྱི་གནས་སུ་བཀོད། Acharya Aryadeva left Acharya Avashvagosh in embarassment.

ཁ་ཁུ་སིམ་པོ། peaceful/silence/ quiet/ remote གངས་རི་ཏེ་སེའི་གཡས་ གཡོན་ཆང་མ་ཁ་ཁུ་སིམ་པོ་ཞེ་དྲག་ཡོད་རེད། The areas around Mt.Kalilash are very quiet and peaceful.

ཁ་ཁྲག་སྣ་ཁྲག Lit.: bleeding mouth; bleeding nose/ Sense implied: to be beaten to a pulp དམག་མིས་ཁ་ཁྲག་སྣ་ཁྲག་མ་ཐོན་བར་དུ་བརྡུངས་སོང་། The soldiers beat him to a pulp.

ཁ་མཁས་ལྕེ་བདེ། a glib talker གློག་བརྙན་ནང་དུ་མི་ཁ་མཁས་ལྕེ་བདེ་མང་པོས་ གཏམ་བཤད་བྱས། Many glib talkers made speeches in the film.

ཁ་མཁས་འདུ་ཆགས། Lit.: to talk sweetly/ to look captivating/ Sense implied: somewhat artificial གནས་གྱུའི་ལས་བྱེད་དུ་མོ་དེ་ཚོ་ཁ་

མཁས་འདུ་ཚགས་ཞེ་དྲག་ཡོད་རེད། Air-hostesses are very gentle in speech and captivating in looks.

ཁ་འགྱུལ་ལུས་འགྱལ། to act upon one's words ཁ་ནས་འགྱལ་བ་ནང་བཞིན་ལུས་ཀྱིས་ཀྱང་འགྱལ་ན་དོན་འགྲུབ་ཡོང་། There shall be success if one acts upon one's words.

ཁ་གྱོང་ཚིག་བཟངས། glib speech ཉམ་ཆུང་ལ་མཚོངས་ཆུང་བྱས་ཏེ་ཁ་གྱོང་ཚིག་བཟངས་མ་གཏོང་། Do not insult simple people by speaking glibly.

ཁ་ཞེ་གཉིས་མེད། Lit.: no difference in speech and thought/ Sense implied: honest and straightforward ནང་པ་ཚོས་དཀོན་མཆོག་ལ་ཁ་ཞེ་གཉིས་མེད་ཀྱིས་དད་པ་བྱེད་པ་རེད། Buddhists maintain unwavering faith in the Triple-Gem.

ཁ་བརྒྱ་ལྗེ་སྟོང་། Lit.: hundred mouths with thousand tongues/ Sense implied: unreliable/worthless speech ཆབ་སྲིད་ཀྱི་མགོ་ཁྲིད་འགའ་ཤས་ཀྱིས་ཁ་བརྒྱ་ལྗེ་སྟོང་གི་གསུང་བཤད་གནང་གི་འདུག Some political leaders make worthless speeches

ཁ་དགྲ་སྣ་དགྲ Lit.: mouth enemy; nose enemy/ Sense implied: enmity དོན་མེད་མི་ལ་ཁ་དགྲ་ར་དགྲ་མ་གསོག Do not create enmity towards strangers.

ཁ་འགྱིག་སོ་འགྱིག wrathful stance དྲག་པོའི་རྣམ་པ་ཅན་གྱི་ཨི་དམ་ཁ་འགའ་ཁ་འགྱིག་སོ་འགྱིག་གནང་སྟེ་བཞེངས་ཡོད། Some wrathful deities are erected in wrathful stance.

ཁ་སྐྱོ་མོ་གྱོད་ཀྱི་གཞི་མ། Lit.: the door of mouth is the source of dispute/ Sense implied: too much talk causes trouble ཁ་སྒོ་མོ་གྱོད་ཀྱི་གཞི་མ་རེད། དབྱངས་གསལ་བྱེད་ཡི་གེའི་གཞི་མ་རེད། The door of mouth is the source of dispute just as the vowels and consonants are the source of letters.

ཁ་ངན་ཁོག་ངན། evil speech and evil mind བློན་པོ་དེ་ཁ་ངན་ཁོག་ངན་ཞེ་དྲག་ཡོད་རེད། That minister is very evil in speech and mind.

ཁ་ངན་གཏམ་ངན། scandalous talk/ to disparage གཞན་ལ་ཁ་ངན་མ་ཟེར། གཏམ་ངན་རང་ལ་ཡོང་། Do not disparage others, you will be defamed. གཏམ་ངན་དེ་སུས་འཁྱེར་འདུག Who brought the bad news?

ཁ་ངན་ཚིག་ངན། abusive words གཞན་ལ་ཁ་ངན་ཚིག་ངན་བཤད་ན་རང་ལ་གནོད་པ་ཡོང་། One will be harmed if one speaks abusively to others.

ཁ་རོམས་གྱོད་འགྲངས། Lit.: quench one's thirst; the stomach is full/ Sense implied: to satisfy someone with food སློང་མཁན་དེ་ལ་ཁ་རོམས་གྱོད་འགྲངས་ཀྱི་ཟས་སྟེར་བའི་རྗེས་སུ་གཏམ་ཞིག་དྲིས། After giving the beggar enough food to fill the stomach and, once his thirst is quenched, you may ask him a question.

ཁ་གཅིག་ཁོག་གཉིས། Lit.: one mouth with two hearts/ Sense implied: to say something and do the otherwise ཁ་གཅིག་ཁོག་གཉིས་ཀྱིས་དོན་མི་འགྲུབ། One cannot succeed when one says something else and acts in the other way round.

ཁ་གཅིག་ལྕེ་གཉིས། Lit.: one mouth with two tongues/ Sense implied: duplicitous speech and double dealing དགྲ་བོས་ཁ་གཅིག་ལྕེ་གཉིས་ཀྱི་ལམ་ནས་དཀྲུགས་ཤིང་བསླངས་པ་རེད། The enemy created discord through double dealing.

ཁ་བཙུས་སྣ་བཙུས། Lit.: to turn away one's mouth and nose/ Sense implied: to show reluctance དགེ་ཕྲུག་གི་བགང་སློབ་ལ་སློབ་ཕྲུག་ཡག་པོ་ཚོས་ནམ་ཡང་ཁ་བཙུས་སྣ་བཙུས་བྱེད་ཀྱི་མ་རེད། Good students will never show reluctance to their teacher's advices.

ཁ་ཆག་སྣ་རལ། Lit.: broken mouth and torn nose/ Sense implied: misfortunes and obstacles མི་མང་མཐུན་པོ་མེད་ན་ཁ་ཆག་སྣ་རལ་རྒྱུན་མར་ཡོང་གི་རེད། The misfortunes will befall always if the people are not on good terms.

ཁ་ཆད་འགྱུར་མེད། unchanging promise ཁ་ཆད་འགྱུར་མེད་དུ་གནས་པ་ནི་མི་ཡི་ཡོན་ཏན་ཁྱད་པར་དུ་འཕགས་པ་ཞིག་རེད། Keeping promises is one of the best qualities of a person.

ཁ་ཆད་བུ་ལོན། the promise becomes a debt མ་ཐུབ་པ་ལ་ཁ་ཆད་མ་གནང་། ཁ་ཆད་བུ་ལོན་དང་འདྲ་བ་ཡིན། Do not make a promise that one cannot fulfill. A promise becomes like a debt.

ཁ་ཆར་བུ་ཡུག snow and rain storm དགུན་ཁ་ཁ་ཆར་བུ་ཡུག་གི་དཀྱིལ་དུ་ལུག་མང་པོ་འཁྱག་ནི་ཤིབ། Many sheep were frozen to death during winter in the midst of snows and rain storms.

36

ཁ་ཆུ་ཟར་ཟར། drooling/ releasing saliva ཕྲུ་གུ་ཆུང་ཆུང་དེ་ཚོ་ཁ་ཆུ་ཟར་ཟར་ འགྲོ་གི་འདུག Those small children are going about drooling.

ཁ་ཆེ་ཡང་སྣ་ཁྲུང་འོག་རེད། Lit.: although the mouth is big, it is under the nose/ Sense implied: to be under the control of someone འཛིན་སྐྱོང་ཇི་ཙམ་དབང་ཆེ་ཡང་ཁྲིམས་ཀྱི་འོད་དུ་འགྲོ་དགོས། དཔེར་ ན་ཁ་ཇི་ཙམ་ཆེ་ཡང་སྣ་ཁྲུག་འོག་ཏུ་ཡིན་པའི་དཔེ་བཞིན་རེད། However powerful an administration may be, it is under the law just as a mouth is under the nose however big it may be.

ཁ་ཆེམས་རླུང་བསྐུར། Lit.: to send someone's will in the air/ Sense implied: to ignore someone's will བཀའན་དྲིན་ཅན་གྱི་ཕ་མ་ རྣམས་ཀྱི་ཁ་ཆེམས་རླུང་ལ་བསྐུར་མི་རུང་། One should not ignore the will of one's kind parents.

ཁ་མཆུ་བོགས་མར་ལེན་པ། Lit.: to take a case on lease/ Sense implied: unnecessarily welcoming trouble/ to file a case on behalf of someone སྔོན་མ་བོད་དུ་མི་ཁ་ཤས་ཀྱིས་ཁ་མཆུ་འབོགས་མ་ལེན་ པ་རེད། In the past some Tibetans take case on lease in Tibet.

ཁ་འཇམ་གཏིང་ནག Lit.: gentle speech with evil motive/ Sense implied: evil person ཚོང་པ་ཁ་འཇམ་གཏིང་ནག་དེ་ཡིས་མི་མང་པོར་མགོ་ བསྐོར་བཏང་བ་རེད། That evil businessman deceived many people.

ཁ་འཇམ་སྦྱེལ་ལད། flattery talk དཔོན་པོ་དེ་ཁ་འཇམ་སྦྱེལ་ལད་བྱེད་མཁན་ལ་ཞེ་ དྲག་ཕྱགས་མཉེས་པོ་ཡོད། That officer likes very much, who flatters.

ཁ་འཛམ་ཚིག་སྙན། smooth and pleasing speech ཉན་ལགས་ནས་སློབ་

སྟོན་གནང་སྐབས་ཁ་འཛམ་ཚིག་སྙན་བེད་སྤྱོད་གནང་གི་འདུག Our teacher
speaks gently and pleasantly in his teaching.

ཁ་རྗེ་དབང་ཐང་། the whole property of someone བོད་མི་ཚོའི་ཁ་རྗེ་དབང་

ཐང་ཚང་མ་རྒྱ་མི་ལ་ཤོར་བ་རེད། Tibetans lost the whole of their
property to the Chinese.

ཁ་ཉུང་ལག་གཙང་། Lit.: less talk and clean hand/ Sense implied:
taciturn and decent ཕྱུ་གུ་ཉུང་དུའི་དུས་ནས་ཁ་ཉུང་ལག་གཙང་དུ་གནས་པ་

ནི་སྐྱེས་བུ་ཆེན་པོའི་རྟགས་རེད། Being taciturn and decent since
childhood is a sign of great men.

ཁ་ཏ་སྐུལ་སླུག to encourage and advise ངའི་གྲོགས་པོས་ང་ལ་ཁ་ཏ་སྐུལ་

སླུག་མང་པོ་གནང་བྱུང་། My friend gave me much encouraging
advice.

ཁ་ཏ་ངན་པ། bad advice རོགས་པ་མི་ངན་ནེ་ཚོས་ཁ་ཏ་ངན་པ་སྤྲོད་ཀྱི་རེད། Evil
companions will give bad advice.

ཁ་ཏ་བཟླབ་བྱ། kind advice རྒྱན་དུ་ཉན་པའི་ཁ་ཏ་བཟླབ་བྱ་ལ་ཉན་དགོས། One
should always listen to the advice of elders.

ཁ་གཏད་དོ་རྒྱ། the opponents རྩེད་འགྲན་གྱི་ཁ་གཏད་དོ་རྒྱ་ནི་ཚོ་རྩེད་མོ་ཞེ་དྲག་

མཁས་པོ་འདུག The opponent players of the match are very
skilful.

ཁ་གཏིང་མེད་པ། ཁ་ཞེ་གཉིས་མེད། Lit.: no difference in speech and thought/ Sense implied: practical and honest རྒྱལ་ཁབ་ཀྱི་དོན་ དུ་ཞེ་གཉིས་མེད་ཀྱི་ལས་དོན་བྱེད་མཁན་ལ་རྒྱལ་གཅེས་པ་ཟེར། He who practically and sincerely works for the nation is called a patriot.

ཁ་དན་ཚིག་དན། Lit.: firm mouth and words/ Sense implied: to keep one's promise/ an adherent of promises སྔོན་གྱི་མི་ རྣམས་ཁ་དན་ཚིག་དན་ལ་གནས་པ་རེད། In olden days people adhered to their pledges.

ཁ་བལྟ་མིག་བལྟ། Lit.: to see mouth and eye/ Sense implied: to guide/care and guidance ཕྲུ་གུ་ཆུང་དུས་ནས་ཁ་བལྟ་མིག་བལྟ་གཟབ་ གཟབ་གནང་དགོས། One should give good care and guidance to a child since childhood.

ཁ་སྟོང་ཚིག་སྟོང་། Lit.: empty mouth and word/ Sense implied: gossip ཁ་སྟོང་ཚིག་སྟོང་བཏང་པ་ལས་ཁ་འདོན་དགོ་སྟོར་བྱེད་པ་དགའ། It is better to engage in prayers than in gossip.

ཁ་སྟོང་ལག་སྟོང་། Lit.: empty mouth and empty hand/ Sense implied: to give nothing/ to let somebody go empty handed ལོ་གསར་སྐབས་སྐུ་མགྲོན་པོ་སུ་བྱུང་ཡང་ཁ་སྟོང་ལག་སྟོང་ལ་གཏོང་མི་ཉན། During Losar one should not turn away one's guest with an empty hand and empty mouth.

ཁ་ཕུག་ཁ་ཕུག at once/ straightforward/ in time ལས་ཀ་ཚང་མ་ཁ་ ཕུག་ཁ་ཕུག་ལ་གནང་དགོས། All work should be done in time.

ཁ་ཐུག་གདོང་ཐུག Lit.: meeting face to face/ Sense implied: to meet unexpectedly དེ་རིང་ཁྲོམ་ལ་གྲོགས་པོ་རྙིང་པ་ཞིག་དང་ང་ཁ་ཐུག་གདོང་ཐུག་བརྒྱབ་བྱུང་། Today I unexpectedly met an old friend of mine in the market.

ཁ་ཕོག་དོན་གནས། practical སྔོན་དུས་ཀྱི་མི་རྣམས་མནའ་གན་མ་བཞག་ཀྱང་ཁ་ཕོག་དོན་ལ་གནས་པ་བྱེད་མཁན་ཤ་སྟག་ཡིན། In ancient times people would stick to their word although no affidavits were kept.

ཁ་ཕོག་ལག་བཞག practical ལས་དོན་གང་ཡིན་ཡང་ཁ་ཕོག་ལག་བཞག་ཅིག་བྱེད་དགོས། One should be practical in every work one does.

ཁ་འཐོར་བ། Lit.: scattered/ Sense implied: disintegration གླང་དར་མའི་རྗེས་སུ་བོད་ཀྱི་རྒྱལ་སྲིད་ཁ་འཐོར་བ་རེད། The Tibetan nation disintegrated politically after the King Lang Darma.

ཁ་དན་རྒྱབ་བསྒྱུར། to break one's promise/ to violate the pledge མཛའ་བའི་གྲོགས་པོ་རྣམས་ཀྱིས་ཁ་དན་རྒྱབ་བསྒྱུར་བྱེད་མི་རུང་། One should not break one's promises to intimate friends.

ཁ་དན་ཚིག་ལ་གནས་པ། able to keep one's promises རྩ་མཐུན་གྲོགས་པོ་ཡིན་ན། ཁ་དན་ཚིག་ལ་གནས་དགོས། If you are an intimate friend, you should keep your words.

ཁ་དིག་ལྡི་ལྡིབས། to stammer ཕུ་གུ་དེ་སྐྱེས་པའི་དུས་ནས་ཁ་དིག་ལྡི་ལྡིབས་བྱེད་ཀྱི་འདུག The child is stammering since his birth.

40

ཁ་དྲག་དབང་ཤེད། exploitations by those who are in power དཔོན་ དན་དེ་ཚོས་ཁ་དྲག་དབང་ཤེད་སྤྱད་དེ་མི་སེར་ལ་བཟབས་མནར་མང་པོ་བཏང་སོང་། The evil officers greatly exploited their subjects misusing their power.

ཁ་བདེ་པོ་མི་ཡི་དཔོན་པོ་ཡིན། ལག་བདེ་པོ་མི་ཡི་གཡོག་པོ་ཡིན། An eloquent speaker is people's master and a craftman is people's servant.

ཁ་བདེ་ལག་བདེ། articulate and dexterous དོན་གྲུབ་ནི་ཁ་བདེ་པོ་ཡིན་པ་མ་ ཟད་ལག་ཀྱང་བདེ་པོ་འདུག Dhondup is not only articulate but dexterous as well.

ཁ་འདོན་དགེ་སྦྱོར། reciting prayers and engaging in virtues བསོད་ ནམས་གསོག་པའི་སླད་དུ་ཁ་འདོན་དགེ་སྦྱོར་ལ་བཙོན་དགོས། One should engage in prayer recitations and virtuous actions for the accumulation of merit.

ཁ་འདྲིས་ཁོག་འདྲིས། a close familiarity ཡུན་རིང་མཉམ་དུ་འདྲིས་ན་ཁ་འདྲིས་ ཁོག་འདྲིས་ཡོང་གི་རེད། A close familiarity will arise when people acquaint one another for a long time.

ཁ་ནང་གི་རྨ། ཁ་ནང་ན་གསོ། Lit.: a sore in the mouth is cured by itself/ Sense implied: resolved internally རྒྱལ་ཁབ་ནང་ཁྲལ་གྱི་མི་ མཐུན་པ་དེ་ལ་ནང་འགྲིགས་བྱེད་དགོས་པ་ཡིན། དཔེར་ན་ཁ་ནང་གི་རྨ་ཁ་ནང་ན་གསོ་བ་ བཞིན། The disharmony within a nation should be compromised internally just as sore in the mouth is cured by itself.

ཁ་ནས་མུ་ཏིག་ཕོར་དོགས་པ། Lit.: to doubt that pearls will drop out from the mouth/ Sense implied: one who doesn't want to share one's knowledge/ This proverb is used when someone is reluctant to share one's knowledge.

ཁ་ཐན་ཚིག་ཐན། verbal help or advice གྲོང་གསེབ་གཅིག་པའི་མི་རྣམས་དུག་ དུ་ཁ་ཐན་ཚིག་ཐན་གྱི་རོགས་རེས་བྱེད་པ་རེད། People of the same village always help one another.

ཁ་ཕོག་རྣ་ཕོག Lit.: to hurt at the mouth and nose/ Sense implied: to hurt many people unintelligently བདེན་པ་བཤད་ པའི་སྐབས་སུ་གཞན་ལ་ཁ་ཕོག་རྣ་ཕོག་ལས་ཀྱིས་ཚགས་ཨོང་། Someone's feeling gets hurt when the truth is spoken out.

ཁ་འཁངས་ལག་འཕྱིས། to blame ནོར་འཁྲུལ་རང་གིས་བྱས་ཏེ་ཁ་འཁངས་ལག་ འཕྱིས་གཞན་ལ་བྱས་ན་མ་རབས་རེད། Having committed the mistake by oneself, if one blames other people, it is an impolite manner.

ཁ་ལྗིད་པོ། Lit.: heavy mouth/ Sense implied: taciturn ཁོང་ཁ་ལྗིད་ པོ་ཡོད་རེད། སྐད་ཆ་དྲིས་ན་མ་གཏོགས་བཤད་ཀྱི་མ་རེད། He is taciturn in nature. He will not speak unless he is asked.

ཁ་སྦྲང་རྩི་ཁོག་སྨྱུག་ཆ། ཁ་སྦྲང་རྩི་ཁོག་ཚེར་མ། ཁ་སྦྲང་རྩི་ཁོག་རལ་གྲི། ཁ་འོ་མ་ཁོག་ཚེར་མ། see ཁ་འཛེམ་གཏིང་ནག Lit.: the mouth is honey and the heart is ink/ the mouth is honey and the heart is thorn/ the mouth is honey and the heart is sword/ the mouth is milk and the heart is is thorn/ Sense implied: bad hearted person with sweet speech ཁ་སྦྲང་རྩི་ཁོག་སྨྱུག་ཚའི་མི་ལ་དོགས་གཟོན་གྱིས། Beware of a bad hearted person with sweet speech.

42

ཁ་མ་འཛིས་ན་ཆམ་པ་འགོས་དོགས་མེད། Lit.: if mouth is not shared, one cannot catch the cold/ Sense implied: To show that there is a connection due to which there is influence.

ཁ་མང་ལྗེ་མང་། Lit.: many mouths and many tongues/ Sense implied: talkative ཁ་མང་ལྗེ་མང་གི་གཏམ་ལ་ཡིད་རྟོན་མེད། A talkative's version is not reliable.

ཁ་མང་ན་དགྲ་སྲུང་། too much talk creates enemity དབྱར་ཁ་ལྕགས་དང་ དགུན་ཁ་རྫ། དབྱར་དགུན་མེད་པར་དམར་པོའི་ལྗེ་ལ་བདག་པོ་རྒྱོབས། ཁ་མང་ན་དགྲ་ སྲུང་། Take care of iron in summer and clay-pots in winter. However take care of the mouth both summer and winter as too much talk creates enemy.

ཁ་མང་ལག་མང་། Lit.: many mouths and many hands/ Sense implied: refers to public's མི་མང་གི་ཁ་མང་ནི་དུག་ཡིན། མི་མང་གི་ལག་ མང་ནི་གསེར་ཡིན། Public mouths are poison whereas their hands are gold.

ཁ་མ་འགུལ། ཨོག་མ་འགུལ། Lit.: to move the chin but not the mouth/ Sense implied: to blame others by gesture/ This is gesture performed by someone who is not satisfied with somebody.

ཁ་མིག་ཡར་བལྟ། to follow good examples ཁ་མིག་མར་བལྟ། to follow bad examples ཁ་མིག་ཡར་བལྟ་བྱེད་དགོས་མར་བལྟ་མ་བྱེད། Follow the good examples, not the bad examples.

ཁ་མེད་དམིགས་མེད། in great number/ a lot of མི་སྐྱ་དེ་ལ་དངུལ་ཁ་མེད

དམིགས་མེད་གནས་སོང་། I had to pay a lot of money for the lithium statue.

ཁ་ཚམ་ཚིག་ཙམ། merely in words ཁ་འདོན་བསྐྱར་བའི་སྐབས་སུ་ཁ་ཚམ་ཚིག་ ཙམ་མིན་པར་བསམ་བློ་བཏང་དགོས། Recitation of prayers should not be mere utterance of words, rather one should think as well.

ཁ་རྩོད་ཙིག་རྩོད། dispute/ minor disagreement སྤུན་མཆེད་ནང་ཁྱུལ་ཁ་རྩོད་ ཚིག་རྩོད་བྱུ་མི་རུང་། There should not be disputes among the relatives.

ཁ་ཚ་དགོས་གཏུགས། urgent need/ succour རྒྱ་གར་གཞུང་གི་བོད་མི་སྐྱབས་ བཅོལ་བ་རྣམས་ལ་ཁ་ཚ་དགོས་གཏུགས་ཀྱི་རོགས་རམ་མང་པོ་གནང་བ་ལ་ཐུགས་རྗེ་ཆེ། Thanks to the government of India for providing succour help to the Tibetan refugees.

ཁ་ཚེར་ཚེར། to smile or giggle ཁོང་གིས་དུག་པར་ང་ལ་ཁ་ཚེར་ཚེར་གནང་གི་ ཡོད། He always smiles at me.

ཁ་ལ་ངོས་ལེན། to receive or give acceptance ང་ལྷ་སར་འབྱོར་དུས་ངའི་ གྲོགས་པོས་ང་ལ་ཁ་ལ་ངོས་ལེན་ཡག་པོ་བྱས་བྱུང་། When I arrived in Lhasa my friend welcomed me and treated me very well.

ཁ་ཡོད་ལག་ཡོད། real and practical ཨ་མི་རི་ཁའི་གཞུང་དེ་ཁ་ཡོད་ལག་ཡོད་ཀྱི་ དམངས་གཙོའི་གཞུང་ཞིག་རེད། The U.S.A. government is a real democratic government.

ཁ་གཡེང་མིག་གཡེང་། to be inattentive and distracted འཛིན་གྲར་ཁ་

གཡེང་མིག་གཡེང་བྱེད་ན་སློབ་སྦྱོང་ལེག་པོ་ཤེས་ཀྱི་མ་རེད། One will not understand the lesson if one is inattentive in the class.

ཁ་རེ་ཁ་ཐུག straightforward/direct ང་མི་ཁ་རེ་ཁ་ཐུག་ཚ་པོ་ལ་དགའ་པོ་ ཡོད། I like those who are very straightforward.

ཁ་འཕས་ཁ་འས། a few/ some བོད་མི་ཁ་འཕས་ཁ་འས་ཡག་པོ་འདུག་ཁ་འཕས་ཁ་འས་ ཁྱད་ཚར་འདུག Some Tibetans are good whereas others are strange.

ཁ་འཕའི་པགས་པ་ག་ནས་འཐེན་འཐེན་རེད། Lit.: one can stretch a deer's skin in any direction one likes/ Sense implied: many interpretations can be given རྒྱ་གར་མཁས་པའི་གསུང་དེ་ཚོ་ཁ་འཕའི་ པགས་པ་འཐེབ་པ་ནང་བཞིན་འགྲེལ་བཤད་ག་ནས་རྒྱབ་རྒྱབ་རེད། The works of Indian Masters can be interpreted in many ways just as a deer skin can be stretched in any direction one wants.

ཁ་བཤད་ཆུ་ཡི་སྦུ་བ། ལག་ལེན་གསེར་གྱི་ཐིགས་པ། Lit.: speech is like froth and practice is like golden drops/ Sense implied: very rare in practice/ This is used when one says too much and does nothing. ཁ་གསང་ན་གོ་བདེ། ལམ་གསང་ན་འགྲོ་བདེ། If someone is frank it is easier to understand and if the road is opened it is easier to go.

ཁ་གསང་གོ་བདེ། if one is frank it is easier to understand/ This is used when someone does not make clear indication.

ཁ་གསལ་ཆོག་གསལ། very clear གནས་ལགས་ནས་སློབ་སྟོན་གནང་སྐབས་འགྱུར་

བཤད་ཁ་གསལ་ཚིག་གསལ་གསུང་གི་འདུག The teacher explains very clearly while teaching.

ཁ་དཀྲིས་བསྐོན་འཇུག་གས། to blame and accuse མའོ་ཙེ་ཏུང་གི་ཆབ་སྲིད་ནོར་ འཁྲུལ་རྣམས་མི་བཞི་ཕྱོག་ཁག་ཁག་ལ་ཁལ་དཀྲི་བསྐོན་འཇུག་གས་བྱས་པ་རེད། Mr. Mao blamed the gang of four for his political mistakes.

ཁག་ཁག་སོ་སོ། separate and distinct ཆོས་དང་འཇིག་རྟེན་ཁག་ཁག་སོ་སོ་རེད། Religion and worldly life are two separate entities.

ཁང་རོ་གྱང་གོག ruined buildings/ ruins གནས་ས་མང་ཆེ་བར་ཁང་རོ་གྱང་ གོག་མང་པོ་མཐོང་རྒྱུ་ཡོད། At most of the holy sites, we can see many ruins.

ཁམ་གཅིག་སྲོག་བསྐྱེལ། to lose one's life for a morsel of food

ཁལ་བོང་བུས་འཁྱེར་ནས་རྒྱ་ལམ་སྐྱོད་པ་ན་དོན་མེད། Lit.: There is no reason for the road to suffer since it is the donkey that carries the load./ Sense implied: inappropriate complaint

ཁའི་དེ་བཞིན་གཤེགས་པས་ལུས་ཀྱི་སྒྲིབ་པ་མི་དག Merely saying Tathagata will not purify the physical obscurations. (It is a sarcastic remark to those who recite blindly without thinking over the text.)

ཁས་བླངས་རྒྱབ་བསྐྱར། to violate the promise བཀྲོག་ཏུ་བྲལ་བའི་དཀའ་ངལ་ ཕྲད་ན་མ་གཏོགས་ཁས་བླངས་རྒྱབ་བསྐྱར་གནང་མི་རུང་། One should not violate one's promise unless inevitable problems are encountered.

ཁས་བླངས་ལག་བསྟར། to implement a promise བྱང་ཆུབ་སེམས་དཔའ་ རྣམས་ཀྱིས་གཞན་དོན་དུ་ཁས་བླངས་པ་རྣམས་ངེས་པར་ལག་བསྟར་བྱེད་པ་རེད། Bodhisattvas definitely implement their promises made for the welfare of others.

ཁས་ལེན་འགན་ཁུར། responsibilities ལས་ཀ་འདིའི་ཁས་ལེན་འགན་ཁུར་ཚང་མ་ ཁོང་གིས་གནང་བ་རེད། He took all the responsibilites of this work.

ཁས་ལེན་ངོས་ལེན། to accept/ to recognise རྒྱ་གར་གཞུང་ནས་ཁྱེད་རང་གི་ ཙོངས་མཆན་དེ་ལ་ཁས་ལེན་ངོས་ལེན་གནང་གི་འདུག The govenment of India gives recognition to your visa.

ཁུག་ཁྱུག་ཀྱོག་ཀྱོག nooks and crannies དེ་རིང་ཁུག་ཁྱུག་ཀྱོག་ཀྱོག་ཡོད་ཚད་ལ་ གཙང་མ་བཟོ་གི་ཡིན། Today we will clean all the nooks and crannies.

ཁུངས་བསྐྱེལ་དག་བུད། convincing proof རང་གི་ངོས་ནས་ཁུངས་བསྐྱེལ་དག་ བུད་ཐུབ་ཀྱི་མེད་ན་གཞན་ལ་སྐྱོན་བརྗོད་མ་གནང་ན་ལེགས། It is better not to criticise others when one doesn't have convincing proof.

ཁུངས་བསྐྱེལ་རྟེས་སྤྲོད། to submit proof རང་གི་ལས་མཇུག་རྣམས་ཁྱངས་ བསྐྱེལ་རྟེས་སྤྲོད་ཡག་པོ་གནང་སྟེ་ས་གནས་གཞན་དུ་ཕེབས་གལ་ཆེ། It is important to handed-iver the proof of having completed one's work before going to another place.

ཁུངས་བསྐྱེལ་ར་སྤྲོད། evidences བོད་རང་བཙན་ཡིན་པའི་ཁུངས་བསྐྱེལ་ར་སྤྲོད་ཀྱི་ ཡིག་ཆ་ཁག་མང་པོ་ཡོད། There are many historical evidences of Tibet being an independent nation.

ཁུངས་དག་སྤུས་གཙང་། good finishing/ work of quality ཚེམ་བུ་བ་དེ་
ཚོས་ནམ་ཡང་ལས་ཀ་སྤུས་དག་བྱེད་ཀྱི་མ་རེད། The tailors never do their
work qualitatively and with good finishing.

ཁུངས་དེད་རྩད་གཙོད། to search or to trace the origin མི་གསོད་མཁན་
དེ་ཁུངས་དེད་རྩད་གཙོད་ཐུབ་ན་ངེས་པར་བརྙེད་ཀྱི་རེད། If one can make a
search for the murderer, definitely he can be found.

ཁུངས་ཡོད་ལུང་ཡོད། something that has evidence to prove ཁུངས་
ཡོད་ལུང་ཡོད་ཀྱི་ཅེད་ཚོམ་རྣམས་ལ་ཆན་རིག་དང་མཐུན་པའི་ཅེད་ཚོམ་ཟེར།
Scientific articles are those that have evidence to prove.

ཁེ་ཆེ་ཉེན་ཆུང་། greater benefit and less risk དེབ་ཀྱི་ཚོང་ཁང་ཞིག་བཙུགས་
ཐུབ་ན་ཁེ་བཟང་ཆེ་ལ་ཉེན་ཁ་ཆུང་བ་ཡོད། If one can open a book-shop,
there is greater benefit than risk.

ཁེ་ཉེན་གོ་འཛོལ། to mistake profit for loss and vice versa ཁེ་ཉེན་གོ་
འཛོལ་མི་ཡོང་བའི་ཆེད་རྩིས་ལག་པོ་རྒྱབ་དགོས། In order not to mistake
profit for loss and vice versa, one should calculate well.

ཁེ་འདོད་གྲགས་འདོད། desire for wealth and fame རང་ཉེད་ལ་རྣམ་དཔྱོད་
མེད་ན་ཁེ་འདོད་གྲགས་འདོད་བྱེད་པས་ཅི་ལ་ཕན། What is the use of aspiring
for wealth and fame when one does not possess the skill to
acquire them.

ཁེ་ཕན་གང་ཆེ། whatever is more advantageous ཁྱེད་རང་ལ་ཁེ་ཕན་
གང་ཆེ་བ་དེ་གནང་རོགས་གནང་། Please do whatever is more
advantageous to you.

ཁ་ཕན་བསམ་ཤེས། to understand the benefit སྤྱི་ཚོགས་ཀྱི་ཁ་ཕན་བསམ་ཤེས་ལ་དགོངས་ཏེ་ཕྱིར་རང་འདི་གར་ཕེབས་རོགས། You are requested to come here with the thought of benefitting the society.

ཁ་གཅོང་། ཁབ་གཅོང་། apart/ separate བོད་དེ་རྒྱལ་ཁབ་གཞན་ལས་ཁ་གཅོང་དུ་བསྡད་པའི་རྐྱེན་གྱིས་རྒྱལ་ཁབ་གཞན་དང་འབྲེལ་བ་མ་བྱུང་བ་རེད། Tibet having remained apart from the rest of the countries, could not develop relations with other countries of the world.

ཁེངས་སྐྱུངས་བག་ཡོད། humbleness with conscientiousness སྐྱེས་བུ་དམ་པ་རྣམས་ཧ་ཅང་ཁེངས་སྐྱུངས་བག་ཡོད་དང་ལྡན་པ་ཞ་སྤྱག་རེད། Great and noblemen are very humble and conscientious.

ཁོག་པའི་སྙིང་དང་དཔྲལ་བའི་མིག Lit.: heart of the body and eye of the forehead/ Sense implied: very dear and precious པགོང་ས་མཆོག་ནི་བོད་མི་ཚང་མའི་ཁོག་པའི་སྙིང་དང་དཔྲལ་བའི་མིག་རེད། His Holiness the Dalai Lama is the heart and eye of every Tibetan.

ཁོག་པའི་ནད་ལ་ནད་མེད་ན། གདོང་ལ་ཟིགས་པ་ཆགས་དོན་མེད། Lit.: if there is no illness inside, there is no reason to have black spots on one's face/ Sense implied: If someone is innocent, there is no need to feel guilty

ཁོག་ཡངས་ཕམ་ཁུར། to accept defeat patiently (positive) ལས་དོན་ཆེན་པོ་འགྲུབ་པའི་ཆེད་དུ་ཁོག་ཡངས་ཕམ་ཁུར་གནང་དགོས། One needs to accept defeat patiently in order to fulfil a big task.

ཁོང་ཁྲོ་སློང་མཁན་མེད་ན། བཟོད་པ་སུ་ལ་སྒོམ། If there is no one to make you angry, to whom would you practice patience?

ཁོག་ཡངས་དཀྱིལ་ཆེ། broad minded and brave རྒྱལ་ཁབ་ཀྱི་དབུ་ཁྲིད་ནི་ ཁོག་ཡངས་ལ་དཀྱིལ་ཆེ་བ་དགོས་པ་ཡིན། The head of a state should be broad minded as well as brave.

ཁོང་དཀྱིལ་འཁོར་བཞེངས་ཀྱི་འདུག Lit.: He is constructing a mandala./ Sense implied: One who is deeply engrossed in thought.

འཁྱགས་དུས་གོས་དང་ལྟོགས་དུས་ཟས། clothes when it is cold and food when hungry བཀའ་དྲིན་ཅན་གྱི་ཕ་མ་ནི་འཁྱགས་དུས་གོས་དང་ལྟོགས་ དུས་ཟས་སྟེར་མཁན་དེ་རེད། It is kind parents who give clothes when one is cold and food when one is hungry.

འཁྲུགས་སློང་ཆེད་བཟོ། to intentionally stir up trouble ཕྱི་གཟར་ཁལ་ཆེ་ བ་ཕྱི་ནས་འཁྲུགས་སློང་ཆེད་བཟོ་བྱས་པ་ལ་བརྟེན་ནས་བྱུང་། Most of the civil wars were outcome of the disturbances intentionally created by outside forces.

འཁྲུལ་སྣང་བདེན་འཛིན། holding/taking a mistaken appearance for truth/to grasp truth at the illusory appearance/ It is a philosophical thinking.

མཁས་པའི་སྡིག་པ་ཕྱི་ཡང་ཡང་། བླུན་པོའི་སྡིག་པ་ཡང་ཡང་ཕྱི། Lit.: although it is a big sin, it is small for the wise; although it is a small sin, it is big for the idiot/A heavy negativity is light for the wise but a light negativity is heavy for the stupid   Sense implied: A holy man knows the remedy for the sin whereas an idiot does not.

གཉིད་འདི་ཉིད་མེད་པ། in a helpless situation dilemma སློབ་སྦྱོང་ཡག་པོ་མ་གནང་ན་ཡིག་ཚད་སྐབས་ག་ཉིད་འདི་ཉིད་མེད་པ་ཆགས་ཀྱི་རེད། One will be in a helpless situation during the examination if one does not study properly.

ག་ཟེར་འདི་ཟེར་མེད་པ། to have no control over one's talk ཆང་བཏུང་སྟེ་ར་བཟི་བའི་སྐབས་སུ་ག་ཟེར་འདི་ཟེར་མེད་པ་ཆག་གི་རེད། When someone is intoxicated, he has no control over his speech.

ག་རེ་འདུག་ནའང་། whatever is there ཁོང་གི་ཕྱག་ཏུ་ག་རེ་འདུག་ནའང་གཞན་ཕན་གྱི་ཆེད་དུ་ཡིན་པ་རེད། Whatever is there in his hand is for the benefit of others.

ག་རེ་ཡིན་ནའང་། anyhow/ in any case/ whatever it may be ཁྱེད་རང་གི་བུ་ལོན་དེ་ག་རེ་ཡིན་ནའང་ཟླ་བ་གཅིག་གི་ནང་ལ་འཇལ་གྱི་ཡིན། Any how I will return your loan within a month.

ག་རེ་ཡིན་ཟེར་ནའང་། no matter what one claims to be ཁྱེད་རང་ག་རེ་ཡིན་ཟེར་ནའང་ཁྱེད་རང་ལ་དེབ་མི་གཡར་ཐག་གཅོད་ཡིན། No matter what you claim to be I will definitely not lend the book.

ག་རེ་ཡོད་ནའང་། anything that is available ཁོང་ལ་ག་རེ་ཡོད་ན་ཡང་རང་གི་གྲོགས་པོ་ལ་ཕྱེད་ཀ་སྤྲོད་ཀྱི་རེད། He gives half of anything that he has to his friends.

ག་ལེར་ག་ལེར། slowly/ gently ལས་ཀ་ག་ལེར་ག་ལེར་བྱས་ན་དུས་ཐོག་ལ་ཚར་གྱི་
མ་རེད། One cannot finish one's work in time if one does it slowly.

ག་ས་ག་ནས། from everywhere/ from all directions དུ་རམ་ས་ལ་ལ་
རྒྱལ་ཁབ་ག་ས་ག་ནས་མི་མང་པོ་ཡོང་གི་འདུག Many people come to Dharamsala from every different countries of the world.

ག་ས་ག་ལ། all over/ everywhere སྐུ་ལོ་པ་གོང་ས་མཆོག་ཕྱི་རྒྱལ་ག་ས་ག་ལ་
ཆིབས་བསྒྱུར་གནང་བ་རེད། Last year His Holiness the Dalai Lama visited many countries abroad.

གང་ཅིའི་ཐད་ནས། by all means/ in all respects རྒྱ་གར་གཞུང་ནི་གང་ཅིའི་
ཐད་ནས་རྒྱ་ནག་གཞུང་ལས་དྲག་གི་རེད། The Indian government is better than the government of China in all respects.

གང་དགའ་ཅི་ལེགས། whatever is good རྒྱལ་ཁབ་ཀྱི་དོན་དུ་གང་དགའ་
ཅི་ལེགས་ཤིག་གནང་རོགས་གནང་། Please do whatever is good for the country.

གང་མགྱོགས་ཅི་མགྱོགས། as soon as possible བོད་མི་ཆིག་སྟོང་ཐམ་པ་གང་
མགྱོགས་ཅི་མགྱོགས་ཨ་མི་རི་ཁ་ལ་གཏོང་གི་རེད། One thousand Tibetans shall be sent to U.S.A. as soon as possible.

གང་ལྡོག་ལྡོག to do as much as one can do བོད་མི་ཚོས་རང་གི་རྒྱལ་ཁབ་
ཀྱི་དོན་དུ་ནུས་པ་གང་ལྡོག་ལྡོག་འདོན་པ་གནང་བ་རེད། Tibetans do as much as they can do for their country.

52

གར་བདང་གོ་ཆོད། an efficient person དཔེ་མཛོད་ཀྱི་དྲུང་ཆེ་དེ་གར་བདང་གོ་
ཆོད་གཅིག་འདུག The secretary of the Library is an efficient person.

གར་བཀླ་འདི་བཀླ་མེད་པ། desperately looking everywhere རང་གི་ཕྲུ་
གུ་བརླགས་པའི་ཕ་མ་དེ་མིག་གར་བཀླ་འདི་བཀླ་མེད་པར་བྱེད་ཀྱི་འདུག The mother who lost her child is desperately looking everywhere.

གང་ལྟར་ཡང་སྐྱིང་། any how གང་ལྟར་ཡང་སྐྱིང་རྒན་ལགས་ཕེབས་པ་དེ་ཡག་པོ་
བྱུང་སོང་། Any how it is good that the teacher has come.

གང་ཐུབ་ཅི་ཐུབ། as best as one can རྒྱ་གར་གཞུང་ནས་བོད་མི་སྐྱབས་བཅོལ་བ་
ཚོ་ལ་རོགས་རམ་གང་ཐུབ་ཅི་ཐུབ་གནང་ཡོད། The government of India provided their best to help the Tibetan refugees.

ག་ཆོད་ཐུབ་ཐུབ། as much as possible བཀྲ་ཤིས་ཀྱིས་རང་གི་གྲོགས་པོ་ལ་རོགས་
རམ་ག་ཆོད་ཐུབ་ཐུབ་གནང་གི་འདུག Tashi helps his friend as much as possible.

གང་འདོད་འདོད། whatever one likes གཞུང་གི་དངོས་པོ་ཁྱེད་རང་སྤྱེར་ནས་གང་
འདོད་འདོད་གནང་ན་ཡག་པོ་མ་རེད། It is not good to do whatever you like with the government property.

གང་སྟབས་བདེ་བ། whatever is convenient ཕྱག་ལས་གང་སྟབས་བདེ་བ་དེ་
ཁྱེད་རང་ནས་སྟོན་ལ་གནང་རོགས་གནང་། Please do whatever is convenient to you first.

གང་དྲག་ཅི་དྲག to do one's best བོད་གཞུང་ལ་ངས་གང་དྲག་ཅི་དྲག་ཞུས་པ་
ཡིན། I did my best for the Tibetan government.

གང་འདྲ་ཅིག་ཡིན་ནའང་། whatever it may be བོད་རང་བཙན་གྱི་དོན་དུ་དཀའ་
ངལ་གང་འདྲ་ཅིག་ཡིན་ན་ཡང་གདོང་ལེན་བྱེད་དགོས་པ་ཡིན། We should
struggle for our independence whatever the problems we
might face.

གང་བྱུང་མང་བྱུང་། གང་བྱུང་མང་བྱུང་བྱེད་པ། གང་བྱུང་མང་བྱུང་བཤད་པ།
unrestraint/ to act without decency/ to speak without
decency སློབ་གྲྭའི་ནང་དུ་གང་བྱུང་མང་བྱུང་བྱེད་ན་སློབ་གྲྭ་ནས་ཕྱིར་འབུད་བྱེད་ཀྱི་
རེད། If you do whatever comes to your mind in the school
you will be dismissed from the school.

གང་མཚམས་ཤིག་ནས། after a while/after sometime ཕྱིན་རང་ཨ་རིར་
འབྱོར་ནས་གང་མཚམས་ཤིག་ནས་སྐྱིད་པོ་ཚོར་གྱི་རེད། After a while you will
feel happy when you reach the United States.

གང་གཟབ་གཟབ། with great care དགེ་རྒན་དེ་ཚོས་སློབ་ཕྲུག་རྣམས་ལ་གང་གཟབ་
གཟབ་བསླབ་གནང་གི་འདུག The teachers are teaching the students
with great care.

གང་ལ་གང་མཚམས། quite good ཁོང་ཁང་པ་གང་ལ་གང་མཚམས་ཡག་པོ་ཞིག་གི་
ནང་ལ་བཞུགས་འདུག He stays in a quite good house.

གང་ཤེས་ཅི་ཤེས། to the best of one's knowledge/whatever one
knows དགེ་རྒན་ལགས་ཀྱིས་གང་ཤེས་ཅི་ཤེས་སློབ་སྟོན་གནང་གི་འདུག The teacher
is teaching to the best of his knowledge.

54

གང་ས་གང་ལ། everywhere ངའི་གྲོགས་པོ་འཛམ་གླིང་གང་ས་གང་ལ་འགྲོ་མྱོང་ ཡོད། My friend has the experience of having gone everywhere in the world.

གང་ས་ཅི་ཐད། in every field ཨ་མེ་རི་ཁ་ནི་རྒྱ་ནག་ལས་གང་ས་ཅི་ཐད་ནས་དྲག་ག ཡོད། The U.S.A.is better than China in every field.

གང་བསམ་པ་དེ་བཤད་པ། to say whatever is in the mind གང་བསམ་ པ་དེ་ཤོད་མཁན་ལ་གསང་བ་ཤོད་མི་རུང་། One should not disclose the secret to someone who says whatever comes to his mind

གབ་རེས་ཡིབ་རེས། hide and seek ང་ཆུང་ཆུང་ཡིན་དུས་གབ་རེས་ཡིབ་རེས་མང་ པོ་རྩེད་མྱོང་། When I was small I played the hide and seek game a lot.

གར་འགྲོ་འདིར་འགྲོ་མེད་པ། to wander everywhere ཚེ་རིང་གར་འགྲོ་ འདིར་འགྲོ་མེད་པ་ཕེབས་ཀྱི་རེད། Mr.Tshering roams everywhere without purpose.

གར་སོང་ཆ་མེད། not to know where one has gone གར་སོང་འདིར་ སོང་མེད་པ། not to know where one has gone/ out of sight སློབ་ གྲྭ་ཕྱིན་ནས་ཁོང་རང་གར་སོང་ཆ་མེད་ཆགས་སོང་། Nothing is known about him (where he has gone) since he left the school.

གར་སོང་རྗེས་མེད། no trace of one's whereabout མཚན་ལ་ཀུན་མ་ བསླེབས་ཀྱང་ཞོགས་པ་གར་སོང་རྗེས་མེད་དུ་གྱུར་འདུག Although a thief entered the house at midnight, there was no trace of his whereabouts in the morning.

གལ་འགངས་ཆེན་པོ། extremely important ཡིག་ཆ་འདི་བོད་རང་བཙན་བསྒྲུབ་པ་ལ་གལ་འགངས་ཤིན་ཏུ་ཆེན་པོ་ཡིན། This document is extremely important to prove Tibetan Independence.

གལ་ཆེ་དོན་དམ། to take great care སློབ་ཕྲུག་ཚོའི་ཤེས་ཡོན་ལ་གལ་ཆེ་དམ་དོན་གཟིགས་སྐྱོང་གནང་གལ་ཆེ། One should give great care of to the student's education.

གལ་ཆེ་དུས་གཏུགས། important and urgent དེང་གི་དུས་སུ་བོད་ཀྱི་སྐད་ཡིག་སྦྱོང་རྒྱ་དེ་ནི་གལ་ཆེ་དུས་གཏུགས་ཀྱི་གནས་སྟངས་ཤིག་ཏུ་ཆག་ཡོད། It has become important and urgent to study Tibetan language these days.

གལ་གནད་ཆེན་པོ། very important སློབ་ཕྲུག་གཅིག་ལ་རང་གི་ལག་འཁྱེར་གལ་གནད་ཆེན་པོ་ཞིག་དགག་ཆག་ཡོད། A degree has become very important for a student.

གལ་པོ་ཆེ་ལ་ནན་ཏན་དང་། དམ་པའི་ཆོས་ལ་བརྒྱ་ཆོར། Lit.: to emphasize the important ones and to make a hundred repetitions of a spiritual practice/ Sense implied: to emphasize ཁྱེད་རང་གིས་མཁྱེན་གསལ་རེད། ཡིན་ན་ཡང་གལ་པོ་ཆེ་ལ་ནན་ཏན་དང་དམ་པའི་ཆོས་ལ་བརྒྱ་ཆོར་གྱི་ཆེད་དུ་ཡང་བསྐྱར་ཞུས་པ་ཡིན། It was clear to you, however as to emphasise this I told you again.

གུས་བཀུར་ཡི་རང་། to respect and admire རང་གི་སློབ་དཔོན་ལ་གུས་བཀུར་ཡི་རང་གནང་བ་ནི་བོད་ཀྱི་གོམས་གཤིས་བཟང་པོ་ཞིག་རེད། It is the Tibetan custom to respect and admire one's master.

གུས་བཙི་དགའ་ཞེན། respected and beloved *v* གོང་ས་སྐྱབས་མགོན་ཆེན་ པོར་འཛམ་གླིང་ནང་པ་ཡོངས་ཀྱིས་གུས་བཙི་དགའ་ཞེན་ཉིན་ཏུ་ཆེན་པོ་ཞུ་གི་ཡོད། His Holiness the Dalai Lama is respected and beloved by all Buddhists throughout the world.

གོ་རྒྱུ་ཐོས་རྒྱུ་མེད་པ། to hear nothing about someone བཀྲ་ཤིས་ལགས་ སློབ་གྲྭ་ཐོན་པའི་རྗེས་སུ་གོ་རྒྱུ་ཐོས་རྒྱུ་མེད་པ་ཆགས་སོང་། Since Tashi left the school, nothing has been heard about him

གོ་རྒྱུ་ཆོར་རྒྱུ་མེད་པ། nonsense དོན་དག་གོ་རྒྱུ་ཆོར་རྒྱུ་མེད་པའི་བཀའ་མོལ་དེ་འདྲ་ མ་གནང་། Please do not talk such nonsense.

གོ་དོན་ལེགས་རྟོགས། to understand very well སངས་རྒྱས་ཀྱི་གསུང་རབ་ གོ་དོན་ལེགས་རྟོགས་ཡོང་བ་ལས་སྟ་པོ་མ་རེད། It is not easy to understand well the meaning of the Buddha's teaching.

གོ་བ་ལོག་སྒྲུབ། misinterpretation ཆད་མའི་གཞུང་ལུགས་པོ་མ་ཤེས་ན་སངས་རྒྱས་ ཀྱི་གསུང་ལ་གོ་བ་ལོག་སྒྲུབ་ཡོང་ཉེན་ཡོད། There is a danger of misinterpretating Buddha's teaching if one does not know the presentation of valid cognitions properly.

གོ་མྱོང་ཐོས་མྱོང་། Lit.: to have heard or experience/Sense implied: to have familiarity with རྒན་པོ་གོ་མྱོང་ཐོས་མྱོང་མང་པོ་ཡོད་ པ་ལ་གྲོས་རིས་ན་ལེགས་བཤད་བཟད་ཐོབ་ཀྱི་རེད། One will get a good lesson if one asks an experienced old man.

གོ་ལ་མ་གོ། not hearing clearly/ to have half heard བགག་མོལ་གོ་ལ་ མ་གོ་གནང་ན་ཕན་ཐོགས་མེད། It is useless to engage in discussion that is not heard clearly.

གོང་མཐོར་འགྲོ་ཐབས། means of promoting or advancing/ improving ཤེས་ཡོན་ཡར་རྒྱས་གོང་མཐོར་འགྲོ་ཐབས་སུ་དེབ་སྣ་ཚོགས་སློག་དགོས་པ་ཡིན། It is necessary to read many different books as a means of improving one's educational standard.

གོང་ནས་གོང་དུ། higher and higher/ to promote དཔལ་འབྱོར་གྱི་འཕེལ་རྒྱས་བསྐྱེན་གོང་ནས་གོང་དུ་སྤེལ་བ་ལ་དེང་དུས་ཀྱི་དཔལ་འབྱོར་གྱི་འགྲོ་སྟངས་ཤེས་དགོས་པ་ཡིན། In order to promote economic development, it is necesary to know the modern economic methods.

གོང་བུ་གཅིག་གྱུར། Lit.: to become one solid/ Sense implied: unity/ integrity/ solidarity བོད་མི་ཡོངས་རྫོགས་མཐུན་བསྒྲིལ་གོང་བུ་གཅིག་གྱུར་བྱུང་ན་རང་བཙན་ལོན་པར་ཕན་ཐོགས་ཆེ། It is very useful to have solidarity among the Tibetans for acheiving their Independence.

གོང་བུའི་ནུས་པ། the power of unity/ the spirit of solidarity རྒྱ་ནག་གིས་བོད་རྒྱ་ཆེའི་མང་ཚོགས་ཀྱི་གོང་བུའི་ནུས་པ་གཏོར་ཐབས་བྱས་ཡོད། Chinese have tried to destroy the spirit of Tibetan solidarity.

གོམ་པ་མདུན་སྤོས། Lit.: to step a forward/ Sense implied: to advance ལས་འགུལ་ཡར་རྒྱས་ཡོང་བ་ལ་གོམ་པ་མདུན་ནས་མདུན་དུ་སྤོ་དགོས་པ་ཡིན། It is necessary to advance step by step for the progress of a project.

གོམ་པ་སྔོན་སྤོས། Lit.: to step earlier/ Sense implied: to be ahead འཕྲུལ་ཆས་ཐོག་རྒྱ་ནག་ལས་ཉི་ཧོང་གོམ་པ་གང་སྔོན་སྤོས་བྱས་ཡོད། Japan has taken a step ahead of China in the field of technology.

གོམ་པ་རིམ་བགྲོད། progressing step by step ཆབ་སྲིད་ཀྱི་ནང་དུ་གོམ་པ་རིམ་བགྲོད་གནང་ཐུབ་ན་ཉི་མ་གཅིག་ཏན་ཏན་རྒྱལ་ཁ་ཐོབ་ཐུབ་ཀྱི་རེད། If one progress step by step in politics, one day one will gain victory.

གོམས་པ་ལངས་ཤོར། spoiled habits ཐ་མག་འཐེན་རྒྱུ་སོགས་ལ་གོམས་པ་ལངས་ཤོར་མ་ཆག་པ་གནང་དགོས། One should not indulge in bad habits, like smoking and so forth.

གོམས་གཤིས་ངན་པ། bad habits གོམས་གཤིས་ངན་པ་ཆུང་དུས་ནས་སྤོང་རྒྱུ་ཞེ་དྲག་གལ་ཆེན་པོ་རེད། It is very important to abandon bad habits from childhood.

གོམས་གཤིས་བཟང་པོ། good habits མི་ཚང་ཡ་རབས་ཀྱི་ཕྲུ་གུ་དེ་ཚོ་གོམས་གཤིས་བཟང་པོ་ཞེ་དྲག་ཡོད་རེད། Children from a good family have good habits

གོམས་སྲོལ་རྙིང་པ། old custom བོད་ཀྱི་ལུགས་སྲོལ་རྙིང་པ་ལ་ཆང་སའི་སྔོན་དུ་བུའི་ཁྱིམ་ཚང་ནས་བུ་མོའི་མགོ་ལ་གཡུ་ཞིག་འདོགས་སྲོལ་ཡོད། In the age-old custom of Tibet, a would-be bride is garlanded a torquoise by the boy's family as an engagement gift.

གོས་ལ་གོན་མཁས་བྱས་ན་གོན་རྒྱུ་རྒྱུན་མི་ཆད། ཟས་ལ་ཟ་མཁས་བྱས་ན་ཟ་རྒྱུ་རྒྱུན་མི་ཆད། If one carefully wears clothes, the clothes will never be worn out and if one eats moderately, the food will never run out.

གྱོང་ཕོག་གུན་གསབ། compensation for the loss ལམ་ཟུར་དུ་ཡོད་པའི་ཁང་པ་རྣམས་གཞུང་གིས་བཤིག་པ་སོང་ཙང་གཞུང་ནས་གྱོང་ཕོག་གུན་གསབ་གནང་གི་རེད།

Because the government demolished the houses on the sides of the road, the govt. will give compensation for the loss.

གྱོད་ཚ་པོ། a pretender/ malingerer མི་འདི་ལས་ཀ་བྱེད་དུས་གྱོད་ཚ་པོ་ཞེ་དྲག་འདུག This man malingers at the time of work.

གྲ་རྒྱས་ཕུན་སུམ་ཚོགས་པ། very excellent/ abundance in everything ཚོས་བྱེད་དགེ་འདུན་པ་རྣམས་ལ་གྲ་རྒྱས་ཕུན་སུམ་ཚོགས་པ་མེད་ན་ཡང་འགྱིགས། It doesn't matter for a practitioner even if the facilities are not very excellent.

གྲ་སྒྲིག་ཨྱང་བསར། ever ready/ fully prepared ང་ཚོ་བོད་ལ་འགྲོ་རྒྱར་གྲ་སྒྲིག་ཨྱང་བསར་ཨྱིན། We are fully prepared to go to Tibet.

གྲགས་པ་ཕུལ་བྱུང་། excellent reputation ནོ་བེལ་གཟེངས་དྲགས་ཐོབ་པའི་སྐྱེས་བུ་རྣམས་སུ་གྲགས་པ་ཕུལ་བྱུང་ཐོབ་ཡོད། The noble laureate have gained excellent reputation.

གྲངས་ལས་འདས་པ། countless མི་གྲངས་ལས་འདས་པ་དམག་གི་སྐབས་སུ་བསད་ཡོད། Countless people were killed during the war.

གྲལ་རིམ་འཐབ་རྩོད། class struggle དམངས་གཙོའི་རྒྱལ་ཁབ་ནང་གྲལ་རིམ་འཐབ་རྩོད་རྩ་བ་ནས་མེད། There is no class struggle in a democratic country.

གྱུང་ག་དོད་པོ། alert/ alive སྲུ་སྲུང་བ་རྣམས་ཐག་ཏུ་གྱུང་ག་དོད་པོ་དགོས་པ་ནི་ཨྱིན་ཏུ་གལ་ཆེན་པོ་རེད། It is very important for security guards to be always alert and vigilant.

60

གྲུབ་མཐའ་སྐྱོན་མེད། flawless philosophical school རྒྱུ་མཚན་ཡང་དག

ལྡན་པའི་གྲུབ་མཐའ་རྣམས་གྲུབ་མཐའ་སྐྱོན་མེད་རེད། A philosophical school
with valid reasonings is called a flawless philosophical school.

གྲུབ་མཐའ་རིས་མེད། Lit.: irrespective of the sects/ Sense implied:
ecumenical གྲུབ་མཐའ་རིས་མེད་ལ་སློབ་སྦྱོང་གནང་རྒྱུ་གལ་ཆེན་པོ་རེད། It is
important to study (faith) irrespective of the sects.

གྲུབ་མཐའ་འཐེན་འཁྱེར། biased attitute toward the philosophical
schools/ sectarian གྲུབ་མཐའ་ལ་འཐེན་ཁྱེར་བྱེད་ན་རང་རྒྱུད་ལ་ཉམས་རྟོགས་
སྐྱེ་གི་མ་རེད། Sectarian people cannot actualise realisation.

གྲོགས་ཁ་ནང་བསྐྱབས་པ་ལྕེ་ཡིས་ཕུལ། Lit.: the favour that is coming
to the mouth is pushed away by the tongue/ Sense
implied: to reject an opportunity/to miss an opportunity
ལས་ཀ་ཡག་པོའི་འདུ་ཐོབ་ཀྱང་རང་གིས་མ་བྱེད་པ་ནི་གྲོགས་ཁ་ནང་བསྐྱབས་པ་ལྕེ་ཡིས་

ཕུལ་ཟེར་བ་དང་མཚུངས་སོ།། Not availing of a good job opportunity
of job resembles the favour that has come to the mouth being
pushed away by the tongue.

གྲོགས་མེད་གཅིག་པུ། Lit.: to have no friend/Sense implied:
alone/ loneliness འཆི་བའི་དུས་སུ་གྲོགས་མེད་གཅིག་པུར་འགྲོ་དགོས། One
has to go alone at the time of death.

གྲོང་པའི་བ་ཡི་ཡང་མྱ་ངན་ཞག་གསུམ། Lit.: to mourn three days
even for the death of one's neighbour's cow/ Sense
implied: to respect or share other's suffering, such as
not playing radios and so forth during the misfortune

61

བོད་དུ་གྲོང་པའམ་ཁྱིམ་མཚེས་ཀྱི་བ་ཕྱི་བ་ཡིན་ན་ཡང་ཤུ་ངན་ཤག་གསུམ་བྱེད་པ་རེད། Tibetan people even mourn three days at the death of one's neighbour's cow.

གྲོས་འདྲི་ཞུད་ཞིབ། to consult and examine ལས་དོན་འདིའི་སྐོར་གཞན་ལ་ གྲོས་དེ་ཞུད་ཞིབ་གནང་ན་ཡག་པོ་མཁྱེན་གྱི་རེད། One will gain a good understandiing of the work if one examines it and consults others.

གྲོས་མི་ལ་དྲིས། ཐག་རང་གིས་གཅོད། consult others and make one's own decision

གླང་ཆེན་རྒྱབ་ཁལ་བེའུ་ལ་འགེལ། Lit.: to load a calf with an elephant load/ Sense implied: to over load somebody/exploitation ཕྲུ་གུ་ལོ་བཅུ་བཞི་ལ་ངལ་རྩོལ་སྤྱལ་བ་ནི་གླང་ ཆེན་རྒྱབ་འཁེལ་བེའུ་ལ་འཁེལ་བ་དང་གཅིག་པ་ཡིན། Engaging in the labour at the age of fourteen is to over load or exploit children.

སྐྱིད་ཁའི་ཉིན་ལས་ལྟོགས་པ་མེད། གཟབ་སྟོས་ཉིན་ལས་གྲང་བ་མེད། There is no greater hunger than at a picnic; there is no greater cold than in the new dress/

གླུ་ཡིན་བྲོ་འཁྲབ། to sing and dance ལོ་གསར་སྐབས་ཀུན་གཞན་ཆང་མས་གླུ་ ཡིན་བྲོ་འཁྲབ་བྱེད་ཀྱི་རེད། Everyone will dance and sing during Losar.

སྐྱེན་པ་ཀླུ་ཆུགས། a fool's persuasion ལས་དོན་གང་ཡིན་ན་ཡང་སྐྱེན་པ་ཀླུ་ ཆུགས་བྱ་མི་རུང་། One should not engage in a fool's persuasion whatever kind of job it may be.

སློ་བར་མ་ཕན་མཆིན་པའི་དུག Lit.: it did not help the lungs but it poisoned the liver/ Sense implied: Instead of help it became a harm to somebody.

སློ་བུར་ཐོབ་རྒྱག suddenly ངའི་གྲོགས་པོ་སློ་བུར་ཐོབ་རྒྱག་འགའ་མི་ཉག་ནས་འབྱོར་སོང་། My friend suddenly returned from Ga Mi-nyag.

སློ་བུར་དྲག་གནོན། sudden represion/sudden attack དགྲ་ཕྱོགས་ནས་སློ་བུར་དྲག་གནོན་ག་དུས་བྱེད་མིན་ཤེས་ཁག་པོ་རེད། It is difficult to know when there will be sudden repression by the enemy.

དགའ་སྐྱོ་ཟུང་འབྲེལ། དགའ་སྐྱོ་འཛིས་མ། a mixture of joy and sorrow ལོ་མང་པོའི་རྗེས་ལ་མར་རང་གི་བུ་ཕྲག་ན་དགའ་སྐྱོ་ཟུང་འབྲེལ་ཡོང་གི་རེད། There will be a mixture of joy and sorrow when a mother meets her son after a long time.

དགའ་དགའ་སྐྱིད་སྐྱིད། དགའ་དགའ་སྟོ་སྟོ། དགའ་མགུ་ཡི་རང་། happily/joyfully/ rejoicingly བོད་མི་ཆང་མ་ལོ་གསར་སྐབས་དགའ་དགའ་སྐྱིད་སྐྱིད་ངང་སྤྱོད་ཀྱི་རེད། All Tibetans live happily during Losar.

དགའ་སྐྱོམ་ཆོག་ཤེས། to be happy and be contented/to be satisfied and pleased རང་ལ་གང་ཡོད་པ་དེ་ལ་དགའ་སྐྱོམ་ཆོག་ཤེས་བྱེད་པ་ཉམས་ལེན་རེད། It is a religious practice to be satisfied with what one has.

དགའ་སྟོན་རྟེན་འབྲེལ། celebration ངའི་གཅེན་མོའི་ཆང་སའི་དགའ་སྟོན་རྟེན་འབྲེལ་སང་ཉིན་རེད། Tomorrow is my sister's marriage celebration.

དགའ་པོ་ཉེ་པོ། close friends and well wishers ང་ཚོ་ཆུང་ཆུང་ནས་ཕན་ ཚུན་དགའ་པོ་ཉེ་པོ་རེད། We were close friends from childhood on.

དགའ་སྤྲོ་འཁོལ་བ། bubbled over with joy གནས་ཚུལ་བཟང་པོ་དེ་གོ་ནས་ བོད་མི་ཚང་མ་དགའ་སྤྲོ་རབ་ཏུ་འཁོལ་སོང་། All Tibetans bubbled with joy when they heard the good news.

དགའ་མིན་དགའ་མདོག to be biased མང་ཚོགས་ཀྱི་དབུ་ཁྲིད་ནི་དགའ་མིན་དགའ་ མདོག་མི་བྱེད་མཁན་དེ་འདྲ་དགོས་པ་ཨིན། Public leaders should be unbiased

དགེ་རྒན་བཟང་པོའི་དགེ་ཕྲུག ཕ་མ་བཟང་པོའི་བུ་ཕྲུག Lit.: students of a good teacher; children of a good parents/ Sense implied: A student will be as his teacher and a child will be as his parents/ an example of goodness/ This is used to appreciate someone's children or students.

དགེ་འདོན་སྐྱོན་སེལ། constructive suggestions and criticism གསར་ འགོད་པ་དྲང་པོ་ཡོད་ན་དགེ་འདོན་སྐྱོན་སེལ་གནང་དགོས། One should give constructive suggestion and criticism if the news writers are honest.

དགེ་སྡིག་དཀར་ནག Lit.: white virtues and black non-virtues/ Sense implied: good and bad/positive and negative མཁས་ པས་ལས་དགེ་སྡིག་དཀར་ནག་ནམ་ཡང་ནོར་གྱི་མ་རེད། Scholars will never mistake the positive and negative action.

དགེ་བཤད་སྡིག་བཀྲོལ། Lit.: to explain virtues and to release

(from) non-virtues/ Sense implied: to show what is right and wrong དགེ་བའི་བཤེས་གཉེན་གྱི་ལས་འགན་ནི་དགེ་བསྡུད་སྡིག་བསྒྲལ་གནང་རྒྱུ་དེ་ཡིན་པ་རེད། It is the duty of the spiritual master to show what is right from wrong.

དགོངས་པ་གཅིག་པ། same opinion, assertion, thought and interpretation བཀའ་འགྱུར་དང་བསྟན་འགྱུར་གྱི་དགོངས་པ་གཅིག་པ་རེད། The interpretations of the Kangyur and Tangyur are same.

དགོངས་དག་ཞུགས་བཞིན། to beg one's pardon honestly/to ask for forgiveness ཁ་སང་དུས་ར་བཀྱབ་པ་ནང་བཞིན་ཡོང་ཐུབ་མ་སོང་། དགོངས་དག་ཞུགས་བཞིན་ཞུ་གི་ཡོད། Yesterday I could not come to our appointment for which I beg pardon.

དགོངས་པ་དཔྱིས་ཕྱིན་པ། complete thought སངས་རྒྱས་ཀྱི་དགོངས་པ་དཔྱིས་ཕྱིན་པ་མི་ཕལ་པས་ཤེས་ཐུབ་ཀྱི་མ་རེད། An ordinary man cannot understand the complete thought of Buddha.

དགོངས་པ་རང་ཞུས། Lit.: no way but to resign ཁོང་གིས་གཞུང་དངུལ་བར་བཅོས་བྱས་ཚང་དགོངས་པ་རང་ཞུས་བྱེད་དགོས་ཐུག There is no way but to resign for he was involved in the misuse of government money.

དགོངས་རྫོགས་རྗེས་དྲན། death anniversary ནང་པ་ཆོས་མས་སངས་རྒྱས་ཤཀྱ་ཐུབ་པའི་དགོངས་རྫོགས་ལོ་བསྒྱུར་རྗེས་དྲན་ཞུ་བ་རེད། All Buddhists annually commemorate the Mahaparinirvana of Buddha Shakyamuni.

དགོངས་བཞེད་ཆད་མེད། to give great consideration ཨ་མེ་རི་ཁ་གཞུང་

གིས་བོད་མི་ཚོ་ལ་དགོངས་བཞེད་ཆེན་མེད་གནང་ཡོད་རེད། The united States government gave great consideration to the Tibetans.

དགོས་མཁོའི་ཅ་ལག necessary things/ necessity སྐྱིད་ཁའི་སྔོན་ལ་དགོས་ མཁོའི་ཅ་ལག་ཆང་མ་ནོས་ཤོག Buy all the necessary things before the picnic.

དགོས་མཁོ་སྟེང་རེས། self-suffient ཉེ་ཧོང་ནི་དགོས་མཁོ་སྟེང་རེས་ཀྱི་རྒྱལ་ཁབ་ གཅིག་རེད། Japan is a self-sufficient nation.

དགོས་འདོད་ཀུན་འབྱུང་། a wish fulfilling gem ནོར་བུ་དགོས་འདོད་ཀུན་ འབྱུང་ལ་གསོལ་བ་ཅི་བཏབ་ཀྱང་འགྲུབ་ཀྱི་རེད། Whatever prayer one makes before the wish-fulfilling gem will be fulfilled.

དགོས་པ་དགེ་ཚན། purpose/significance/benefit ཚོས་སྐྱངས་ནས་དགོས་ པ་དགེ་མཚན་ག་རེ་ཡོད་རེད། What is the purpose of studying dharma.

དགོས་མེད་མཛེས་ཚོས། unnecessary decoration/ elaboration ཤྲ་ ཁག་ནང་དུ་དགོས་མེད་མཛེས་ཚོས་དེ་འདྲ་མཐོང་རྒྱུ་མེད། One cannot find unnecessary decorations in a monk's quarter.

དགྲ་ག་དུས་ཡོང་དང་བུ་ནམ་སྐྱེས་མི་ཤེས། Lit.: nobody knows when the enemy will come or a son will be born/ Sense implied: everything is so uncertain or one should be ever ready

དགྲ་གཉེན་གོ་ལྡོག to mistake an enemy from a friend and vice

versa དགྲ་གཉེན་གོ་སློག་གི་བསམ་ཚུལ་དེ་ཉེན་ཁ་ཆ་པོ་རེད། The thought of taking an enemy for a friend and vice versa is very dangerous.

དགྲ་གཉེན་དབྱེ་འབྱེད། to distinguish enemy from friend སངས་རྒྱས་ལ་དགྲ་གཉེན་དབྱེ་འབྱེད་ཀྱི་ཕྱགས་བསམ་མེད། Buddha does not distinguish an enemy from friend.

དགྲ་གཉེན་མགོན་གསུམ། an enemy, a friend and a protector མི་ཡིན་པའི་ཆ་ནས་དགྲ་གཉེན་མགོན་དསུམ་མ་ནོར་བ་བྱེད་དགོས་རེད། Being humans one should not mistake an enemy, a friend and a protector.

དགྲ་འདུལ་གཉེན་སྐྱོང་། to conquer one's enemy and protect one's friends གཞུང་གི་སྲིད་བྱུས་ནི་དགྲ་འདུལ་གཉེན་སྐྱོང་གི་སྲིད་བྱུས་ཤིག་ཡིན། The government policy is to conquer one's enemy and protect one's friends.

དགྲ་བོའི་བྲན་གཡོག Lit.: enemy's servant/ Sense implied: slave དགྲ་བོའི་བྲན་གཡོག་བྱེད་པ་ལས་ཤི་བ་དགའ། It is better to die than to become a slave of one's enemy.

དགྲ་མ་ཡོང་གོང་ནས་མཚོན་ཆ། Lit.: the arms should be ready before the enemy arrives/ Sense implied: making preparations in advance

དགྲ་མིས་བསད་པའི་མགོ་ལག Lit.: the head and arms of an enemy killed by others/ Sense implied: to claim credit for other's work དགྲ་མིས་བསད་པའི་མགོ་ལག་ལ་རང་གི་བྱས་རྗེས་སུ་ངོམས་པ་ནི་ཐ

67

འལ་རེད། Claiming credit for other's work is a very low deed.

མགོ་བསྐོར་བརྐུས་བཅོས། to deceive and insult གཞན་ལ་མགོ་བསྐོར་དང་བརྐུས་བཅོས་མ་གཏོང་། Do not deceive and insult others.

མགོ་ཆག་ཆག་ཁྲག་ཤོན། Lit.: to bleed from a cracked head/ Sense implied: to be beaten until one bleeds ར་བཞི་སྐྱབས་མགོ་ཆག་ཁྲག་ཤོན་བྱུང་ན་ཡང་ཏུ་གོ་གི་མ་རེད། In the state of intoxication, one will not know even if one has been beaten bloodedly.

མགོ་མཇུག་བར་གསུམ། from the beginning to the end སྙིང་རྗེ་ནི་བྱང་ཆུབ་ཀྱི་སེམས་བསྐྱེད་པར་མགོ་མཇུག་བར་གསུམ་དུ་གལ་ཆེ་བ་ཡིན། Compassion is very important for the generation of Bodhicitta from the beginning to end.

མགོ་བདེ་པོས་ཞྭ་མོ་བརྐྱགས། Lit.: a clever man losing his hat/ Sense implied: the defeat of a clever man

མགོ་འབུལ་ལུས་འབུལ། Lit.: to offer one's head and body/ Sense implied: to surrender everything after the defeat of a war དམག་བརྒྱབས་ནས་ཕམ་ན་དགྲ་ལ་མི་འདོད་བཞིན་དུ་མགོ་འབུལ་ལུས་འབུལ་ཞུ་དགོས་རེད། If the war is defeated one has to surrender everything to the enemy against one's wish.

མགོ་མེད་མཇུག་མེད། Lit.: no beginning; no end/ Sense implied: disorder/lack of discipline or incomplete ལས་ཀ་མགོ་མེད་མཇུག་མེད་དེ་འདྲ་བྱེད་ན་སུས་ཀྱང་ཡིད་ཆེས་བྱེད་ཀྱི་མ་རེད། If you do such incomplete work no one will trust you.

མགོ་རྡུལ་རྣ་བས་མ་ཚོར། Lit.: unknown to the ear about the rotten head/ Sense implied: very careless/ not knowing what is happening nearby

མགོ་ལ་མེ་འོར་ཡང་ཕྱུར་ལོང་མེད་པ། Lit.: no time to rub one's head even if it catches fire/ Sense implied: to be very busy ཆང་ སའི་རྗེས་ལ་མགོ་ལ་མེ་འོར་ཡང་ཕྱུར་ལོང་ཡོང་གི་མ་རེད། After marriage one will not have time to rub one's head even it catches fire.

མགོ་ལས་རྨ་ཆེ་བ། Lit.: a sore bigger than the head/ Sense implied: to commit a serious blunder ལས་འགུལ་གྱི་འཆར་གཞི་ ནོར་ན་མགོ་ལས་རྨ་ཆེ་བ་བཟོ་ཉེན་ཡོད་རེད། If one makes a mistake in the planning of project, it might become a blunder, like making a sore bigger than the head.

མགོན་མེད་སྐྱབས་མེད། Lit.: without protector and refuge/ Sense implied: in a critical situation/ poor and down trodden དཀོན་མཆོག་གསུམ་ནི་མགོན་མེད་སྐྱབས་མེད་རྣམས་ཀྱི་མགོན་སྐྱབས་རེད། The Three-Jewels are the protector of all the poor and down trodden people.

མགྱོགས་མགྱོགས་བྱས་ན་འགོར་འགོར། work done in haste always takes more time/ Whenever one does work in hurry, it is normally not done in a good way. Therefore one has to it again. Then of course it will take more time to complete the work. In such cases we use this expression.

འགོ་སྟོད་ལ་ཇ་གསར། infatuation with novelty in the beginning ལས་ཀར་མགོ་སྟོད་ལ་ཇ་གསར་བྱས་ཀྱང་མཇུག་སྐྱེལ་མཁན་དཀོན་པོ་རེད། People

69

are infatuated with the novelty of a project in the beginning but it is rare to find someone who will complete it.

མགོ་འདོན་འཚོ་སྐྱོང་། to care for & to bring up ཕ་མས་ཕྲུ་གུར་མགོ་འདོན་ འཚོ་སྐྱོང་གནང་བ་རེད། Parents care for and bring up their children

འགྱེལ་བའི་ཐོག་ལ་རྡོག་རྗེས། Lit.: to stamp on the fallen/ Sense implied:to torture and insult someone in difficulty/ This is used when someone in difficulty is tortured and insulted. ཁོང་རང་ན་བའི་སྐྱང་ལ་ལས་ཀ་ནས་ཕྱིར་འབུད་པ་ནི་འགྱེལ་བའི་ཐོག་ལ་ རྡོག་རྗེས་རེད། On the top of being ill, he was dismissed from the job. This is to torture someone in difficulty.

འགྲན་ཟླ་བྲལ་བ། Lit.: matchless/ Sense implied: incomparable/ excellent ཁོང་གསུང་བཤད་གནང་རྒྱུ་ལ་འགྲན་ཟླ་དང་བྲལ་བ་རེད། He is excellent in giving speeches.

འགུལ་ལམ་སུམ་མདོ། intersection/road-crossing (meeting place of three roads) འགུལ་ལམ་སུམ་མདོར་ཇ་ཁང་ཡག་པོ་གཅིག་འདུག There is a good tea-stall at the intersection of three roads.

འགྲོ་བཟོ་སྟོད་མཁས། wise manner of living in a society སྐྱེ་ཚོགས་ ནང་འགྲོ་བཟོ་སྟོད་མཁས་ཤེས་ན་གྲུང་པོ་ཡིན། One who knows the wise manner of living in a society is called wise person.

འགྲོ་སྟངས་སྤྱོད་སྟངས། how to manage in one's life ཕ་མས་རང་གི་ཕྲུ་ གུར་འགྲོ་སྟངས་སྤྱོད་སྟངས་སློབ་སྟོན་གནང་གི་རེད། Parents guide their children in how to manage their lives.

70

འགྲོ་བདེ་སྡོད་བདེ། very convenient to go or stay མི་གཅིག་པུ་ཡིན་ན་འགྲོ་ བདེ་སྡོད་བདེ་ཞེ་དྲག་རེད། It is very convenient to go or stay if you are alone.

འགྲོ་བའི་མི་ལ་སྡོད་པའི་སེམས་མེད། a traveller has no mind to stay/ somewhat sarcastic remark

འགྲོ་རོགས་འདུག་རོགས། a companion or a friend ང་ལ་འགྲོ་རོགས་ འདུག་རོགས་ཞི་མི་གཅིག་མ་གཏོགས་མེད། I have no one but a cat as my friend or companion.

རྒན་མོ་གསེར་འཁུར་གྱི་དུས། Lit.: time of an old woman who carries gold at her back/ Sense implied: time free of social menace/ This proverb is used to indicate the good old days when even an old woman could travel safely with gold at her back.

རྒན་ཁ་གཞོན་ཉན། the young obedient to the old རྒན་ཁ་གཞོན་ཉན་བྱེད་ ན་ཡ་རབས་རེད། It is well mannered to be obedient to elders.

རྒས་དུ་རྒས་དུ། to become older and older ང་ཚོས་མ་ཤེས་པ་མ་གཏོགས་ཏེ་ མ་རེ་རེ་ནས་རྒས་དུ་རྒས་དུ་འགྲོ་གི་ཡོད་པ་རེད། Although we are not aware of it, we are becoming older day by day

རྒོལ་འཛིང་སྨུ་མཐུད། continuous fight དགྲ་པོ་རྒྱ་ནག་ལ་རྒོལ་འཛིང་སྨུ་མཐུད་ ནས་བྱེད་ན་ཉི་མ་གཅིག་ང་ཚོ་ལ་རྒྱལ་ཁ་ཐོབ་ཀྱི་རེད། If we continuously fight against the Chinese, one day we will certainly get the victory.

རྒྱ་མཚོ་སྐམ་ནུས་ན་སྦྱལ་པ་ཤི་ནུས། Lit.: if the ocean can dry, frogs can die/ Sense implied: if the higher ones can sacrifice why not the lower ones

རྒྱ་མཚོ་རྒྱུ་ཐིག་གི་འབྲེལ་བ། Lit.: relation of a drop in the ocean/ Sense implied: to make karmic connection བླ་མ་བཟང་པོ་དང་རྒྱ་མཚོ་རྒྱུ་ཐིག་གི་འབྲེལ་བ་གནང་རྒྱུ་གལ་ཆེན་པོ་རེད། It is important to make a karmic connection with a good lama.

རྒྱ་མཚོར་རྡོ་རྡུགས། Lit.: to throw a stone in the ocean/ Sense implied: not to give any kind of response/ indifferent བོད་པ་གཅིག་ཡིན་པའི་ཆ་ནས་བོད་དོན་སྐོར་ལ་རྒྱ་མཚོར་རྡོ་རྡུགས་ནང་བཞིན་བྱེད་ན་ཡག་པོ་ཡོད་པ་མ་རེད། As a Tibetan it is not good to remain indifferent towards the Tibetan cause.

རྒྱུ་ཐུབ་མ་འདུས་པ། unmanageable རྒྱུ་ཐུབ་མ་འདུས་པའི་ལས་ཀ་ལ་ལག་པ་མ་ཆང་། Do not touch an unmanageable work.

རྒྱབ་གཅིག་མཆོངས་གཅིག Lit.: to hit and jump at one time/ Sense implied: not to have a second thought བོད་རང་བཙན་གྱི་དོན་ལ་ཐུག་དུས་བོད་མི་ཆང་མས་བསམ་བློ་རྒྱག་གཅིག་མཆོངས་གཅིག་དགོས་པ་ཡིན། For the Independence of Tibet, no Tibetan should have a second thought.

རྒྱགས་པ་རིལ་རིལ། pudgy/ fat and short/stout གར་མཁན་རྒྱགས་པ་རིལ་རིལ་དེ་སྙིང་རྗེ་པོ་མི་འདུག The pudgy dancer is not beautiful.

རྒྱབ་སྐྱོར་ཡོད་མེད། to have support or not ལས་འགུལ་ཆག་ཚུད་མིན་རྒྱབ་

སྐོར་ཡོད་མེད་ལ་རག་ལུས་པ་རེད། The success of a project depends upon whether one has support or not.

རྒྱབ་རྟེན་དབང་གཉེན། to have support, power and friendship སྔོན་མ་རྒྱ་ནག་ལ་ཨུ་རུ་སུའི་རྒྱབ་རྟེན་དབང་གཉེན་ཡོད། Chinese had support, power and friendship with Russia in the past

རྒྱབ་མདུན་རྫོ་སློག insincere/hypocrisy ལས་ཀ་རྒྱབ་མདུན་རྫོ་སློག་བྱེད་རྒྱུ་ཡོད་མ་རེད། One should not be insincere in one's work.

རྒྱལ་བསྟན་སླར་གསོ། revival of Buddhism བོད་རང་བཙན་ཐོབ་པའི་རྗེས་སུ་རྒྱལ་བསྟན་སླར་གསོ་ཐུབ་ངེས་ཡིན། It is definite that the revival of Buddhism is possible after the Tibetan Independence.

སྐུ་སྐར་དབུས་ན་ཟླ་བ་འཁར། Lit.: the moon rising among the stars/ Sense implied: the moon outshines the other stars/ This is used to show someone is matchless. སངས་རྒྱས་ཤཱཀྱ་ཐུབ་པ་སྟོན་པ་ཐམས་ཅད་ཀྱི་མཆོག་ཏུ་གྱུར་པ་དེ་རེད། དཔེར་ན་སྐུ་སྐར་དབུས་ན་ཟླ་བ་བཞིན་ནོ། Shakya Thupba was the best teacher just like moon among the stars.

རྒྱུ་རྫས་རྗེས་འབྲངས། Lit.: one who follows wealth and gifts/ Sense implied: very greedy/ རྒྱུ་རྫས་རྗེས་འབྲངས་ཁོ་ན་བྱེད་ན་རྒྱུ་མ་གཏོགས་གང་ཡང་ཐོབ་ཀྱི་མ་རེད། If you just follow wealth, you will get nothing except wealth.

རྒྱུ་ཆ་མཁོ་སྒྲུབ། to procure necessities/ collections required for project དགོན་པ་བཞེངས་རྒྱུའི་རྒྱུ་ཆ་མཁོ་སྒྲུབ་ཀྱི་ཆེད་དུ་ང་ལ་མི་གཉིས་དགོས། I need two persons for the procurement of necessities for the construction of a monastery.

རྒྱུ་མ་ཆད་ནས་གསོན་རེ། Lit.: hoping to be alive though the intestines are torn/ Sense implied: hope to the last བོད་རང་ བཙན་གྱི་དོན་དུ་རྒྱུ་མ་ཆད་ན་ཡང་གསོན་རེ་བྱེད་དགོས་པ་ཡིན། Even when someone is nearing death, he should have hope for Tibetan Independence.

རྒྱུ་རྐྱེན་མེད་པ། without causes and conditions རྒྱུ་མེད་རྐྱེན་མེད་ལས་ ཆོས་གཅིག་ཀྱང་བྱུང་བ་མེད། No phenomenon arises without causes and conditions.

རྒྱག་པ་ལེབ་བརྡང་། Lit.: beating indiscriminately/ Sense implied: equal treatment (with respect to punishment) without judging what is right or wrong བདག་དཔྱད་མ་གནང་ བར་རྒྱག་པ་ལེབ་བརྡང་གནང་ན་ཡག་པོ་མ་རེད། It is not good to beat indiscriminately without investigation.

སྒོང་བརྐུས་ན་བྱ་དེ་བརྐུ། Lit.: One who steals an egg will steal a hen too/ There is a Tibetan way of saying that to steal an egg is a sign one will become a thief when one becomes an adult. (Just to express this we use this proverb.)

སྒོང་ངས་རྟ་འཕྱགས། lit : an egg suppports (lifts) a horse/ Sense implied: the strength of honesty or justice/ an example of justice

བརྒྱ་ཁ་གཅིག་གཙོད། Lit.: a hundred mouths over-powered by one/ Sense implied: minority rule/ minority in power

བརྒྱ་འགྲོ་སྟོང་འགྲོ། Lit.: to go by hundreds and thousands/ Sense implied: a sign to show many to and fro travellers

རྒྱ་བོད་ཀྱི་བར་ལ་འགྲུལ་པ་བརྒྱ་འགྲོ་སྟོང་འགྲོ་ཡོད་པ་རེད། There are hundreds and thousands of travellers between Tibet and China.

བརྒྱ་ཆ་བརྒྱ་ཐམ་པ། hundred percent ཁོང་གི་གསར་འགྱུར་དེ་བརྒྱ་ཆ་བརྒྱ་ཐམ་པ་ བདེན་པ་རེད། His news is hundred percent true.

བརྒྱ་ནང་ནས་བསྒྲུགས། སྟོང་ནང་ནས་བདམས། Lit.:to pick out and select from among hundreds and thousands/ Sense implied: best selected candidates

བརྒྱ་ཕྲག་སྟོང་ཕྲག Lit.: hundreds and thousands/ Sense implied: many/ in large number རྒྱ་མིས་བོད་མི་སྟོང་ཕྲག་མང་པོ་དམར་གསོད་བཏང་ བ་རེད། The Chinese killed thousands of Tibetans.

བརྒྱ་བཤད་སྟོང་བཤད། Lit.: to say hundreds and thousands/ Sense implied: beating around the bush ལས་ཀ་ཡག་པོ་མ་བྱེད་ན་ བརྒྱ་བཤད་སྟོང་བཤད་བྱེད་པས་ཕན་ཐོགས་གང་ཡང་མེད། If one does not work sincerely it is of no use in beating around the bush.

བསློ་བ་རྣར་གཅོན། Lit.: irritating to the ear/ Sense implied: not listening to གཞུང་གི་བཀའ་ལ་བསློ་བ་རྣར་གཟོན་བྱེད་ན་ཉེན་ཁ་ཆེན་པོ་ ཡོད། There is a great danger if one (does not listen to the government's order) takes government's order irritating to the ear.

ང་འགྲོ་ཁོ་འགྲོ། Lit.: I will go/ He will go/ Sense implied: to have a rush of volunteers སྔོན་མ་ཡིན་ན་ལས་ཀ་བྱེད་དུས་ང་འགྲོ་ཁོ་འགྲོ་ ཟེར་ནས་དང་བླངས་མང་པོ་ཡོང་གི་ཡོད། In the past there used to be many volunteers for work; saying that I will do; he will do.

ང་རྒྱལ་ཁེངས་དྲེགས། proud and arrogant ང་རྒྱལ་ཁེངས་དྲེགས་བྱེད་ན་ཡོན་ དན་ཐོབ་ཀྱི་མ་རེད། One cannot gain knowledge with pride and arrogance.

ང་རྒྱལ་ཞེ་སྡང་། arrogance, hatred and anger ང་རྒྱལ་ཞེ་སྡང་བྱེད་པས་ དོན་མི་འགྲུབ། One cannot serve ones purpose with hatred, arrogance and anger.

ངང་རྒྱུན་རིང་པོ། tolerant people/ quiet people བོད་མི་རྣམས་སྤྱིར་སྐྱངས་ ངང་རྒྱུན་བཟང་པོ་ཡོད་པ་རེད། In general Tibetans are quiet people

ངང་རྒྱུན་སྒུང་སྒུང་། short tempered ངང་རྒྱུན་སྒུང་སྒུང་བྱེད་ན་དོན་ཆེན་འགྲུབ་ཐུབ་ ཀྱི་མ་རེད། One cannot accomplish great things with a short tempered mentality.

ངང་རྒྱུད་བཟང་པོ། good nature བུ་མོ་ངང་རྒྱུན་བཟང་པོ་རྣམས་ཡིད་ལ་འགྲོ་པོ་ཞེ་ དྲག་ཡོང་། Good natured girls are very attractive.

ངན་པ་ཁ་བསྒྲིལ། to unite the evil persons ངན་པ་ཁ་བསྒྲིལ་ན་བཟང་པོ་བདེ་ མི་ཆགས། If evil persons unite there is no peace for good people.

ངན་པར་རོ་བསྟུང་། to flatter evil persons ངན་པར་རོ་བསྟུང་བྱེད་པ་ནི་འཛིན་ སྐྱོང་གི་སྐྱོན་ཆེ་ཤོས་གཅིག་རེད། One of the most serious shortcomings of an administration is to flatter evil persons

ངན་པ་གཉའ་རྗེངས། evil persons becoming very strong or proud/ This is used when there is disorder in a society where the evil persons become very strong.

ངན་པ་ཆོར་མ་བཅད་ན། བཟང་པོ་སྐྱོ་བ་མི་སྐྱེ། If evil persons are not defeated, the good people cannot feel happiness.

ངན་པ་ལངས་ཤོར། indulged in bad habit/bad habit ཆང་རག་འཐུང་ རྒྱར་ངན་པ་ལངས་ཤོར་མ་ཆག་པ་གནང་དགོས། One should not indulge in the bad habit of drinking alcohol

ངན་པས་རང་བསྟོད། ཁ་ཏས་སྐྱོ་བསྟོད། Lit.: Evil persons praise themselve as crows praise their feathers./ This proverb is used to appraise for self-praise

ངན་བྱས་རོ་གསོ། to appraise one's own evil deeds མི་སྡུག་ཅག་རྣམས་ ཀྱིས་ངན་བྱས་ལ་རོ་གསོ་གཏོང་གི་རེད། Evil people will appraise their evil deeds.

ངན་བྱས་སྣ་དགུ Lit.: nine various evil deeds/Sense implied:

77

exploitations or atrocities deeds རྒྱ་མིས་བོད་པར་ངན་བྱུས་སྣ་ཚོགས་བཏང་བ་རེད། Chinese exploited Tibetans in various evil deeds.

ངན་ལན་ངན་འཇལ། ངན་ལན་དན་སློན། tit for tat བློ་སྦྱོང་གི་ཉམས་ལེན་ནང་ལ་ངན་ལན་ངན་འཇལ་གྱི་བསླབ་བྱ་གསུངས་ཡོད་པ་མ་རེད། Tit for tat instruction is not said in the thought transformation texts.

ངན་ལན་བཟང་འཇལ། opposite of tit for tat/ to repay the evil with kindness ངན་ལན་བཟང་གིས་འཇལ་དགོས་པ་དེ་བློ་སྦྱོང་གི་ཉམས་ལེན་ནང་དུ་གསུངས་ཡོད་པ་རེད། To repay the evil with kindness is said in the practice of thought transformation.

ངན་སེམས་རྒྱུན་བཅངས། to have always evil thought/always harbouring bad thought ངན་སེམས་རྒྱུན་འཆང་བྱེད་ན་རང་གི་བསོད་ནམས་རང་གིས་ཟད་འགྲོ་གི་རེད། If one always harbour bad thought one's fortune will diminish naturally.

ངང་ངམ་ཤུགས་ཤུགས། natural urge/ involuntarily/ automatically/spontaneously ང་རང་ཚོ་ལ་བསམ་བློ་ངན་པ་ཉམས་ངང་ངམ་ཤུགས་ཀྱིས་སྐྱེ་གི་རེད། Bad thoughts spontaneously arise in us.

ངར་ཤུགས་ཆེན་པོ། full of anger and spirit/angry and forceful

ངལ་བ་ཁྱད་བསད། meeting the challenge of hardship with courage/willingly bearing hardships སློབ་སྦྱོང་གནང་དུས་ངལ་བ་ཁྱད་དུ་བསད་དེ་དཀའ་ལས་བརྒྱན་དགོས། One should put effort to meet the hardship with courage at the time of learning.

ངལ་བ་སྟོང་ཟད། attempt becoming useless བསམ་བློ་ཡག་པོ་མ་བཏང་ན་ ངལ་བ་སྟོང་ཟད་དུ་འགྲོ་སྲིད་པ་རེད། If one does not think properly, there is a possibility that one's attempt might become useless.

ད་འབོད་འོ་དོད། a cry in lamentation/crying desperately for help དཀའ་ངལ་འཕྲད་དུས་དུ་འབོད་འོ་དོད་བྱེད་པས་ཅི་ལ་ཕན། What is the use of crying desperately for help when one is in calamity?

ངོ་རྒོལ་སྐྱེར་ལངས། uprising/ demonstrations against somebody/rebellion བོད་རྒྱལ་ཁབ་ཀྱིས་ངོ་རྒོལ་སྐྱེར་ལངས་ཐེངས་སོ་ལྔ་པ་ དེ་དལོ་འཁེལ་གྱི་འདུག The 35th national uprising of Tibet falls this year.

ངོ་དགའ་སྐྱེལ་ལད། sycophancy/ flattery ང་ངོ་དགའ་སྐྱེལ་ལད་བྱེད་མཁན་ལ་ དགའ་པོ་མེད། I don't like those who flatter.

ངོ་ཆེན་ངོ་ཆུང་། nepotism/favouritism འཛམ་གླིང་གི་སྤྱི་ཚོགས་ཆང་མར་ངོ་ ཆེན་ངོ་ཆུང་བྱེད་མཁན་མང་པོ་ཡོད་རེད། In every society of the world, there are people who indulge in nepotism.

ངོ་གཉེར་མ། མིག་མཆི་མ། Lit.: wrinkled face and tearful eyes/ Sense implied: an indication of suffering and unhappiness གཞིས་ལུས་བོད་མི་མང་ཆེ་བ་ངོ་གཉེར་མ་དང་མིག་མཆི་མས་ ཁེངས་འདུག Most of the Tibetan faces in Tibet are full of tears and wrinkles.

ངོ་བོ་དབྱེར་མེད། inseparable nature རང་གི་རླ་མ་དང་ཡི་དམ་ངོ་བོ་དབྱེར་མེད་དུ་

བསྟེན། One should cultivate the inseparable nature of one's Lama and the deity.

རོ་ཚ་ཁ་སྐྱེངས། embarrassment རྫུན་ཐེར་འདོན་བྱེད་དགོས་བྱུང་ན་རོ་ཚ་ཁ་སྐྱེངས་ ཆག་གི་རེད། If the need arises to point out the lie, it would be very embarassing.

རོ་ཚ་ཁྲེལ་མེད། lack of embarrassment and shame རོ་ཚ་ཁྲེལ་མེད་ཀྱི་ མི་རྣམས་ལ་སྤྱི་ཚོགས་ཀྱི་ནང་དུ་ས་ཆ་མེད། There is no place in a society for those people who lack embarassment and shame.

རོ་ཚ་ཁྲེལ་གཞུང་ཡོད་པ། to have a sense of embarrassment and shame རོ་ཚ་ཁྲེལ་གཞུང་ཡོད་པ་རྣམས་ལ་ཡ་རབས་ཟེར། He who has a sense of embarrassment and shame is called decent.

རོ་ཚ་སྙིན་པོ། shy/not open སློབ་སྦྱོང་གནང་དུས་རོ་ཚ་སྙིན་པོ་གནང་རྒྱུ་ཡོད་མ་རེད། One should not feel shy at the time of study.

རོ་ཚ་དམའ་འབེབས། to defame and humiliate གཞན་ལ་རོ་ཚ་དམའ་ འབེབས་མ་བྱེད། Do not defame and humiliate others.

དངོས་བརྒྱུད་ཅི་རིགས། either directly or indirectly གཞན་ལ་དངོས་ བརྒྱུད་ཅི་རིགས་ཀྱི་སྐྱ་ནས་ཕན་པ་བསྒྲུབ་དགོས། One should help others either directly or indirectly.

དངོས་དངོས་རྗེན་རྗེན། very clearly ཁོང་ལ་དངོས་དངོས་རྗེན་རྗེན་བཤད་ན་ཡང་ ད་གོ་གི་མི་འདུག He does not understand even when told very clearly.

80

དངོས་ཐོག་བདེན་འཚོལ། seeking truth from facts དངོས་ཐོག་བདེན་འཚོལ་གྱི་སྲིད་བྱུས་ལ་བརྟེན་ནས་གནས་ཚུལ་ཆང་མ་གསལ་པོ་ཤེས་ཐུབ་ཀྱི་རེད། With the policy of seeking truth from facts, one can understand the whole issue.

དངོས་མཐོང་བདེན་རྟོགས། seeing the facts/understanding the truth ཁྱེད་རང་བོད་ལ་ཕེབས་ན་བོད་ཀྱི་གནས་ཚུལ་དངོས་མཐོང་བདེན་རྟོགས་ཡོང་གི་རེད། You will see and understand the true condition of Tibet if you pay a visit to Tibet.

དངོས་གནས་དྲང་གནས། really/ truly ཁོང་དངོས་གནས་དྲང་གནས་མི་ཡག་པོ་གཅིག་རེད། He is really a good person.

དངོས་ཡོད་ཉམས་མྱོང་། actual experience/practical experience ཁྱེད་རང་གི་བཀའ་མོལ་ཆང་མ་དངོས་ཡོད་ཉམས་མྱོང་དང་མཐུན་གྱི་འདུག All your talk accords the actual the experience.

དངོས་ཡོད་གནས་ཚུལ། the actual situation/ the real picture དངོས་ཡོད་ལས་བཀལ་བ་དེ་ཚོང་ཚོས་ཁས་ལེན་བྱེད་ཐུབ་ཀྱི་མ་རེད། We cannot agree those that are beyond actual situation.

དངོས་ཤུགས་བརྒྱུད་གསུམ། by all means ངས་ཁྱེད་རང་ལ་དངོས་ཤུ་བརྒྱུད་གསུམ་གྱི་ཐོག་ནས་རོགས་པ་བྱེད་ཀྱི་ཡིན། I will help you by all means.

མངོན་གསལ་དོད་པོ། very conspicous གསང་བའི་ལས་ཀ་དེ་ཚོ་མངོན་གསལ་དོད་པོ་རང་བྱེད་མི་རུང་། It is not suitable to perform the secret work very conspicously.

ངམ་སྟོན་ཁྲོམ་བསྐོར། a march or demonstration བོད་མི་ཚོས་ལོ་ལྟར་ གསུམ་བཅུའི་དུས་དྲན་ཉིན་ངམ་སྟོན་ཁྲོམ་བསྐོར་བྱེད་པ་རེད། Every year on 10th March, Tibetans stage demonstrations.

སྔ་རྗེས་བར་གསུམ། Lit.: before, after and in between/ Sense implied: throughout the process སྙིང་རྗེ་ནི་སེམས་བསྐྱེད་ཀྱི་སྔ་རྗེས་ བར་གསུམ་དུ་གལ་ཆེ་བ་ཡིན། Compassion is important throughout the process of bodhicitta.

སྔ་བལྟས་ཕྱིས་བསམ། to look back and think for the future ལོ་ ཆུང་དུས་སྔ་བལྟས་ཕྱི་བསམ་ཞེ་དྲག་ཤེས་ཀྱི་མ་རེད། At tender age, one cannot look back and think for the future

སྔ་པོ་སྔ་པོ། very early དམག་མི་ཚོ་ཞོགས་པ་སྔ་པོ་སྔ་པོ་ལངས་དགོས་རེད། Soldiers have to get up early in the morning.

སྔ་ལངས་ཕྱིས་ཉལ། Lit.: to rise up early in the morning and to go to bed late at night/ Sense implied: to be very hard working མི་ལེ་ལོ་ཅན་ཚོས་ནམ་ཡང་སྔ་ལངས་ཕྱིས་ཉལ་བྱེད་ཀྱི་མ་རེད། Lazy people will never get up early in the morning and go to bed late at night.

སྔ་རབས་ད་རབས། past and present events/old and modern account ངའི་གྲོགས་པོ་ལ་སྔ་རབས་ད་རབས་མང་པོ་བཤད་རྒྱུ་ཡོད་རེད། My friend has many old and modern accounts to narrate.

སྔར་སྲོལ་རྒྱུན་འཛིན་གས། continuing the old tradition སྔར་སྲོལ་བཟང་ པོ་རྒྱུན་འཛིན་གས་སུ་གནས་རྒྱར་དགའ་པོ་ཡོད། I am happy for continuing the good old tradition.

སྤྱར་མེད་རྒྱས་སྤྲོས། unprecedented lavishness སྤྱར་མེད་རྒྱས་སྤྲོས་ནི་ཡག་ ཏགས་རྩ་བ་ཉིད་ནས་མིན། The unprecedented lavishness is not at all a good sign.

སྤྲོ་ཐིང་ཐིང་། completely blue ས་ཁྲའི་ཐོག་ལ་སྤྲོ་ཐིང་ཐིང་དེ་མཚོ་ཁྲི་ཤོར་རྒྱལ་མོ་ རེད། The shimmering blueness on the map is Kokonor lake.

སྤྲོ་ལོ་འཕུར་བ། to be disgraceful ཆང་འཐུང་ན་སྤྲོ་ལོ་འཕུར་ཡོང་། If one drinks wine, one might display one's disgrace.

བསྤྱོགས་བཤེར་འཛིན་བཟུང་། to check and arrest བལ་ཡུལ་དང་རྒྱ་གར་ས་ མཚམས་སུ་བསྤྱོགས་བཤེར་འཛིན་བཟུང་མང་པོ་བྱེད་ཀྱི་འདུག Many checks and arrests are made at the Indo-Nepal border.

སྤྱོན་འགོག preventive measure བྱུས་ཉེས་མ་བྱུང་གོང་ནས་སྤྱོན་འགོག་བྱེད་ དགོས། One should apply a preventive measure before one meets misfortune.

སྤྱོན་འགྲོའི་ཆ་རྐྱེན། prerequisites ཨ་རི་ར་མ་འགྲོ་གོང་ནས་སྤྱོན་འགྲོའི་ཆ་རྐྱེན་མང་ པོ་ཞིག་ཚང་དགོས། Many prerequisites have to be fulfilled before going to U.S.A.

སྤྱོན་དང་པོ། at first སྤྱོན་དང་པོར་ང་ཕྱིན་པ་ཡིན། I went first.

སྤྱོན་མ་ནང་བཞིན། as before དེང་སང་མི་ཆང་མ་སྤྱོན་མ་ནང་བཞིན་ཡག་པོ་ཡོད་པ་མ་ རེད། Today people are not as good as they were before.

སྤྱོན་མེད་གསར་བསྐྲུན། invention སྤྱོན་མེད་གསར་བསྐྲུན་ཐུབ་པ་དེ་ནི་ཞིབགས་སྤྱས་ ཆེན་པོ་ཞིག་རེད། An invention is a great contribution.

ཚ་ཚོ་ལབ་སློང་། clamour/ too much talk/ gossip ཚོགས་འདུར་ཚ་ཚོ་མང་པོ་
མ་གནང་། Do not gossip too much in the meeting.

ཚ་ཟིང་དགུ་ཟིང་། a great nuisance མི་འདིས་ཚ་ཟིང་དགུ་ཟིང་བཟོ་གི་འདུག
This man makes a great nuisance.

ཚ་ལེ་ཙོ་ལེ། gibberish མི་འདི་ལ་གནས་ཚུལ་ཚ་ལེ་ཙོ་ལེ་མ་གཏོགས་བཤད་རྒྱུ་མི་འདུག
This man has nothing to say except gibberish.

ཅི་ཟེར་ཁ་ཉན། ཅི་ཟེར་བཀའ་བསྒྲུབ། Lit.: listening to whatever one
says/ Sense implied: very obedient རྒྱུས་རྣ་མེད་ཀྱི་གདམས་ངག་
ནང་ལ་ཅི་ཟེར་བཀའ་བསྒྲུབ་ཀྱི་མན་ངག་ལ་ནན་ཏན་གསུངས་ཡོད། In the
instruction of highest Tantra, the instruction of listening to
whatever one (Lama) says is emphasised.

ཅི་ལྕོགས་ཅི་ནུས། to do one's best ངའི་གྲོགས་པོས་ང་ལ་ཅི་ལྕོགས་ཅི་ནུས་ཀྱི་
རོགས་པ་གནང་བྱུང་། My friend did his best to help me.

ཅི་ཐུབ་གང་ཐུབ། ཅི་དྲག་གང་དྲག as much as one can do/as best
as one can ཁོང་གིས་ཅི་ཐུབ་གང་ཐུབ་བྱེད་ཀྱི་འདུག དེ་ལས་ལྷག་པ་ཁོང་ལ་གང་
ཡང་བྱེད་རྒྱུ་ཡོད་པ་མ་རེད། He does his best. He cannot do more
than this.

ཅི་དྲན་གང་དྲན། whatever one remembers/ whatever comes to

mind ཚོགས་འདུའི་ནང་ལ་ཅི་དྲན་གང་དྲན་ཚང་མ་གསུང་རྒྱུ་ཡོད་པ་མ་རེད། One should not tell whatever comes to mind in the meeting.

ཅི་འགྲོས་མོལ་འགྲོས། casual talk/chit chat ཅི་འགྲོས་མོལ་འགྲོས་ཐོག་ལ་དུས་ ཚོད་མང་པོ་བཏང་ན་རྒྱུད་ཆུད་རེད། If one spends more time in casual talk, it is a waste of time.

ཅི་བྱ་གཏོལ་མེད། ཅི་བྱེད་འདི་བྱེད་མེད་པ། ཅི་བསམ་འདི་བསམ་མེད་པ། in dilemma/ not knowing what to do next/ སྐྱོ་བྱུར་དུ་ཕྱིན་ནན་བྱུང་ ན་ཅི་བྱ་གཏོལ་མེད་དང་ལུས་ཀྱི་རེད། If misfortunes come all of a sudden, one will be in a state of dilemma.

ཅི་མཛད་ལེགས་མཐོང་། to consider good whatever someone does/ This proverb shows how to relate, especially a tantric disciple, to a spiritual master.

གཅན་གཟན་ཤ་ལ་རྔམ་པ་ལྟར། Lit.: like wild beast pouncing on meat/ Sense implied: very greedy ནོར་གྱི་དོན་དུ་གཅན་གཟན་ཤ་ལ་ རྔམ་པ་ལྟར་རྒྱུགས་རྒྱུ་མེད། One should not run after wealth just as a wild beast pouncing on meat.

གཅིག་ཀྱང་མ་ལུས་པ། Lit.: leaving not even one/ Sense implied: all དེབ་གཅིག་ཀྱང་མ་ལུས་པ་ཉོ་དགོས། One should buy all the books leaving none.

གཅིག་སྐྱེས་གཉིས་སྐྱེས། to give birth one after another ངའི་ཨ་མ་ལ་ ཕྲུ་གུ་གཅིག་སྐྱེས་གཉིས་སྐྱེས་བྱུང་སྟེ་དེང་སང་ཕྲུ་གུ་ལྔ་ཡོད། My mother had her five children one after another.

85

གཅིག་གིས་གཉིས་ཚོད། killing two birds with one stone/being able to perform two works at a time by one person.

གཅིག་བརྒྱུད་གཉིས་བརྒྱུད། through one after another སངས་རྒྱས་བཙོམ་ལྡན་འདས་ནས་གཅིག་བརྒྱུད་གཉིས་བརྒྱུད་བྱས་ཏེ་སེམས་བསྐྱེད་ཀྱི་འཕྲིན་རྒྱུད་ད་ལྟ་བར་དུ་གནས་ཡོད། From Buddha Shakyamuni onward the transmission of bodhicitta has continued through one to the next.

གཅིག་མཇུག་གཉིས་མཐུད། Lit.: one following the other/ Sense implied: continuation བོད་མི་རྣམས་གཅིག་མཇུག་གཉིས་མཐུད་བྱས་ཏེ་རྒྱ་གར་དུ་འབྱོར། Tibetans came to India continuously one after another.

གཅིག་འདུས་གཉིས་འདུས། gathering one by one ཁྲོམ་དུ་འགྱུལ་པ་གཅིག་འདུས་གཉིས་འདུས་བྱས་ནས་མི་ཚོགས་ཆེན་པོ་ཆག་འདུག A big crowd is formed at the market having gathered travellers one by one.

གཅིག་པ་གཅིག་རྐྱང་། absolutely same/ very identical ང་ཚོའི་དམིགས་ཡུལ་རྣམས་གཅིག་པ་གཅིག་རྐྱང་རེད། Our objectives are absolutely the same.

གཅིག་ཕན་གཅིག་གྲོགས། helping one another/ mutual help འཛམ་གླིང་གི་རྒྱལ་ཁབ་ཕན་ཚུན་གཅིག་ཕན་གཅིག་གྲོགས་བྱེད་དགོས་རེད། Nations of the world should help one another.

གཅིག་མིན་གཉིས་མིན། always saying no ག་དུས་ཡིན་ནའང་གཅིག་མིན་གཉིས་མིན་ཟེར་ན་ཡག་པོ་མི་འདུག It is not good to give always negative response.

86

གཅིག་ཡིད་གཅིག་ཆེས། to trust one another གཅིག་ཡིད་གཅིག་ཆེས་ཀྱི་ གྲོགས་པོ། trust worthy friend གཅིག་ཡིད་གཅིག་ཆེས་ཀྱི་གྲོགས་པོ་དཀོན་པོ་ རེད། Trust worthy friends are very rare.

གཅིག་ལན་གཉིས་སློག Lit.: to hit back two for one blow/ Sense implied: disobedient རྒན་རབས་ལ་གཅིག་ལན་གཉིས་སློག་བྱེད་ན་ཡག་པོ་མ་ རེད། It is not good to hit back (talk) the elders.

གཅིག་ཤེས་ཀུན་གྲོལ། to know all by knowing one བླ་མའི་མན་ངག་ལ་ བརྟེན་ན་གཅིག་ཤེས་ཀུན་གྲོལ་ཡོང་གི་རེད། One will know everything by relying upon the instruction of one's master.

གཅེས་འཛིན་བདག་སྲུང་། to uphold and preserve རང་གི་སྐད་ཡིག་རང་ གིས་གཅེས་འཛིན་བདག་སྲུང་བྱེད་དགོས་པ་ཨིན། One should uphold and preserve one's own language.

བཅུས་རིལ་ཚ་པོ། naughty persons མི་བཅུས་རིལ་ཚ་པོ་ལ་སུས་ཀྱང་དགའ་པོ་ བྱེད་ཀྱི་མ་རེད། No one will like naughty persons.

བཅོས་མིན་སྙིང་རྗེ། genuine compassion གཞན་གྱི་སྡུག་བསྔལ་ལ་སྙིང་རྗེ་བཅོས་ མིན་སྐྱེ་དགོས། One should generate genuine compassion for others' suffering.

གཅིག་ཤེས་ཀུན་གྲོལ། to know all by knowing one བླ་མའི་མན་ངག་ལ་ བརྟེན་ན་གཅིག་ཤེས་ཀུན་གྲོལ་ཡོང་གི་རེད། One will know everything by knowing one relies upon the instruction of one's master.

གཅེས་འཛིན་བདག་སྐྱོང་། to uphold and preserve རང་གི་སྐད་ཡིག་རང་ གིས་གཅེས་འཛིན་བདག་སྐྱོང་བྱེད་དགོས་པ་ཡིན། One should uphold and preserve one's own language.

བཅུས་རིལ་ཚ་པོ། naughty persons མི་བཅུས་རིལ་ཚ་པོ་ལ་སུས་ཀྱང་དགའ་པོ་ བྱེད་ཀྱི་མ་རེད། No one will like naughty persons.

བཙས་མིན་སྙིང་རྗེ། genuine compassion གཞན་གྱི་སྡུག་བསྔལ་ལ་སྙིང་རྗེ་བཙས་ མིན་སྐྱེ་དགོས། One should generate genuine compassion for others' suffering.

ཆང་ངེ་ཆུང་ངེ། Lit.: small things/ Sense implied: insignificant/less important གནས་ཚུལ་ཆང་ངེ་ཆུང་ངེ་ལ་དུས་ཚོད་མང་ པོ་གཏོང་རྒྱུ་ཡོད་མ་རེད། One should not spend more time on insignificant matters.

ཆ་འཛོག་འཕེར་བ། reliable ཁོང་ནི་སྤྱི་ཚོགས་ཀྱི་ནང་ན་ཆ་འཛོག་འཕེར་བའི་མི་ཞིག་ རེད། He is a reliable person in society.

ཆ་འཛོག་ཡིད་ཆེས། to recognize and trust བོད་གཞུང་ལ་བོད་མི་ཚང་མས་ ཆ་འཛོག་ཡིད་ཆེས་བྱེད་པ་རེད། All Tibetans recognize and trust the Tibetan government.

ཆ་མཐུན་ལུགས་མཐུན། according to custom and tradition སྤྱི་ཚོགས་ ཀྱི་ནང་དུ་ཆ་མཐུན་ལུགས་མཐུན་གནང་རྒྱུ་གལ་ཆེན་པོ་རེད། It is important to live according to the society's custom and tradition.

ཆ་མིན་ལ་ཐོ། wrong pair ལྷམ་དེ་ཆ་མིན་ལ་ཐོ་རེད། The shoes are wrongly paired.

ཆ་ལེ་ཚོ་ལེ། carelessly/ messily རང་གི་ལས་ཀ་ཆ་ལེ་ཚོ་ལེ་བྱེད་ན་གྲུབ་འབྲས་ བཟང་པོ་ཡོང་གི་མ་རེད། One will not achieve good result if one is careless in one's work.

ཆག་སྒོ་བྱུང་ན་མགོ སྐུ་གི་བྱུང་ན་མཐབ། Lit.: problems hit the

(responsible) heads and famine hits the poor/ Sense implied: Whenever there is problem, the head is hit and he is in trouble but whereas whenever there is famine, the poor and down trodden are hit and caught up.

ཆག་ཆོག་ཆོག delicate/ fragile/ easily breakable དཀར་ཡོལ་ཆག་ཆོག ཆོག་རེ་འདྲ་མ་ཉོ། Do not buy easily breakable cups.

ཆག་རྡུང་རྣག་རྡུང་། hodge-podge/ a mess/ whatever one desires སློབ་གྲྭའི་ནང་ལ་ཆག་རྡུང་རྣག་རྡུང་བྱེད་ཆོག་གི་མ་རེད། One cannot do whatever one desires in a school.

ཆགས་སྡང་ཕྱོགས་རིས། ཆགས་སྡང་ཕྱོགས་ལྷུང་། partiality/ bias སྐུ་ཞབས་ཇེ་གྷོ་མོ་ནི་ཆགས་སྡང་ཕྱོགས་རིས་ཅན་གྱི་མི་ཞིག་རེད། Mr.John Dove is partial and prejudiced.

ཆགས་ས་བརྟེན་ས་མེད་པ། homeless/ destitute རྒྱ་མིས་བོད་མི་ཚོར་རང་གི་ལུང་པར་ཆགས་ས་བརྟེན་ས་མེད་པར་བཟོས་པ་རེད། The Chinese made the Tibetans homeless and destitute in their own country.

ཆང་རིན། payment for the drink/ Sense implied: tip at the end of a business ཆོག་མཆན་ཐོབ་རྒྱར་ཆང་རིན་སྒོར་བརྒྱ་ཐམ་པ་ཕྱེར་སོང་། I had to give Rs.100.00 as a tip in order to get the permission.

ཆང་ལན་ཆུ་འཇལ། Lit.: giving water in return for wine/ Sense implied: to repay kindness with ill treatment ཆང་ལན་ཆུ་ཡིས་འཇལ་ན་མི་གཤིས་ངན་པའི་རྟགས་རེད། To repay kindness with ill-treatment is a sign of bad nature.

90

ཆབ་ཆབ་བཙོ་བཅུད། Jack of all trades, and master of none ངས་ཆབ་ཆོབ་བཙོ་བཅུད་ཤེས་ཀྱི་ཡོད། I am jack of all trades, and master of none.

ཆབ་སྲིད་འཕྱགས་བསྐུན། political development ཆབ་སྲིད་འཕྱགས་བསྐུན་ ཡག་པོ་གཅིག་ཡོང་བ་ལ་ཡུལ་མི་ཚོར་ཤེས་ཡོན་དགོས་པ་ཡིན། Citizens should be well educated to have good political development in a country.

ཆམ་པར་ཕན་ཡང་ཡ་མར་གནོད། Lit.: though it helps cold, it harms the sinus/ Sense implied: although it helps this, it harms that.

ཆར་པ་ཆུ་གྲོགས་དང་ཉི་མ་མེ་གྲོགས། Lit.: rain is a friend of water and the sun is a friend of fire/ Sense implied: to help oneanother རྟེན་འབྲེལ་དང་སྟོང་ཉིད་གཉིས་ཆར་པ་ཆུ་གྲོགས་དང་ཉི་མ་མེ་གྲོགས་ ཀྱི་ཚུལ་དུ་གནས་པ་རེད། There is a harmony in the philosophy of dependent arising and emptiness just as rain helps water and sun helps fire.

ཅིག་བསྒྲིལ་གྱི་ནུས་པ། the power of unity རྒྱལ་ཁབ་ཀྱི་འཕྱགས་བསྐུན་གྱི་ལས་ ཀ་རྣམས་ཅིག་བསྒྲིལ་གྱི་ནུས་པ་ལ་བརྟེན་ནས་བསྒྲུབ་ཐུབ་པ་ཡིན། The development of nation is possible through the power of unity.

ཆུ་དཀྲོགས་ནས་མར་མི་ཐོན། Lit.: churning water produces no butter/ Sense implied: useless attempt/futile effort

ཆུ་མགོ་གངས་ལ་ཐུག Lit.: the source of water lies in the snow/

Sense implied: reliable source/ reliable origin ཆུ་མགོ་གངས་ ལ་ཐུག་པ་ནང་བཞིན་ཆོས་ཀྱི་ཁུངས་དེ་སངས་རྒྱས་ལ་ཐུག་པ་ཡིན། The source of Dharma is in Buddha just as the source of water is in the snow.

ཆུ་བརྒྱ་ཟམ་གཅིག Lit.: one hundred streams flowing under one bridge/ Sense implied: to be under the control of a single authority.

ཆུ་ཐིགས་བསགས་པའི་རྒྱ་མཚོ། Lit.: an ocean, a collection of water drops/ Sense implied: a collection of small things make a big thing དགེ་བ་རྣམ་ཆུང་ཡིན་ན་ཡང་སྤང་ཆུང་བུ་མི་རུང་། ཆུ་ཐིགས་བསགས་ པའི་རྒྱ་མཚོའི་དཔེ་རེད་ཅེ་མ་གཅིག་བསོད་ནམས་རྒྱ་ཆེན་པོ་གསོག་ཐུབ་ཀྱི་རེད། Even the virtue is of small type one should not ignore it as it was said in the saying that a collection of water makes the ocean.

ཆུ་ཕོན་ཟམ་བརྗེད། Lit.: to forget the bridge when the water is crossed/ Sense implied: to forget other's kindness ཆུ་ཕོན་ ནས་ཟམ་པ་བརྗེད་པ་ནང་བཞིན་གཞན་གྱི་བཀའ་དྲིན་བརྗེད་རྒྱུ་ཡོང་པ་མ་རེད། One should not forget others' kindness just as one gets the bridge after crossing the river.

ཆུ་དྭངས་ན་གསལ། Lit.: to see fish in the clean water/ Sense implied: very clear/ no need to ask or to doubt. ཆུ་དྭངས་ མའི་ནང་ན་ཉ་གསལ་བ་ནང་བཞིན་ཁོང་གི་བཀའ་སློབ་རྣམས་ཤིན་ཏུ་གསལ་པོ་འདུག His speches are very clear just as one sees fish in the water clearly.

ཆུ་དྲོད་འཛམ་གྱིས་ཤ་མི་འཚོས། Lit.: tepid water cannot cook meat/

Sense implied: loose disciplines do not work

ཆུ་རྦུ་གར་འཐིད། Lit.: wherever the start of water leads/ Sense implied: sloppy/ one who is easily misled by others/ to listen to others person without investigations རྒྱུན་པོ་ཆུ་རྦུ་ གར་འཐིད། A stupid who is easily influenced by others.

ཆུ་མ་བདེན་ན་ཉ་མི་བདེ། དཔོན་མི་བདེ་ན་གཡོག་མི་བདེ། Lit.: if the water is disturbed, the fish are also disturbed and if the master is in trouble, the servants are also in trouble

ཆུ་མ་ཡོང་གོང་ནས་རགས། Lit.: to build dams before the flood comes/ Sense implied: precautionary measures ཡིག་ཚད་མ་ ཡོང་གོང་ནས་སློབ་སྦྱོང་ཡག་པོ་གནང་དགོས། དཔེར་ན་ཆུ་མ་ཡོང་ནས་རགས་རྒྱབ་པ་ ནང་བཞིན་རེད། One should study properly before the examination just as a dam is built before the flood.

ཆུ་ལན་ཆང་འཇལ། Lit.: to give wine in return for water/ Sense implied: to return kindness even for a small thing

ཆུ་ལེན་བུམ་སྟོང་། Lit.: went to get water but returned with the empty vessel/ Sense implied: unsuccessful attempt/failure སློབ་གྲར་བཏང་ནས་སློབ་སྦྱོང་ཡག་པོ་མ་གནང་ན་ཆུ་ལེན་བུམ་སྟོང་ནང་བཞིན་ཆགས་ཀྱི་ རེད། Having been sent to school, if one does not study properly it would resemble returning with a empty vessel.

ཆུང་བཀྲས་ཆེར་སྐྱག one who insults poor and down trodden/ Sense implied: evil and timid.

ཆུང་འདྲིས་བྲམས་པ། Lit.: a childhood friend, be it a boy or girl/ Sense implied:childhood lover དུས་རྟག་ཏུ་ཆུང་འདྲིས་བྲམས་པ་ཡང་ ཡང་དྲན་གྱི་འདུག I always remember my childhood lover.

ཆེ་ཆུང་མཚམས་པོ། a suitable size ཁང་པ་འདི་མི་གཉིས་ལ་ཆེ་ཆུང་མཚམས་པོ་ འདུག This house is of a suitable size for two people.

ཆེ་ཐག་ཆོད། enormous/ too big/ big enough ཁང་པ་འདི་མི་གཅིག་ལ་ཆེ་ ཐག་ཆོད་འདུག This house is big enough for one person.

ཆེ་བཞག་ཆུང་བསྒྱུར། ཆེ་བཞག་ཆུང་བཀོལ། to make a small sacrifice for big cause.

ཆེ་རུ་ཆེ་རུ། to grow bigger and bigger ཕྲུ་གུ་ཆེ་རུ་ཆེ་རུ་འགྲོ་དུས་སྤོད་པ་ངན་ རུ་ངན་རུ་འགྲོ་གི་འདུག When the children grow bigger and bigger they become impudent.

ཆོག་ཆོག readiness ང་འགྲོ་ཆོག་ཆོག་ཡིན། I am ready to go.

ཆོག་ཤེས་ཚུལ་མཐུན། moderately content བྱ་བ་ཆེ་ཆུང་གང་ཡིན་ནའང་ཆོག་ ཤེས་ཚུལ་མཐུན་གནང་གལ་ཆེ། It is important to be moderately contented with whatever the work might be, big or small.

ཆོས་ཀྱི་བག་ཆགས། Lit.: predisposition of dharma/ Sense implied: spiritual inclination དད་པ་ཡོད་པ་ནི་ཆོས་ཀྱི་བག་ཆགས་ཡོད་ པའི་རྟགས་རེད། To have faith is a sign of spiritual inclinations.

94

ཆོས་བརྒྱུད་འདྲ་མིན། various religious traditions ཆོས་བརྒྱུད་འདྲ་མིན་ སྒོར་སློབ་སྦྱོང་གནང་རྒྱུ་གལ་ཆེན་པོ་རེད། It is important to study various religious traditions.

ཆོས་ལྡན་རྒྱལ་ཁབ། religious nation གནའ་དུས་རྒྱ་གར་ནི་ཆོས་ལྡན་རྒྱལ་ཁབ་ ཡག་པོ་ཞིག་རེད། In the past India was a very good spiritual nation.

ཆོས་རར་ཆོས་དང་། གཞས་རར་གཞས། Lit.: to debate at the debate ground and to sing at the singing event/ Sense implied: to be very mindful of what things should be done where and when

ཆོས་སྲིད་གཉིས་ལྡན། spiritual and temporal པགོང་ས་མཆོག་ནི་བོད་ཆོས་ སྲིད་གཉིས་ལྡན་གྱི་དབུ་ཁྲིད་དམ་པ་ཞིག་རེད། His Holiness the Dalai Lama is the spiritual and temporal leader of Tibet.

འཆད་རྩོད་རྩོམ་གསུམ། teaching, debate and composition འཆད་རྩོད་ རྩོམ་གསུམ་ལ་མཁས་ན་མཁས་པ་རེད། He is a scholar who is skillfull in teaching, debate and composition.

འཆི་མཉམ་གསོན་མཉམ། to live and die together གྲོགས་པོ་ཕོ་སྟོབས་ཁྲུབ་ཅེར་ ན་འཆི་མཉམ་གསོན་མཉམ་ཁྲུབ་པ་ཞིག་དགོས། A trustworthy friend is one who can live and die together.

ཇ་དང་དགེ་རྒན་ཚ་ན་དགའ། Lit.: Tea and teacher should be hot. Sense implied: It's is better if the tea is hot and a teacher is strict.

ཇ་འདྲེན་ཆང་འདྲེན། Lit.: serving tea and wine/ Sense implied: warm hospitality མགྲོན་པོ་ནང་དུ་བསླེབས་པ་དང་ཇ་འདྲེན་ཆང་འདྲེན་གནང་རོགས་གནང་། When guests arrive home, please serve them tea and wine.

ཇ་ཞིམ་པོ་མར་གྱི་བཀའ་དྲིན་རེད། Lit.: Tea tastes fine due to butter./ Sense implied: something that is good due to other's kindness

ཇ་ལན་ཆུ་འཇལ། བཟང་ལན་ངན་འཇལ། Lit.: giving water in return for tea and treating ill in return for the goodness one has done/ungrateful

ཇི་མ་ཇི་བཞིན། exactly same ཡིག་ཚད་ལ་དཔེ་ཕྱུས་ཇི་མ་ཇི་བཞིན་བྱེད་ཐུབ་ཐབས་མཁན་དཀོན་པོ་རེད། It is very rare to be able to copy exactly the same in the examination.

ཧྲུས་མེད་ཧྲུས་ཁྲི། to intervene or interfere ཧྲུས་མེད་ཧྲུས་ཁྲི་བྱས་ན་དཀའ་ངལ་ཆག་གི་རེད། It will become a problem if someone interferes in other's work/Poking one's nose in other's business will become a problem.

ཇེ་དན་ཇེ་སྡུག becoming worse and worse ཁོས་ཨ་རག་བཏུང་ནས་ནད་ གཞི་ཇེ་དན་ཇེ་སྡུག་ཏུ་ཕྱིན་སོང་། By taking alcohol, his illness has gone from bad to worse.

ཇེ་བཟང་ཇེ་ལེགས། to became better and better སློབ་གྲར་ཚུད་ནས་སྤུ་གུ་ དེ་ཇེ་བཟང་ཇེ་ལེགས་སུ་གྱུར་སོང་། Since the boy got admission to the school, he has became better and better.

མཇིང་པ་གཡག་ལས་སྦོམ་པ། Lit.: a neck thicker than a yak's/ Sense implied: a very proud and haughty person.

འཇམ་མཁས་སྒྱུ་བྱེད། polite and skillful deception གཡོ་སྒྱུ་ཅན་གྱི་འཇམ་ མཁས་སྒྱུ་བྱེད་ལ་མགོ་བསྐོར་མ་ཐེབས་པ་བྱེད་དགོས། One should not be trapped by the skillful ways of deceptive people.

འཇམ་ཞིང་ཞིང་། pin drop silence གྲོང་གསེབ་ཁག་ཏུ་མཚན་ལ་འཇམ་ཞིང་ཞིང་ ཡོད་རེད། There is pin drop silence at night in the villages.

འཇིག་རྟེན་ཁ་རྒྱུན། common sayings/ proverb འཇིག་རྟེན་ཁ་རྒྱུན་དུ་དཔོན་ ལ་མི་སྐྲག་དབང་ལ་སྐྲག་ཟེར་བ་ཡིན། There is a common saying that one is not afraid of a leader, but of his power.

འཇུ་ན་སྨན་དང་། མ་འཇུ་ན་དུག If digested, it is a medicine, if not it is a poison ཟས་དེ་འཇུ་ན་སྨན་དང་མ་འཇུ་ན་དུག་རེད If the food is digested, it is a medicine if not it is a poison.

འཇོན་པོ་ནོད་པོ། very efficient (at certain context it is used as sarcastic remark)

རྗེས་མ་རྗེས་མ། after a long time/ later on ཁོང་གི་བརྩོན་འགྲུས་ལ་བལྟས་

ན་རྗེས་མ་རྗེས་མ་མཁས་པ་ཆགས་པར་ཐེ་ཚོམ་མི་འདུག If we take notice of his diligence there is no doubt of his becoming a good scholar later on/eventually.

རྗེས་ལུས་ཐེབས་དོགས། doubt of lagging behind ཁྱེད་རང་སློབ་སྦྱོང་ལ་

རྗེས་ལུས་ཐེབས་དོགས་མི་འདུག There is no danger of lagging behind at your studies.

རྗེས་སུ་ཡི་རངས། rejoicing/appreciation དགེ་བ་ལ་རྗེས་སུ་ཡི་རངས་བྱེད་པ་

ནི་དགེ་བ་གསོག་པའི་ཐབས་དམ་པ་ཡིན། Rejoicing at the virtues is the best means to earn merits.

ལྗིད་རྡེག་རྡེག heavy/ sluggish དོག་ཁྲིས་འདི་ལྗིད་རྡེག་རྡེག་འདུག This luggage is heavy.

བརྗེད་ངས་ལེ་ལོ། forgetfulness and laziness ཡོན་ཏན་གྱི་ཚོམ་ཀུན་ནི་བརྗེས་

ངས་དང་ལེ་ལོ་རེད། Forgetfulness and laziness are the thieves of knowledge.

བརྗོད་དུ་མེད་པ། inexpressible ཡིག་ཚད་ཁྱང་དང་པོ་ལོན་པར་བརྗོད་དུ་མེད་པའི་

དགའ་བ་ཚོག He felt inexpressible joy for securing the first position in the examination.

ཉ་གོ་རུང་མས་མི་ཚོད། Lit.: a turnip cannot substitute a fish/ Sense implied: X cannot be substituted by Y

ཉ་རུང་མཉམ་བསྲེ། Lit.: to mix turnip with fish/ Sense implied: indiscrimate/ in mess.

ཉ་སྟོང་བཅུད་གསུམ། fifteenth, thirtieth and the eighth of a lunar calendar/ Tibetans consider these dates auspicious.

ཉ་སྟོང་བཅུད་གསུམ་ལ་མཆོད་རྟེན་ལ་བསྐོར་བ་བྱེད་ཀྱི་ཡོད། I circumambulate the stupa on the fifteenth, thirtieth and eighth of a lunar calendar month.

ཉ་སྤུ་མེད་ལ་རལ་པའི་ཁྲལ། Lit.: to tax hairless fish with matted hair/ Sense implied: hopeless expectation from someone.

ཉ་ཕག་སྒོང་གསུམ། fish, pork and egg ནང་པ་ཚོས་ཉ་སྟོང་བཅུད་གསུམ་ལ་ཉ་ ཕག་སྒོང་གསུམ་སྒོང་བ་རེད། Buddhists abstain from fish, pork and egg on the fifteenth, thirtieth and the eighth of every month of lular calendar.

ཉ་བསད་ནས་ཁྱི་ལ་སྦྱིན་པ་གཏོང་བ། Lit.: killing fish to give to the dogs/ Sense implied: to help someone by harming another ཉ་བསད་ནས་ཁྱི་ལ་སྦྱིན་པ་གཏོང་བ་ཚོས་ཀྱི་ཉམས་ལེན་མིན། Killing a fish in order to give food to dogs, is not a religious practice.

ཉན་ཞེས་གོ་ཞེས། Lit.: one who listens carefully with understanding/ Sense implied: obedient or sensible person གཞོན་པས་རྒན་པ་ལ་ཉན་ཞེས་གོ་ཞེས་བྱེད་ན་ཡག་པོ་ཡོད་རེད། It is good that the youngers should listen to the elders.

ཉམ་ཆུང་ཚུལ་ལྡན། simple and disciplined ཉམ་ཆུང་ཚུལ་ལྡན་གྱི་མི་ལ་ཀུན་གྱིས་སྔོན། Everyone admired a person of disciplined and simple nature.

ཉམ་ཐག་ཝུ་ཐུག poor and desperate condition ཉམ་ཐག་ཝུ་ཐུག་གི་མི་ལ་ངེས་པར་རོགས་པ་བྱེད་དགོས། He who is poor and in desperate condition must be helped.

ཉམས་ལེན་ཁྲུ་སྒོ། process of practice དགེ་བའི་བཤེས་གཉེན་མཆོག་ནས་ཉམས་ལེན་ཁྲུ་སྒོ་གང་ཡིན་བཀའ་སློབ་གནང་རོགས་གནང་། May I request the spiritual master to guide me in the process of my practice.

ཉལ་ས་བྱུང་ན་རྐྱོང་ས། Lit.: when one finds a place for rest, needs more space to stretch out one's legs/ Sense implied: greedy/ demanding more and more (sarcastic remark).

ཉི་མ་གང་འཁྱོལ། just to pass away the time ལས་ཀ་ཉི་མ་གང་འཁྱོལ་བྱེད་ན་འགྲིགས་ཐབས་མེད། Just to pass time with one's work is not acceptable.

ཉི་མ་གཅིག་ལ་ལོ་གཅིག་གི་སྣང་བ། Lit.: one day appears as long as one year/ Sense implied: to feel the day extremely boring/loneliness

ཉིན་གཅིག་ཟས་གཅིག one meal a day སྨྱུང་གནས་སྐབས་ཉིན་གཅིག་ལ་ཟས་གཅིག་ལས་མང་བ་ཟ་ཆོག་གི་མ་རེད། When fasting, one cannot eat more than one meal a day.

ཉིན་མཚན་མེད་པ། Lit.: throughout day and night/ Sense implied: to do continuously ཚོང་པ་ཁ་ཤས་དངུལ་གྱི་དོན་དུ་ཉིན་མཚན་མེད་པར་ལས་ཀ་བྱེད་ཀྱི་ཡོད་རེད། Some businessmen work day and night to earn money.

ཉིན་མོའི་སྐར་མ། Lit.: day star/ Sense implied: very rare བླ་མ་བཟང་པོ་འདི་འདྲ་མཇལ་རྒྱུ་ཉིན་མོའི་སྐར་མ་རེད། It is very rare to meet such a good lama.

ཉིན་མོའི་མི་དང་མཚན་མོའི་ཁྱི། Lit.: man at day and dog at night/ Sense implied: to keep watch over all things ངའི་ཁྱི་ནག་པོ་དེ་ཉིན་མོའི་མི་དང་མཚན་མོའི་ཁྱི་ཡིན། My black dog is man at day and dog at night. ངས་ལོ་མང་པོའི་རིང་མི་ཚང་འདིའི་ཉིན་མོའི་མི་དང་མཚན་མོའི་ཁྱི་བྱས་ནས་དཀའ་ལས་བརྒྱབས་པ་ཡིན། For many years I worked hard as a member of the family during day and as a watch dog during night.

ཉིན་མཚན་བསྟོས་མེད། regardless of day and night ཕ་མ་ཆོས་རང་གི་ཕྲུ་གུའི་དོན་དུ་ཉིན་མཚན་བསྟོས་མེད་ལས་ཀ་བྱེད་པ་རེད། Parents work regardless of day and night for their children.

ཉིན་མཚན་དུས་དྲུག Lit.: six times day and night/ Sense implied: always ཕ་གོང་ས་མཆོག་གིས་ཉིན་མཚན་དུས་དྲུག་ཏུ་བོད་རང་བཙན་གྱི་དོན་དུ་སྐུ

ལས་བགྲུན་གྱི་ཡོད་པ་རེད། His Holiness the Dalai Lama always works hard for the independance of Tibet.

ཉིན་ཞག་སྤྲུགས་གཅིག one whole day ཉིན་ཞག་སྤྲུགས་གཅིག་གི་སྡོམ་པ་བསྲུང་རྒྱུ་དཀའ་ངལ་ཆེན་པོ་མ་རེད། It is not difficult to observe one whole day precept.

ཉི་ཚོ་མེད་པ། without ill-health/ well, fine ལྷ་ཡི་དྲིན་ལ་བརྟེན་ནས་ཉི་ཚོ་མེད་པར་གནས་ཡོད། I am fine due to the kindness of god.

ཉི་དུ་ཉི་དུ། becoming closer and closer དེང་སང་ང་ཚོ་གཉིས་ཉི་དུ་ཉི་དུ་འགྲོ་གི་ཡོད། These days two of us are becoming closer and closer to each other.

ཉེས་མེད་ཁ་གཡོག to blame the innocent གཟབ་གཟབ་མ་བྱེད་ན་གཞན་གྱིས་མ་ཉེས་ཁ་གཡོག་བྱེད་ཀྱི་རེད། If one is not careful, others will put blame on one.

ཉེས་མེད་ཉེས་འགེལ། punishing the innocent ཆོས་ལྡན་རྒྱལ་ཁབ་ཏུ་ཡང་ཉེས་མེད་ཉེས་འགེལ་བྱེད་པ་ཡོད། Even in religious countries, one finds punishment of the innocent.

གཉའ་གནོན་བཤུ་གཞོག oppression and exploitation བྱིས་པར་སློབ་སྦྱོང་སྤྲད་མི་ཆོག་པ་དེ་གཉའ་གནོན་བཤུ་གཞོག་ཆེན་པོ་ཞིག་རེད། It is a serious exploitation and oppression to deprive children of education.

གཉིད་མ་ཉལ་གོང་ནས་གཉིད་ལམ་བཤད། Lit.: to tell one's dreams before one sleeps/ Sense implied: to be extremely imaginative

གཉེན་སྒྲིག་རྟེན་འབྲེལ། marriage celebration ལོ་གསར་སྐབས་ལ་གཉེན་སྒྲིག་
རྟེན་འབྲེལ་མང་པོ་བྱེད་པ་རེད། Many marriage ceremonies are conducted during New-Year festival.

མཉམ་ཤི་མཉམ་གསོན། to live and die together/ to share joy and sorrow together until death སྔོན་གྱི་རྒྱལ་བློན་ཁ་ཤས་མཉམ་ཤི་མཉམ་ གསོན་བྱེད་པ་རེད། In the past, some kings and ministers lead a life of living and dying together.

རྙིང་པ་རྙིང་རྒྱང་། ancient/very old/ totally worn out ང་ཚོ་ལྷ་ཁང་རྙིང་ པ་རྙིང་རྒྱང་གཅིག་ལ་ཕྱིན་པ་ཡིན། We went to a very old temple.

རྩོག་ཁ་ལྱང་པ་གང་། full of disputes ཨ་མའི་རོ། ཁྱོས་རྩོག་ཁ་ལྱང་པ་གང་ བཟོས་སོང་། Bull shit ! He created all these problems.

སྙན་གྲགས་ཀྱི་བ་དན། the banner of fame/ soaring reputation ༸གོང་ས་མཆོག་གི་མཆན་སྙན་གྲགས་ཀྱི་བ་དན་ཕྱོགས་ཐམས་ཅད་དུ་ཁྱབ། His Holiness the Dalai Lama's banner of fame spreads in all directions.

སྦྱགས་དོར་བཅུད་ལེན། Lit.: to leave the dirts and derive the essence/ Sense implied: avoid mistakes and to uphold essence ནམ་དཔྱོད་ཡོད་ན་སྦྱགས་དོར་བཅུད་ལེན་ལ་མཁས་དགོས་པ་ཡིན། One should avoid mistakes and uphold essence, if one is wise.

སྙིང་རྗེ་རྒྱུན་རིང་ན་ཁོང་ཁྲོ་རྒྱུན་མི་ཆད། Lit.: If the time for compassion is too long then the anger will never end./ Sense implied: There should be limit for forgiveness also.

སྣུན་སྣུན་ཚ་ཚ། to fall ill often ངའི་ཨ་མ་ལགས་སྣུན་སྣུན་ཚ་ཚ་འབྱལ་པོ་རེད། My mother often gets sick.

དག་དག་སིག་སིག stone broke ལོ་གསར་སྐབས་པོ་བག་ཐེད་དེ་དངུལ་ཆང་མ་
དག་དག་སིག་སིག་བཟོས་པ་ཡིན། I'm stone broke from gambling during the new year.

དུན་དུན་ཏིག་ཏིག very sure/ careful བུ་ལོན་གན་རྒྱ་དུན་དུན་ཏིག་ཏིག་མ་བཟོས་
ན་རྗེས་མ་རྩོག་ཁྲ་ཡོང་གི་རེད། If the agreement of loan is not made carefully, there will be controversies in the future.

དོག་ཙམ་དོག་ཙམ། little by little ཆང་རག་དང་པོ་དོག་ཙམ་དོག་ཙམ་བཏུང་སྟེ་རྗེས་
སུ་ཆང་གྱི་ར་ཆགས་ཀྱི་རེད། In the beginning, alcohol is taken little by little and later on one becomes an alcoholic.

གདན་བཞུགས་དགེ་འདུན། permanent resident monks གནས་ཆུང་
དགོན་དུ་གདན་བཞུགས་དགེ་འདུན་བཅུ་གྲངས་ཡོད། There are about ten permanent resident monks at Nechung Monastery.

གདན་སྡོད་མི་མང་། local or permanent resident ལྷ་སར་གདན་སྡོད་མི་
འབོར་འབུམ་ཁ་ཤས་ཡོད། As for the population of the local residents in Lhasa, there are several hundred thousand people.

གཏམ་གྱི་མགོ་དེ་སྒྲ་ཡང་། གཏམ་གྱི་མཇུག་དེ་མི་སྒྲ། Lit.: Although the beginning of a talk is easy, the completion of a talk is not easy/ Sense implied: Easier said than done/ Though it is easy to start a talk it is, however, not easy to end a talk.

གདམ་ངན་མི་ཁ། back biting/ bad reputation དྲང་པོ་དྲང་ཤག་བྱེད་ན།
གདམ་ངན་མི་ཁ་ཡོང་དོགས་མེད། If someone acts honestly there will not be any bad reputation.

104

གཏམ་ངན་རྐྱང་འཕྲིར། spreading bad rumours གཏམ་ངན་རྐྱང་འཕྲིར་མ་ བྱུང་གོང་ནས་བྱ་བ་ངན་པ་འདི་འགོག་དགོས། One should stop this bad activity before the spread of bad rumours.

གཏམ་དོན་གཉིས་མེད། to lose both wealth and fame མིག་དམར་འོས་ ཤོག་འོར་སྟེ་ད་ལོ་གཏམ་དོན་གཉིས་མེད་བྱུང་སོང་། Having been defeated in the election, Migmar lost both wealth and fame this year.

གཏའ་མ་འཛིག་ལེན། to keep and take mortgage གན་རྒྱ་གཞིར་བཟུང་ གཏའ་མ་འཛིག་ལེན་གནང་དགོས། The keeping and taking of mortgages should be done in accordance to the agreement.

བཏང་འགྲོ་བཞག་སྤྲོད་འཐེར་བ། one who is efficient in many tasks ང་ཚོའི་དྲུང་ཆེ་མཆོག་ནི་བཏང་འགྲོ་བཞག་སྤྲོད་འཐེར་བའི་མི་ཞིག་རེད། Our secretary is very efficient in all tasks.

བྱེད་བྱེད་བྱུག་བྱུག to boast of having done this or that ཁྱེད་ རང་གི་བྱེད་བྱེད་བྱུག་བྱུག་བཤད་ཀྱང་སུས་ཀྱང་ཡིད་ཆེས་བྱེད་ཀྱི་མ་རེད། Nobody will trust you although you may boast of having done this or that.

རྟ་རྒན་ལམ་རྒྱུས་ཆེ། མི་རྒན་ཉམས་མྱོང་ཆེ། Lit.: An old horse has more experience over the roads, and an old man has more life experience/ Sense implied: the older the man, the greater experience he has.

རྟ་ར་བརྒྱ་གཤག Lit.: splitting a horse's tail into a hundred strands/ Sense implied: over cautious ལས་དོན་ཆུང་ཆགས་ལ་དྲ་ ར་བརྒྱ་གཤག་གནང་དགོས་དོན་མེད། There is no need to be overly cautious over petty things.

རྟ་གཅིག་གིས་སྣ་གཉིས་འཁྲིགས་ཐབས་མེད། Lit.: one horse cannot

carry two saddles/ Sense implied: one man cannot do two jobs at the same time.

རྟ་གཅིག་ལ་ཡོད་ན་སྒ་གཅིག་དགོས། Lit.: one horse needs one saddle/ Sense implied: one thing will necessitate the other.

རྟ་ཕོ་ལ་རྒྱགས་ཤེད་ཡོད་ན་བྱང་ཐང་རྟིང་པ་རེད། Lit.: If a horse has the energy to run fast, he has the whole northern plain to run in/ Sense implied: This proverb is used to test how much one can do (a sarcastic remark).

རྟ་མ་ཚད་གོང་ལ་ཁྲིད་ན་བཟང་། Lit.: It is better to lead a horse before it is tired/ Sense implied: to do something before someone is completely discouraged.

རྟ་ལམ་བོང་བུས་བཀག Lit.: the path of a horse is blocked by a donkey/ Sense implied: This proverb is a sarcastic remark applied to that person who holds a certain post though it does not fit for him; becoming a barrier for future persons applying for the post.

རྟག་པ་ཐེར་ཟུག permanent, a religious terminology འདུས་བྱས་ ཀྱི་དངོས་པོ་རྟག་པ་ཐེར་ཟུག་གཅིག་ཀྱང་མེད། No product phenemenon is permanent.

རྟག་པ་རེ་བཞིན། always/ constantly ང་ཁྱེད་རང་གི་ས་ལ་རྟག་པ་རེ་བཞིན་ཡོང་ ཐུབ་ཀྱི་མི་འདུག I cannot come to your place always.

རྟའི་མགོ་ལ་མཛོའི་རྭ་ཙོ། Lit.: a horn with horn of a dzo/ Sense implied: very unsuitable

ལྟ་རྟོག་སྐུལ་ལྩག to look after/to inspect and to give an encouragement སློབ་གྲྭ་ཁག་ལ་ལྟ་རྟོག་གནང་དུས་དགེ་སློབ་ཡོངས་ལ་སྐུལ་

སློག་གནང་དགོས། When you inspect schools, it is essential to encourage the students and teachers.

ལྟ་སྤྱོད་བཟང་པོ། sound philosophy and conduct སངས་རྒྱས་པ་རྣམས་ཀྱི་ གཞུང་ནས་ལྟ་སྤྱོད་ཤིན་ཏུ་བཟང་པོ་གསུངས་ཡོད། A very sound philosophy and conduct is presented in the Buddhist texts.

ལྟ་བས་མི་ངོམས། Lit.: not feeling enough by seeing/looking at it/ Sense implied: wish to see again and again རྗེ་བཙུན་སྒྲོལ་མའི་ མཛེས་སྡུག་ནི་ལྟ་བས་མི་ངོམ་པ་ཞིག་ཡོད། One never feels enough of seeing the beauty of goddess Tara. The beauty of Tara cannot be satisfied with a mere glance.

ལྟ་བ་མཐོ་པོ། Lit.: high opinion; philosophy/ Sense implied: to be haughty and proud ཆོས་པ་གཡའ་མ་ཞིག་ཡིན་ན་ལྟ་བ་མཐོ་པོ་བྱེད་མི་ རུང་། If you are a true practitioner, you should not be haughty.

ལྟོ་གོས་གཏམ་གསུམ། food, clothing and reputation མི་ཚང་མ་ལྟོ་གོས་ གཏམ་གསུམ་གྱི་ཆེད་དུ་ལས་ཀ་བྱེད་ཀྱི་ཡོད། Every person works for food, clothing and reputation.

ལྟོ་ཆས་ནང་ལ་བཟས། སྒོང་ངེ་ཕྱི་ལ་བཏང་། Lit.: to eat at home and to lay eggs outside/ Sense implied: unfaithful act

ལྟོས་མེད་རྡོག་རོལ། to treat heedlessly ནས་རྒྱང་ལ་ལྟོས་མེད་རྡོག་རོལ་བཏང་ན་ དཔོན་བཟང་གི་དྲི་ཡང་མི་རོ། There is no scent of even good leadership if simple people are ill-treated.

ལྟོས་ས་ལྟོས་འཛོག repatively ལྟོས་ས་ལྟོས་འཛོག་གི་དབང་དུ་བྱས་ན་ཁོང་རང་ ཡག་ཐག་གཅོད་རེད། He is relatively quite good.

107

སྟག་གི་རི་མོ་ཕྱི་དང་མི་ཡི་རི་མོ་ནང་། Lit.: the stripes of a tiger are seen outside and a person's quality is inside/ Sense implied: A person cannot be judged merely through his external/ This is used to say that one cannot judge a person from outer behaviour only.

སྟག་མགོ་སྦྲུལ་མཇུག Lit.: the head of a tiger and the tail of a snake/ Sense implied: impressive in the beginning and disappointing at the end/impressive beginning with poor ending

སྟག་མིས་བསད། གཅུམ་རང་གིས་འཁྱེར། Lit.: A man kills a tiger but you claim the credit./ Sense implied: to steal other's fame or feat.

སྟག་མོ་ལྟོགས་ཟིན་ལྟོགས་ཀྱང་རང་ཤ་མི་ཟ། Lit.: Even if a tigress is starving, she won't eat her flesh/ Sense implied: in order to express something that one will never do.

སྟག་ཤར་གཞོན་པ། smart and energetic young man ད་ལོ་བོད་ནས་སྟག་ཤར་གཞོན་པ་མང་པོ་འབྱོར་སོང་། This year many smart and young men came from Tibet.

སྟབས་བདེ་པོ། convenient ཁ་ལག་བཟོ་རྒྱུར་སྟབས་བདེ་པོ་མི་འདུག་ན་གཡུག་བཞག རོགས་གནང་། Please leave it, if it is not convenient to cook food.

སྟོང་པ་སྟོང་རྐྱང་། completely empty ཞི་མ་ཞེ་མིས་བཏུང་སྟེ་དེ་ཡང་སྟོང་པ་སྟོང་རྐྱང་བཟོས་འདུག The vessel is completely empty as the cat drank the milk.

སྟོང་ཕྲག་ཁྲི་ཕྲག thousands upon thousands ཕྱི་རྒྱལ་ལ་འགྲོ་ན་འགྲོ་གྲོན་སྟོར་མོ་སྟོང་ཕྲག་ཁྲི་ཕྲག་མང་པོ་དགོས་པ་རེད། If one visits abroad, one

needs to have thousands and thousands of rupees for the
expenses.

སྡོད་སྡོད་ཤིག་ཤིག to be mentally and physically relieved ལས་
ཀ་འདི་ཚར་ནས་སྡོད་སྡོད་ཤིག་ཤིག་ཚགས་སོང་། I am relieved at having
finished the work.

སྤོབས་འབྱོར་གཉིས་ལྡན། wealthy and strong ང་ཚོའི་སྦྱིན་བདག་ནི་སྤོབས་
འབྱོར་གཉིས་ལྡན་ཞིག་རེད། Our sponsor is wealthy as well as strong.

བརྟག་དཔྱད་ནན་ཏན། careful examination གནས་ཚུལ་འདི་ཐད་བརྟག་དཔྱད་
ནན་ཏན་བྱས་པ་ཡིན། We did a careful examination of this issue.

བརྟག་དཔྱད་ངོས་འཛིན། recognition of an investigation ཚོགས་ཆུང་གི་
བརྟག་དཔྱད་ལ་ང་ཚོས་ངོས་འཛིན་ཞུ་གི་ཡིན། We will recognise the
investigation of the committee.

བསྟན་འཛིན་གྱི་སྐྱེས་བུ། holy man/holders of the Teaching ནང་པ་
ཚོས་བསྟན་འཛིན་གྱི་སྐྱེས་བུ་ལ་བཀུར་སྟི་བྱེད་པ་རེད། Buddhists respect the
holders of the Teaching.

བསྱན་བཤིག་ཚ་པོ། humorous ང་ཚོའི་བུ་ཆུང་འདི་བསྱན་བཤིག་ཚ་པོ་ཞེ་དྲག་འདུག
Our little son is very humorous.

བསྔོད་ར་གཏོང་འོས། laudable/ commendable དགེ་ལགས་ཀྱིས་བསྔོད་ར་
གཏོང་འོས་གསུང་བཤད་གནང་སོང་། The teacher gave a commendable
speech.

ཐ་སྐྱེད་གསར་བཟོ། coining new terms ཡིག་བསྒྱུར་གྱི་སྐབས་ཐ་སྐྱེད་གསར་
བཟོ་མང་པོ་བྱེད་པ་རེད། Many new terms are coined during translation.

ཐ་བེ་ཐིབ་བེ། gloomy དེ་རིང་གི་གནམ་གཤིས་ཐ་བེ་ཐིབ་བེ་ཞེ་དྲག་འདུག ཆར་པ་བབས་
རེད། Today's weather is very gloomy. It might rain.

ཐ་རེ་ཐོ་རེ། scattered གྲོང་གསེབ་ཀྱི་མི་རྣམས་གྲོང་འཁྱེར་དུ་ཐ་རེ་ཐོ་རེར་གནས་འདུག People from the villages are scattered in the city.

ཐག་ཁྲ་སྦྲུལ་མཐོང་། perceiving a striped rope for a snake མིག་
གསལ་པོ་མེད་ན་ས་ཆེིབ་པའི་སྐབས་སུ་ཐག་ཁྲར་སྦྲུལ་མཐོང་གི་རེད། One will perceive and mistake a striped rope for a snake if one does not have good eye sight, especially when it is dark.

ཐག་རིང་གི་གཉེན་ལས་གྲོང་པའི་དག་དགའ། An enemy neighbour is better than a far away relative.

ཐག་རིང་གི་གཏམ་དེ་ཕྱེད་བདེན་ཕྱེད་མི་བདེན། A far off news is half true and half false.

ཐག་ཐོགས་མེད་པ། without obstruction/ fluently ཁོང་གིས་ལན་ཐག་
ཐོགས་མེད་པར་བཀྱོན་སོང་། He answered fluently/unobstructedly.

ཐང་རེ་ཐེང་རེ། ཐང་རེ་ཐེང་རེ་བྱེད་པ། hesitant/ to be of two minds

ཐན་ནེ་ཐུན་ནེ། bits and pieces ཁྱི་དེ་ལ་ཤ་ཐན་ནེ་ཐུན་ནེ་གཅིག་ཟ་རྒྱུ་ཐོབ་སོང་། The dog got a small bit of the meat to eat.

ཐབ་ཆུང་མེ་ཚ། ཐབ་ཆུང་ཆུང་མེ་ཚ་པོ། Lit.: a small hearth burns strongly/ Sense implied: A small but effective hearth.

ཐབས་བརྒྱ་བྱུས་སྟོང་། Lit.: a hundred ways and thousand plans/ Sense implied: various means ང་ཚོའི་རང་བཙན་གྱི་ཆེད་དུ་ཐབས་བརྒྱ་བྱུས་སྟོང་གནང་དགོས། We have to adopt various means for our Independence.

ཐབས་བྱུས་གང་གཟབ། best possible means ལས་ཀ་འདི་འགྲུབ་པ་ལ་ཐབས་བྱུས་གང་གཟབ་གནང་རོགས་གནང་། Please apply the best possible means to accomplish this work.

ཐབས་ཟད་ཀ་མེད། helpless/ to have no alternative བོད་མི་ཚོས་རྒྱ་མི་ལ་ངོ་རྒོལ་མ་བྱས་ཀ་མེད་ཆགས་པ་རེད། The Tibetans were left with no alternative but to revolt against the Chinese.

ཐབས་ཤེས་སྔ་གཡར། to find means in advance/ to take loan དུ་ལོ་ཚོང་གི་ཆེད་དུ་དངུལ་ཁང་ནས་དངུལ་ཐབས་ཤེས་སྔ་གཡར་ཞུ་གི་ཡིན། This year I shall obtain a loan from the bank for the business.

ཐབས་ཤེས་འབད་བརྩོན། to try and find means མིས་ཐབས་ཤེས་བྱེད་ན་གང་ཡང་མ་ཐུབ་པ་མེད། If man tries with means and effort, there isn't anything that he cannot do.

ཐབས་ཤེས་བཟང་པོ། a very resourceful person མི་འཛོན་པོ་དེ་ཚོ་ཐབས་ཤེས་བཟང་པོ་ཡོད་རེད། An efficient person is a resourceful man.

ཐབས་ཤེས་ཟུང་འབྲེལ། union of method and wisdom ནང་པའི་གཞུང་དུ་ཐབས་ཤེས་ཟུང་འབྲེལ་གལ་ཆེན་པོ་གསུངས་ཡོད། The union of method and wisdom is greatly emphasized in the Buddhist teaching.

ཐབས་ཤེས་ཡོད་རྒུ་རྩལ་སྒྲུགས། Lit.: to search all kind of means/ Sense implied: no effort has been spared ཐབས་ཤེས་ཡོད་རྒུ་རྩལ་སྒྲུགས་ཐུབ་ན་ནམ་མཁའི་བྱ་ཡང་འཛིན་ཐུབ། If one spares no effort, one can catch even a bird in the sky.

ཐམ་མེ་ཐོམ་མེ། unclear mind ཆང་འཐུང་ན་མི་ཐམ་མེ་ཐོམ་མེ་ཆགས་ཀྱི་རེད། One's mind becomes unclear if one takes wine.

ཐུགས་འཁུར་ཆེ་བསྐྱེད། with great dedication ཇེ་བཙུན་པད་མ་མཆོག་ནས་ཐུགས་འཁུར་ཆེ་བསྐྱེད་ཀྱིས་བོད་ཁྱིམ་སློབ་གྲྭ་ཡར་རྒྱས་གཏོང་གནང་མཛད་པ་རེད། With great dedication, Mrs. Jetsun Pema improved TCV Schools.

ཐུགས་ནུས་གང་ལྕོགས། whatever is possible for one's mind ཐུག་ལས་ཐུགས་ནུས་གང་ལྕོགས་གནང་རོགས་གནང་། Please do this work as much as you can.

ཐུད་འཚོ་བ་མར་གྱི་བཀའ་དྲིན་རེད། མར་མེད་ན་ཕྱུར་རའི་པག་གོང་རེད། The fineness of **thue** (Tibetan buttered cheese) is due to butter. Without butter, it would have been a solid piece of cheese and barley flour.

ཐུབ་ཚོད་ཅན་པོ། དབང་ཡོད་ཚ་པོ། one who bullies others ཁོས་གཞན་ལ་
ཐུབ་ཚོད་གཏོང་གི་འདུག He bullies others.

ཐེ་ཚོམ་སོམ་ཉི། doubt དཀོན་མཆོག་ལ་ཐེ་ཚོམ་སོམ་ཉི་མེད་པར་གསོལ་བ་ཐོབ། Pray
to the triple gem without any doubt.

ཐོག་ཐིབས། ཐོབ་རྒྱག་གོ་རྒྱག all of a sudden ཁ་སང་ང་ཐོབ་རྒྱག་གོ་རྒྱག
ཁྲོམ་ལ་འགྲོ་དགོས་བྱུང་། Yesterday, all of a sudden I had to go to
the market. ཚོགས་ཀྱི་དབུས་སུ་ལྷ་མོ་གཡུ་སྒྲོན་མ་ཐོག་ཐིབས་བཀྱོན་སོང་།
Lhamo Youdonma (a female oracle) spontaneously came into
trance in the crowd.

ཐོབ་ཐང་འདྲ་མཉམ། equal rights ཁྲིམས་ཀྱི་མདུན་སར་ཚང་མར་ཐོབ་ཐང་འདྲ་མཉམ་
ཡིན། Everyone is equal in the eyes of law.

ཐོས་བསམ་སློབ་གཉིར། Lit.: to listen, think and learn/ Sense
implied: study and comtemplation དགོན་པར་ཚོས་ཀྱི་ཐོས་བསམ་
སློབ་གཉེར་གནང་བ་རེད། Religious studies and comtemplation are
carried out at the monasteries.

ཐོས་ཆད་གཏམ་མིན། མཐོང་ཆད་ཟས་མིན། Lit.: all that one hears is
not news and all that one eats is not food/ Sense
implied: Don't eat everything and listen to everything.

ཐོས་བསམ་ཕྱོགས་རེ་བ། partial or limited study ཐོས་བསམ་ཕྱོགས་རེ་བས་
མཁས་པ་ཡག་པོ་ཆགས་ཐུབ་ཀྱི་མ་རེད། Partial study cannot make good
scholars.

མཐའ་མེད་མུ་མེད། infinite and boundless ནམ་མཁའི་ཁྱོན་ནི་མཐའ་མེད་མུ་ མེད་རེད། The extent of the sky is infinite and boundless.

མཐར་ཐུག་རྙེད་དོན། the ultimate findings ཆོས་ཀྱི་མཐར་ཐུག་རྙེད་དོན་ནི་རང་ བཞིན་གྱིས་མ་གྲུབ་པ་རེད། The ultimate finding of a phenomena is devoid of inherent existence.

མཐུན་ལམ་དམ་གཙང་། harmonious relationship ལུང་པའི་བདེ་སྐྱིད་ཀྱི་ ཆེད་དུ་མི་རྣམས་མཐུན་ལམ་དམ་གཙང་དགོས་པ་ཡིན། The harmonious relationship is required for the happiness of a country.

མཚོ་ནོན་ཕྲག་དོག jealousy མཚོ་ནོན་ཕྲག་དོག་བྱེད་པས་ཅི་ལ་ཕན། What is the use of getting jealous?

མཐོང་ཐུ་ཐོས་རྒྱ། Lit.: extent of seeing and hearing/ Sense implied: widely read མཁས་པ་ཡག་པོ་ཆགས་པ་ལ་མཐོང་ཐུ་ཐོས་རྒྱ་ཆེན་པོ་ དགོས་པ་ཡིན། In order to become a good scholar, one needs to have read widely.

མཐོང་ཆུང་ཁྱད་གསོད། belittle and disdain ཡ་རབས་རྣམས་ཀྱིས་གཞན་ལ་ མཐོང་ཆུང་ཁྱད་གསོད་བྱེད་ཀྱི་མ་རེད། No decent person will ever belittle and have disdain for others.

འཐེན་འཁྱེར་གར་གོར། partiality and procastination ལུང་ཆན་ཕན་ཆུན་ འཐེན་འཁྱེར་དང་ལས་དོན་ལ་གར་གོར་བྱེད་ན་མཐུན་ལམ་ལ་གནོད་ཀྱི་རེད། It would be detrimental to unity if there were partiality among the region, and procastination in the work.

114

ད་ལྟ་བར་དུ། till today/until now ད་ལྟ་བར་དུ་བོད་ལ་བསྡད་པ་ཡིན། Until now I have lived in Tibet.

དག་ཐེར་ལེགས་བཅོས། reform མ་འོས་རྒྱ་ནག་གི་སྤྱི་ཚོགས་དག་ཐེར་ལེགས་བཅོས་ བཏང་བ་རེད། Mao reformed the Chinese society.

དག་དག་གང་། full/ to fill to the brim ང་ཚོའི་མགྲོན་པོས་ཨ་རག་ཤེལ་དམ་ དག་དག་གང་བཏུང་སོང་། Our guest drank one full bottle of liquor.

དང་རོད། དང་རོད་ཚ་པོ། fashionable/to take care of one's beauty/ tip top ལོ་ན་ཆུང་དུས་དང་རོད་བྱེད་པ་སྤྱི་སྲོལ་རེད། It is common to be fashionable at a young age.

དང་པོ་དང་རྒྱང་། the very first/foremost བོད་མི་ཨ་མི་རི་ཁར་འགྲོ་མཁན་དང་ པོ་དང་རྒྱང་ནི་པ་སངས་རེད། Mr. Pasang was the very first Tibetan who visited United States.

དད་གུས་དག་སྣང་། faith, respect and the pure vision སྐྱེས་བུ་དམ་ པའི་རྣམ་ཐར་ལ་དད་གུས་དག་སྣང་ཆེན་པོ་ཡོད། I have faith and respect in the biographies of the great holy persons.

དད་དད་གུས་གུས། to bow respectfully/devotionally དད་དད་གུས་གུས་ ཀྱི་རྣམ་ཐར་རྒྱང་པས་བཤེས་གཉེན་བསྟེན་ཚུལ་གྱི་ཁ་འབར་མར་མི་འགྱུར། Simply having devotion cannot become a real means of cultivating one's spiritual master.

དམ་བཅའ་འབུལ་བཞེས། oath taking ceremonies སང་ཉིན་བཀའ་བློན་གྱི་ དམ་བཅའ་འབུལ་བཞེས་ཀྱི་ཉི་མ་དེ་རེད། Tomorrow is oath taking ceremony day of the cabinet ministers.

དམ་ཚིག་ཉམས་ཆགས། degeneration of committment/ broken committment ཆོས་སྐྱོང་སྲུང་མར་དམ་ཚིག་ཉམས་ཆག་བསྐང་བའི་དོན་དུ་བསྐང་ གསོ་དང་འཕྲིན་བཅོལ་ཞུ་དགོས། Offer propitiation to the Dharma protector in order to restore the degeneration of committment.

དར་བབ་ལང་ཚོ། youthful life དར་བབ་ལང་ཚོའི་སྐབས་སུ་ཤེས་བྱ་རིག་གནས་ལ་ བརྩོན་དགོས། One should strive for knowledge when one is young.

དལ་འབྱོར་རྙེད་དཀའ། Lit.: leisure and endowment; difficult to find/ Sense implied: human life is diffuicult to obtain ཆོས་ ལྟར་ན་དལ་འབྱོར་གྱི་མི་ལུས་འདི་ཤིན་ཏུ་རྙེད་དཀའ་བ་ཡིན། According to Dharma teaching, precious human birth is very difficult to find.

དལ་སྟོང་སྐྱིད་སྟོང་། free time for leisure དལ་སྟོང་སྐྱིད་སྟོང་གྱིས་མི་ཚེ་འཁྱོལ་ ཐབས་མེད། It is not possible to lead life in leisure and happy relaxation.

དུག་སྦྲུལ་པང་དུ་བླངས་པ། Lit.: taking a viper in one's lap/ Sense implied: taking risk བསྟན་པ་ཆབ་སྲིད་ཀྱི་དོན་དུ་དུག་སྦྲུལ་པང་དུ་བླངས་པ་ ཡིན། I have taken the risk for the spiritual and temporal purpose.

དུས་བདེ་ཞིང་འཛགས། a time of peace and prosperity དུས་བདེ་ཞིང་ འཛགས་ཀྱི་འཚོ་བར་སྤྱོད་སྐབས་ལས་དོན་ལ་བག་ཡངས་ཕྱན་ནུ་ཁྲ་སྲིད། When people lived in the time of peace and prosperity, there was a possibility of discrepancy due to carelessness.

དུས་ཚོད་གཏན་འཁེལ། confirm time ཡིག་ཚོད་ཀྱི་དུས་ཚོད་ད་ལྟ་གཏན་འཁེལ་རྒྱུ་ རེད། The date for examination time is not yet confirmed.

དེ་འདུ་སོང་ཚང་། therefore ཁོང་གཉིས་འབྲེལ་བ་ཡག་པོ་མེད་པ་དེ་འདུ་སོང་ཚང་ ནང་འགྲིག་ཡོང་ཐབས་བྱེད་ཀྱི་ཡོད། As the relationship between two of them is not good, therefore I am mediating for them.

དེང་སང་། དེང་དུས། these days/ modern days དེང་སང་གཞོན་ནུ་མང་པོ་ བོད་ནས་ཡོང་གི་འདུག These days many young men are coming from Tibet.

རོ་གལ་ཆེན་པོ། very important གནས་ཚུལ་ཆུང་ཚག་ལ་ཡང་རོ་གལ་ཆེན་པོ་གནང་ དགོས། One should give special attention and importance to give special attention to even trivial things.

རོ་གལ་ནན་དན། to stress importance བྱེས་པའི་ཤེས་ཡོན་ལ་རྒན་པས་རོ་གལ་ ནན་དན་བྱེད་དགོས་པ་ཡིན། Elders need to give special attention and to emphasize children's education.

རོ་དམ་འཛིན་བཟུང་། to arrest and take into custody རྒྱ་གར་གཞུང་ནས་ སོ་པ་ཡིན་པ་ཏ་གོ་སོང་ན་རོ་དམ་འཛིན་བཟུང་བྱེད་ཀྱི་རེད། If the government of India finds someone as a spy, he will be arrested and taken into custody.

དོ་དོ་ཏན་ཏན། very careful གནས་ཚུལ་ཆུང་ཆུང་ཡིན་ན་ཡང་དོ་དོ་ཏན་ཏན་བྱེད་ཀྱི་ཡོད། I am being very careful even though it is a very insignificant case.

དོགས་ཟོན་བྱེད། beware of ཁྱི་ལ་དོགས་ཟོན་བྱེད། Beware of dogs.

དྲང་པོ་དྲང་གཤགས། faithfully/honestly/sincerely ལས་ཀ་དྲང་པོ་དྲང་གཤག་བྱེད་ཀྱི་ཡོད། I work sincerely.

དྲན་ཤེས་བག་ཡོད། mindfulness, introspection and conscientiousness/ སྡིག་སྤོང་དགེ་སྒྲུབ་བྱ་བ་ལ་དྲན་ཤེས་བག་ཡོད་བསྟེན་དགོས། One has to be mindful, introspective and conscientious in order to abandone negativities and cultivate virtues.

དྲི་བ་དྲིས་ལན། questions and answers/ interview དྲི་བ་དྲིས་ལན་གྱི་སྐབས་སུ་ཚབ་ཚབ་གནང་རྒྱུ་ཡོད་མ་རེད། One should not get nervous at the time of interview.

དྲིན་ཅན་ལག་པར་རྡོ་བརྡབས། Lit.: to hit stone on a kind person's hand/ Sense implied: to be ungrateful དྲིན་ཅན་ལག་པར་རྡོ་བརྡབས་ཀྱི་བྱ་སྤྱོད་ལ་འཇུག་པ་ནི་མི་ཁྲེལ་མེད་དོ་མ་ཞིག་རེད། It is indeed a shameless act to indulge in hitting stone on a kind person's hand.

དྲིན་ལན་ལོག་འཇལ། to repay the kindness with a bad treatement/ ungrateful response ཕ་མ་དང་དགེ་རྒན་ལྟ་བུའི་དྲིན་ཅན་ལ་དྲིན་ལན་ལོག་འཇལ་བྱས་ཚེ་ལ་ཡོག་དེས་པར་འགྱུར་གྱི་རེད། If one is

118

ungrateful to their kind parents and teachers, definitely there will be same treatement to the self also.

དྲེད་མོང་གིས་འཕྱི་བ་འཛིན་པ། Lit.: a brown bear catching mammots/ Sense implied: A man who does things continuously but unattentively. སློབ་སྦྱོང་གནང་དུས་འདྲེ་མོང་གིས་ འཕྱི་བ་འཛིན་པ་ནང་བཞིན་གནང་རྒྱུ་མེད། One should not study like a brown bear catching mammoth.

གདུག་རྩུབ་དགུ་འཛོམས། Lit.: a collection of nine tyrannical acts/ Sense implied: worst torture གདུག་རྩུབ་དགུ་འཛོམས་པའི་གཞུང་འཛིན་ འོག་ནས་ཡང་བདེ་སྐྱིད་ཐོབ་ཐབས་མེད། Never one can obtain happiness under a tyrannical government.

གདུང་སེམས་མཉམ་བསྐྱེད། to share the sadness and disappointment/to share difficulties and hardships སྤྱི་པའི་ ལས་ཀ་ལ་ཚང་མས་གདུང་སེམས་མཉམ་བསྐྱེད་གནང་དགོས་རེད། It is necessary to share the difficulties and hardships for the common cause.

བདག་སྐྱིད་གཞན་སྨོན། happiness for the self and appreciation by others མི་ཚེ་དོན་དང་ལྡན་པ་བྱུང་ན་བདག་སྐྱིད་གཞན་སྨོན་ཡོང་གི་རེད། Successful human life brings happiness for the self and appreciation by others.

བདག་བསྟོད་གཞན་སྨོད། self-praise and belittling others བདག་བསྟོད་ གཞན་སྨོད་བྱེད་པ་རང་ཉིད་ཉམས་པའི་རྒྱུ། It is a cause of downfall to praise oneself and belittle others.

བདག་མེད་ཡིང་བསྐྱུར། totally discarded/ without anybody to

care for/total negligence/ignoring དཀའ་ངལ་འཕྲད་པའི་སྐབས་སུ་ བདག་མེད་ཡིང་བསྐྱར་བྱེད་མཁན་ཕ་སྟུག་རེད། Nobody cares when one is in difficulty.

བདེ་སྐྱིད་ཕུན་སུམ་ཚོགས་པ། very happy and prosperous ཚེ་དང་ མཐུན་པའི་ལས་ཀ་བྱེད་ན་བདེ་སྐྱིད་ཕུན་སུམ་ཚོགས་པ་ཡོང་གི་རེད། If one does work in accordance with the faith, one will be happy and prosperous in one's life span.

བདེན་པ་མཐའ་བསྒྲེལ། to prove the truth in its entirety/to substantiate thoroughly ངས་བཤད་པའི་གཏམ་རྣམས་བདེན་པ་མཐའ་ བསྒྲེལ་བྱ་རྒྱུར་སྲ་སྒྲིག་ཡིན། I am ready to substantiate the truth of what I have said in its entirety.

བདེན་པ་བདེན་ཐུབ། reliable truth/undeniable truth བདེན་པ་བདེན་ཐུབ་ ཀྱི་སྒོ་ནས་ཁུངས་སྐྱེལ་བྱེད་དགོས། One has to prove the facts through reliable truth.

བདེན་པ་ར་སྤྲོད། to point out the facts/to see the truth/evidence to prove the fact བོད་རང་བཙན་གཙང་མ་ཡིན་པའི་བདེན་པ་ར་སྤྲོད་ཉུ་རྒྱུ་ཡོད། We have evidential facts to prove the authenticity of the Independance of Tibet.

བདེན་པའི་གནས་ལུགས། actual situation/ true picture རང་དབང་མེད་ན་ བདེན་པའི་གནས་ལུགས་ཇི་ལྟར་བཤད་ཐུབ། How can one describe the true picture when there is no freedom ?

བདེན་བརྫུན་བརྟག་ཞིབ། to investigate the right and wrong/the

120

truth and falsity བདེན་བརྫུན་བཏགས་ཞིབ་མ་བྱས་པར་ཡིད་ཆེས་བྱེད་ན་གླུགས་ དགས་རེད། It is a sign of stupidity to trust someone without investigating the right and the wrong.

མདའ་གཅིག་གིས་ཤྭ་བ་གཉིས་བསད། Lit.: killing two deers with one arrow/ Sense implied: to have two things done at a time/one stone killing two birds

མདའ་གཞུ་མེད་ན་གཏམ་ངན་མེད། མིག་མེད་ན་ལིང་ཏོག་མེད། Lit.: There will not be bad reputation if there are no bows and arrows and there will not be cataract, if there is no eye./ Sense implied: A man without rank cannot be degraded.

མདོ་སྔགས་ཟུང་འབྲེལ། union of Sutra and Tantra མདོ་སྔགས་ཟུང་འབྲེལ་ གྱི་ལམ་ལ་བརྟེན་ནས་ཉམས་ལེན་བྱེད་དགོས། One needs to practice by way of the path of the union of Sutra and Tantra

འདོད་ཆུང་ཆོག་ཤེས། few desires and contentment འདོད་ཆུང་ཆོག་ཤེས་ ཀྱི་བསླབ་བྱ་འདི་ནི་ནང་པའི་དཔལ་འབྱོར་གྱི་ཉིང་མཚོ་ཡིན། The essense of the Buddhist economy is to be content with few desires.

འདོན་ཁ་ཁྲལ། daily recitation prayers བོད་ཀྱི་དགོན་པར་ཐོག་མར་འདོན་ཁ་ ཁྲལ་སློ་འཛིན་བྱེད་པ་རེད། In the beginning, daily recitation prayers are memorized in the Tibetan monasteries.

འདྲ་འདྲའི་ནང་ནས་མི་འདྲ་བ། Lit.: the unequal among equals/ Sense implied: invincible, dynamic, matchless པགོང་ས་ མཆོག་ནི་རྒྱལ་ཁབ་ཀྱི་དབུ་ཁྲིད་འདྲ་འདྲའི་ནང་ནས་མི་འདྲ་བ་ཞིག་ཡིན་པ་རེད། His

Holiness the Dalai Lama is an incomparable among the leaders of the world./ His Holiness the Dalai Lama is an unequal leader among his equals - the leaders of the world.

འདྲ་དཔེ་རྒྱས་འགེབས། an example applied to many seemingly similar instances although not appropriate

འདྲེ་ཤར་སྒོར་གནས་པ་ལ་གླུད་ནུབ་སྒོར་གཏོང་བ། Lit.: keeping the demon at the eastern gate and giving the ritual cake at the western gate/ Sense implied: to criticise wrong persons/wrong criticism

རོ་སྐམ་ཡང་མི་མི་འབར། ཤིང་རློན་ཡང་མི་འབར། Lit.: even if the rock is dry, it won't burn and the wood will catch fire even it is wet/ Sense implied: possibility and the impossibility depend upon their causal factors

རོ་སྒོར་མོར་མི་དོག་སྐྱེ་མི་སྲིད། Lit.: It is impossible for flowers to grow from pebbles./ Sense implied: An example of impossibility

རོ་ཆུང་ཡང་ལྷགས་པས་ཁྱེར་དོགས་མེད། Lit.: However small a stone may be it cannot be taken away by wind./ Sense implied: unnecessary concern ཕུགས་ཆུང་ཆུང་ཕུགས་གཡེང་མ་གནང་ དང་རོ་ཆུང་ཆུང་ལྷགས་པས་ཁྱེར་དོགས་མེད། ། A humble man should not worry as there is no danger of a stone being carried away by wind.

རོ་ཆུང་ཡང་ཇ་མ་བཅག་ཡོང་། even a small rock can break a clay pitcher/ Sense implied: effectiveness in the work.

རྡོ་དོན་ཡང་སྙིང་། in nut-shell/in essence རྡོ་དོན་ཡང་སྙིང་མི་ཚང་མས་རང་གི་ལས་འགན་ཧུར་ཐག་སྒྲུབ་དགོས། In short everyone has to perform his duty sincerely.

རྡོག་རྩ་ཆིག་བསྒྲིལ། integrity, unity རྡོག་རྩ་ཆིག་བསྒྲིལ་ཡོད་ན་དགྲ་བོས་གནོད་ཐུབ་ཀྱི་མ་རེད། Enemy cannot harm if there is unity in a country.

སྤྱིག་པ་མིག་བཙུམ། to commit non-virtues blindly/ Sense implied: daring and intentional negativities ཆོས་པ་རྣམ་དག་གཅིག་གིས་སྤྱིག་པ་མིག་བཙུམ་ནས་ཡང་བྱེད་ཀྱི་མ་རེད། True dharma practitioners will never commit non-virtues blindly.

སྤྱིག་རང་བསགས་རང་ཁུར། Lit.: one has to take the burden of one's non-virtues/ Sense implied: one is responsible for one's wrong done ལྷས་སྦྱིན་སྤྱིག་པ་རང་ཁུར་དང་ཨ་ནེས་བཙུགས་པའི་ཟམ་པར་ཨ་ནེ་རང་ཉིད་འགྲོ་རྒྱུ་རེད། Lhejin was responsible for his non-virtues and the nuns had to go through the bridges made by them.

སྤུག་རུས་ཆ་པོ། having great fortitude དོན་ཆེན་སྒྲུབ་པ་ལ་སྤུག་རུས་ཆ་པོ་དགོས་པ་ཨིན། A great fortitude is required in order to fulfill a great aim.

སྤུག་བཤད་སྨུག་བཤད། to mumble a curse བུ་མོ་སྦྱོད་ངན་དེ་ཚོས་སྤུག་བཤད་སྨུག་བཤད་ལྷུང་པ་གང་བཤད་སོང་། These indecent girls mumbled a lot of curses.

123

སྡོང་པོ་བསྐྱར་ནས་ཡལ་གར་བཤད་པ། Lit.: talking about the branches leaving aside the main trunk of the tree/ Sense implied: to ignore the root of something/beating around the bush

རྡབ་རྡབ་སིག་སིག to become broke/ having spent all money or emptied ལོ་གསར་ལ་དངུལ་ཆང་མ་རྡབ་རྡབ་སིག་སིག་བཏང་བ་ཡིན། I spent all of my money during Losar (say, by gambling).

བསྡུས་བསྡུས་གཅིག a short one/ brief སྒྲུང་བསྡུས་བསྡུས་གཅིག་གསུང་དང་། Please tell me a short story.

ན་རྒས་རྟེ་རིབ། ageing with sagging eyelids ཕྱན་ད་ཆ་དབང་པོ་ནུས་ཤིང་
ན་རྒས་རྟེ་རིབ་ལ་བརྟེན་བསམ་འཆར་རྒྱས་པོ་ཞུ་མི་ཐུབ། Now that I am aged
with sagged eyelids, I cannot give detailed suggestion.

ན་ན་ཚོ་ཚོ། often getting sick ན་ན་ཚོ་ཚོ་མ་ཡོང་གོང་ནས་འཕྲོད་བསྟེན་ཡག་པོ་བྱེད་
དགོས། One should take good care of one's health before one
gets sick.

ནག་ཉེས་དགུ་འཛོམས། aggregation of nine crimes ནག་ཉེས་དགུ་འཛོམས་
པའི་མི་ལ་བཟང་པོའི་རེ་བ་བྱེད་པ་ནི་གླུགས་པ་རེད། It is stupid to hope for a
good thing from a person who has committed nine crimes.

ནག་ཉེས་ངོས་ལེན། Lit.: confessing or admitting crimes ནག་ཉེས་
ངོས་ལེན་བྱེད་ན་ཁྲིམས་ཐོག་ནས་ཉེས་པ་ཡང་བ་ཡོད་རེད། If someone confesses
his crime, the legal punishment would be lighter.

ནག་ཉེས་ཆེ་ཆུང་། the extent of crime ཁོང་གཉིས་ཀྱི་ནག་ཉེས་ཆེ་ཆུང་ཁྲིམས་ཀྱི་
ཐོག་ནས་ཤེས་ཀྱི་རེད། The extent of their crimes will be known
through the laws.

ནག་པོ་ནག་རྐྱང་། complete black ཨེ་ཤེ་ཡའི་མི་ཚོའི་སྐྲ་ནག་པོ་ནག་རྐྱང་རེད།
The hair of Asian people is completely black.

ནག་མེད་གྱོང་འཁེལ། the innocent loser due to other's blame མི་

ནག་མེད་ལ་མི་བསད་པའི་ཉེས་གྱོང་འཁིལ་སོང་། An innocent person got blamed for the murder.

ནག་ཚུབས་ཚུབས། frowning/ moody ཞོགས་པ་སྟུ་པོ་ནས་གདོང་པ་ནག་ཚུབས་ ཚུབས་བསྟན་ན་སྙིད་པོ་མི་འདུག If you show me a frowning face right in the morning, I am not happy.

ནེ་ཙོའི་མ་ཎི་དང་འདྲ་བའི་ཁ་འདོན་འདོན་པ། reciting prayer like a parrot/prattling like a parrot ཟབ་མོའི་དོན་མ་རྟོགས་ན་ཁྱེད་རང་གི་ འདོན་པ་དེ་ནེ་ཙོའི་མ་ཎི་དང་ཁྱད་པར་མེད། Your recitation of prayers will not be different from that of a parrot reciting OM MA NI PAD ME HUM if you don't understand the profound meaning.

ནང་བགྲུ་མི་ཤེས་ན་ཕྱི་དོན་མི་འགྲུབ། If there is a misfortune/problem at home, one will not be successful outside home

ནང་བགྲུ་ཤེས་ན་ཕྱི་དོན་འགྲུབ་ ནང་བགྲུ་མ་ཤེས་ན་ཕྱིས་དོན་མི་འགྲུབ། If all is well at home, then things will go well outside and vice versa.

ནང་གཏམ་ཕྱིར་སྒྲོལ། disclosing the secret སྤྱི་ཚོགས་ཀྱི་ནང་དུ་ནང་གཏམ་ཕྱིར་ བསྒྲལ་བྱེད་ན་དགུགས་ཤིང་ཆག་གི་རེད། Disclosing a secret of the society to the outside will become a schism.

ནང་དོན་བཀའ་མོལ། private or confidential talk ནང་དོན་བཀའ་མོལ་གང་ བྱུང་ཡང་ང་ལ་ལོན་གནང་རོགས་གནང་། Please inform me whatever the informal discussion may be.

ནང་དོན་རྩོད་རྩོག internal dispute ནང་དོན་རྩོད་རྩོག་སློང་མཁན་སུ་རེད། Who caused the internal dispute ?

ནང་དཔའ་བོའི་དཔའ་གྲལ་མ་ཞིག་ན། ཕྱི་གི་སར་དམག་ལ་སྐྲག་མི་དགོས། When the inner bravery of a warrior is not lost, there is no need to fear the war of king Gesar from the outside.

ནངས་ཚ་ཡོད་ན་གུང་ཚ་མེད། Lit.: If one has salt in the morning, one doesn't have it in the afternoon/ Sense implied: This proverb is used to express the hard life of someone.

ནད་བརྒྱ་སྨན་གཅིག one medication for a hundred sicknesses/ panacea རིན་ཆེན་རིལ་བུ་ནི་ནད་བརྒྱ་སྨན་གཅིག་གི་དཔེ་མཚོན་ཞིག་ཡིན། Rinchen Rilbu (a precious tibetan pill) is an example of a medication that cures a hundred illnesses.

ནད་གཅོང་ནུས་ཐག poor chronic patient བདེ་ལེགས་སྨན་ཁང་ནས་ཐག་ཏུ་ ནད་གཅོང་ནུས་ཐག་ལ་རོགས་རམ་བྱེད་པ་རེད། Delek Hospital always helps the poor and chronic patients.

ནད་བཅོས་སྲོག་སྐྱོབ། to recover from illness and save life དམག་གི་ སྐབས་ནད་བཅོས་སྲོག་སྐྱོབ་ཀྱི་ཆེད་དུ་རྔར་དུ་བཀླ་མཁན་ཡོད། During war there is a separate unit to look after the wounded to save their lives.

ནད་མུག་འཁྲུག་རྩོད་དུས། Lit.: a period of war, starvation and sicknesses/ Sense implied: period of degeneration/bad era

ནམ་མཁའི་མེ་ཏོག Lit.: the sky flower/ Sense implied: a common example of non-existence ནམ་མཁའི་མེ་ཏོག་ནི་མེད་པའི་དཔེ་ཞིག་ཡིན། Sky-flower is an instance of non-existence.

ནམ་རྒྱུན་ནང་བཞིན། as usual དེ་རིང་མཛད་སྒོ་ནི་ནམ་རྒྱུན་ནང་བཞིན་འདུག Today's function looks as usual.

ནམ་རྒྱུན་ཟེར་སྲོལ། common saying or oral interpretation སྤྱི་ཚོགས་ཀྱི་ནང་ནམ་རྒྱུན་ཟེར་སྲོལ་ཁག་ལ་དོ་གལ་ཆེན་པོ་བྱེད་ཀྱི་རེད། Common sayings or oral interpretations are considered important in society.

ནམ་ནག་མཚན་མོ། at mid-night ཡིག་ཚད་སྐབས་ནམ་ནག་མཚན་མོར་ཡང་སློབ་སྦྱོང་བྱེད་ཀྱི་འདུག Students study even at mid-night during the examinations.

ནུས་པས་སླེངས་ཆོད། within the scope of one's ability རང་གི་ནུས་པས་སླེངས་ཆོད་ཧྲུར་ཐག་བྱེད་པ་ཡིན། I did best within the scope of my ability.

གནམ་ཐོག་འཐབ་རྐོལ། air-attack/to attack through planes ཨ་མེ་རི་ཀས་གནམ་ཐོག་འཐབ་རྐོལ་གྱི་ཐོག་ནས་ཨི་རག་ཕམ་པར་བྱས། The United States defeated Iraq through air-attacks.

གནམ་ཐོག་སྲུང་སྐྱོབ། air defence ཨ་མེ་རི་ཀ་ལ་གནམ་ཐོག་སྲུང་སྐྱོབ་ཡོད་པ་དེ་བཞིན་ཨུ་རུ་སུ་ལ་ཡང་ཡོད་པ་རེད། Russia too has an air defence force like that of the U.S.A.

གནས་སྟངས་གཅིག་གྱུར། the same situation or condition བོད་རང་
བཙན་ཤོར་བའི་རྗེས་སུ་བོད་མི་མཐོ་དམན་ཆེན་ཆུང་མ་གནས་སྟངས་གཅིག་གྱུར་ཆགས་པ་རེད། Tibetans of all ranks have fallen in the same condition after losing their independance.

གནས་ངོས་ཚོད་རྩིས། Lit.: to guess someone based upon the situation/ Sense implied: to insult somebody at its weakness/taking advantage of a situation རང་གི་གཞུང་དང་དཔུ་འཁྲིད་ཚོར་གནས་ངོས་ཚོད་རྩིས་ཀྱིས་མཐོང་ཆུང་བརྩི་མེད་བྱེད་མི་རུང་། One should not take advantage of the shortcoming of one's government and leaders.

གནས་ལུགས་གོ་བསྡུར། discussion གནས་ལུགས་གོ་བསྡུར་བྱེད་ན་གནས་ཚུལ་གསལ་པོ་ཆགས་ཀྱི་རེད། The issue will be clear if there will be proper discussion.

གནས་ལུགས་རགས་བསྡུས། a brief report ད་ལམ་གནས་ལུགས་རགས་བསྡུས་ཤིག་སྙན་སྐྱོན་ཞུ་གི་ཡིན། This time I am going to make a brief report.

གནོད་སྐྱོན་ཆབས་ཆེ། a big disaster ཁ་སང་མེར་བསྲེགས་དེས་གནོད་སྐྱོན་ཆབས་ཆེན་བཏང་འདུག Yesterday's arson created a big disaster.

མནར་གཅོད་འཇིགས་སྐྲག fear & oppression ཙོ་གཡོག་མང་པོ་སྟིན་བདག་གི་མནར་གཅོད་འཇིགས་སྐྲག་འོག་མི་ཚེ་སྐྱེལ་ཀྱི་ཡོད། Many slaves spend their lives under the fear & oppression of their masters.

ཉ་ཐོས་བརྒྱ་ལས་མིག་མཐོང་གཅིག་དགའ། Seeing once is better than a hundred hearings.

རྣག་ཐོག་གཅོག་འཐིལ། Lit.: to lance the very centre of the boil/ Sense implied: to point out the mistakes or short-coming རང་གི་སྐྱོན་བརྗོད་པ་དེ་གནད་ལ་འཐིལ་ན་རྣག་ཐོག་གཅོག་འཐིལ་བྱུང་བ་རེད། If someone's criticism rightly hits the target, then it is known as lancing the very centre of the boil.

རྣམ་དཀར་འཕྲིན་ལས། wholesome activity སྐྱེས་བུ་དཀར་པོ་རྣམས་རྣམ་དཀར་ འཕྲིན་ལས་ཀྱི་ལས་ལ་གཏན་དུ་གཞོལ། Good persons are always engaged in the wholesome activity.

རྣམ་དཔྱོད་རྩལ་ལྡན། skillful རྣམ་དཔྱོད་ཀྱི་རྩལ་དང་ལྡན་པའི་མིས་མང་ཚོགས་ཀྱི་མགོ་ འཁྲིད་བྱེད་ཐུབ། A skillful person can lead the people.

རྣམ་གཡེང་བག་མེད། careless and distraction or impoliteness རྣམ་ གཡེང་བག་མེད་ཀྱི་རང་ལ་མི་ཚེ་ཕྱེད་ཀ་རྫོགས། Half of life is wasted in carelessness and distraction.

ན་ཁྱུང་བརྡབས་པ། Lit.: to bang one's nose/ Sense implied: to be disappointed and to get a lesson ཁ་སང་ང་ཁོང་གི་ནང་དུ་ཕྱིན་པ་ཡིན། ཁོང་བཞུགས་མི་འདུག ང་སྣ་ཁྱུང་བརྡབས་སོང་། Yesterday I went to his home. I was disappointed. He was not there.

སྣ་མིན་སྣ་ཚོགས། all sorts/variety གྲོང་འཁྱེར་ཁག་ཏུ་མོ་ཊ་སྣ་མིན་སྣ་ཚོགས་ མཐོང་རྒྱུ་འདུག We see all sorts of cars and vehicles in the cities.

སྣ་ཚོགས་ཐབས་བརྒྱ། hundred ways/hundreds of means ལས་ཀ་ གང་ཞིག་བྱེད་རྒྱུའི་འདུན་པ་ཡོད་ན་སྣ་ཚོགས་ཐབས་བརྒྱ་ལས་ཀྱིས་ཡོང་། Where there is will there are hundreds of ways to do a thing.

སྣ་མཐེབ་སྤྲད་པ། to put a warning finger at the nose ངས་སྐད་ཆ་
བཤད་སྟངས་ནོར་ནས་ཁོང་གིས་སྣ་མཐེབ་སྤྲད་བྱུང་། I made a mistake in the way I spoke for which he pointed a warning finger at my nose.

སྣང་ཆུང་ལྷོད་གཡེང་། negligence and careless ལས་ཀ་གང་འདྲ་ཞིག་ཡིན་ཡང་སྣང་ཆུང་ལྷོད་གཡེང་གནང་མི་རུང་། It is not advisable to be negligent and careless in whatever kind of work it may be.

སྣང་མེད་ཚོར་མེད། indifferent/insensitive སྣང་མེད་ཀྱི་མི་རྣམས་ལ་དགའ་སྡུག་གི་ཚོར་བ་ཅི་ཡང་མེད། An insensitive person doesn't feel joy and sorrow.

སྤུ་བུ་དཀར་པོ་ཚོན་མདོག་གང་ལ་བསྒྱུར་བསྒྱུར་རེད། Lit.: A white wool can be dyed in any colour one wants/ Sense implied: a child can be guided in any direction

སྣུམ་ཟད་མར་མེ། exhaustion of oil in a lamp/dying butter lamp མིའི་མི་ཚེ་ནི་སྣུམ་ཟད་མར་མེ་བཞིན་ཉིན་རེ་ནས་རྫོགས་འགྲོ་བ་རེད། Human life slowly comes to an end day by day just like the exhaustion of oil in a lamp.

སྡོད་ཞབས་བརྡོལ་ལ་ཆུ་བླུགས་པ། Lit.: pouring water into a leaking vessel/pot/ Sense implied: one who doesn't keep in mind what is heard from a teacher; one of the three basic faults of a listener

སྦོན་འཕྲི་སྐོར་བཅོག omission and addition; to alter wherever necessary འདི་རྩོམ་འདི་ལ་སྐོན་འཕྲི་སྐོར་བཅོག་གང་དགོས་བཏང་སྟེ་ཞུས་དག་ གཏོང་རོགས་གནང་། Please edit this article, making ommissions and additions wherever necessary.

132

པ

ཕྲུ་གུ་ཤོར་བ། miscarriage ཕྲུ་གུ་སྐྱེས་པ་ལས་ཕྲུ་གུ་ཤོར་བ་དེ་གཟུགས་པོར་གནོད་སྐྱོན་ཆེ་བ་ཡོད། Miscarriage is more harmful to the health than delivering a child.

པོ་པོ་མོ་མོ། grand-father and grand-mother པོ་པོ་དང་མོ་མོ་གཉིས་གནས་བསྐོར་དུ་ཕྱིན་སོང་། The grand-father and grand-mother went for pilgrimage.

པག་ཁ་ལ་ཟ་བར་ ལམ་ལྟག་ཁུང་དུ་བསྐོར་དོན་མེད། Lit.: There is no need to twist one's arm around one's neck in order to eat a ball of Tsampa/ Sense implied: unnecessary effort.

དཔག་ཏུ་མེད་པ། boundless or inconceiveable ཉི་མའི་འོད་དཔག་ཏུ་མེད་པ་ཕྱོགས་ཐམས་ཅད་དུ་ཁྱབ། The boundless or inconceivable rays of the sun pervades everywhere.

དཔའ་འཁྲུམས་སྙིང་འདར། to be afraid of/ to shiver at the sight of fearful སྡར་མའི་ཚོགས་རྣམས་གཡུལ་གྱི་ངོར་དཔའ་འཁྲུམས་སྙིང་འདར་བྱེད་པ་རེད། Cowardly people lose their heart and shiver at the fearful sight.

དཔའ་ངར་སྤོབས་ལྡན། དཔའ་ངར་བརྟུལ་ཕོད། courageous, powerful and dauntlẻss གླིང་རྗེ་གེ་སར་རྒྱལ་པོ་ནི་དཔའ་བོ་དཔའ་ངར་བརྟུལ་ཕོད་པ་ཞིག་རེད། King Gesar was a very courageous and dauntless warrior.

དཔའ་ཆ་ཐང་པོ། strong, durable and in good condition མོ་ཊ་འདི་ད་

ལྟ་དཔའ་ཆ་ཐང་པོ་འདུག Right now/At the moment this car is in good condition.

དཔར་བསྐྲུན་འགྲེམས་སྤེལ། publication and distribution བོད་ཀྱི་སྲིད་

དོན་རྒྱལ་རབས་དཔར་བསྐྲུན་འགྲེམས་སྤེལ་གནང་མཁན་ཤེས་རིག་དཔར་ཁང་རེད།The Tibetan Cultural Printing Press is the publisher and distributer of the Political History of Tibet.

དཔལ་འབྱོར་འདུ་འགོད། financial dealings/ fund raising ཚོང་པ་

རྣམས་དཔལ་འབྱོར་འདུ་འགོད་ལ་མཁས་པ་ཡིན། Businessmen are expert in fund raising or making money.

དཔལ་འབྱོར་འཕྱུགས་བསྐྱན། economic development རྒྱལ་ཁབ་ཀྱི་དཔལ་

འབྱོར་འཕྱུགས་བསྐྱན་ཆེད་དུ་བཟོ་གྲྭ་བཙུགས་པ་རེད། Many factories are set up for national economic development.

དཔལ་འབྱོར་ལོངས་སྤྱོད། wealth and resources སངས་རྒྱས་ཀྱི་ཚོས་

ལུགས་ལྟར་ན་དཔལ་འབྱོར་ལོངས་སྤྱོད་ཡོང་བ་ལ་སྦྱིན་པ་གཏོང་དགོས། According to Buddhism, one needs to be generous in order to gain wealth and resources.

དཔུང་པ་མཉམ་བཞེས། to shoulder the responsibility equally བོད་

པའི་བུད་མེད་ཚོ་སྐྱེས་པ་དང་མཉམ་དུ་ལས་འགན་དཔུང་པ་མཉམ་བཞེས་བྱེད་པ་རེད། Tibetan women shoulder the responsibility equally with their men.

དཔེ་མི་སྲིད་པ། extremely བྱིད་ཡང་དང་པོ་ལྟོན་པ་དེར་ང་ཚོ་དཔེ་མི་སྲིད་པའི་དགའ་

པོ་བྱུང་། We are extremely happy over your securing first position.

དཔེ་བཟང་ཡར་འགུན། to follow the good example དཔེ་བཟང་པོ་ལ་ཡར་འགུན་བྱེད་ན་ཡག་པོ་ལས་ཀྱིས་ཡོང་། If one follows the good example one will naturally become good.

དཔྲལ་བའི་མིག་དང་ཁོག་པའི་སྙིང་ལྟ་བུ། Lit.: like an eye on our forehead and the heart/ Sense implied: the most precious and the beloved one ཡ་རྒྱལ་བ་ཡིད་བཞིན་ནོར་བུ་ནི་བོད་མི་ཚང་མའི་དཔྲལ་བའི་མིག་དང་ཁོག་པའི་སྙིང་ལྟ་བུ་དེ་ཡིན། His Holiness the Dalai Lama is like the eye of forehead and the heart within every Tibetan.

སྟོབས་པ་ཆེ་བསྐྱེད། with great confidence and courage ཐོན་མི་སམ་བྷོ་ཊས་སྟོབས་པ་ཆེ་བསྐྱེད་ཀྱི་སྒོ་ནས་རྒྱ་གར་དུ་ཕེབས། Thonmi Sambhota had been to India with great courage and confidence.

སྟུང་གི་ཏུ་ཟན་ལུག་རོས་མི་འགྱང་། Lit.: A horse-eating wolf cannot be satisfied with the carcase of a sheep/ Sense implied: very greedy

སྤྱང་ཀིའི་ནུ་ལ་ཆོས་བཤད་པས་མི་ཕན། It is of no use to teach Dharma to a wolf. This proverb is used when someone preaches dharma to an unrecepient who doesn't listen.

སྤྱང་གྱུང་དོད་པོ། active and smart ངའི་གྲོགས་པོ་དེ་སྤྱང་གྱུང་དོད་པོ་ཞེ་དྲག་ཡོད། My friend is very active and smart.

སྤྱང་ཕྲུག་གསོས་ཀྱང་རྫོ་ཁྱི་མི་ཉན། Although one nurtures a wolf-cub, it can not become a watch-dog.

སྤྱང་ཀི་བཟང་ཡང་ལུག་རྫིས་ཉན་མདོག་མེད། Even if a wolf is very nice, a shephered is unlikely to listen/ Sense implied: unreliable/hard to trust someone

སྤྱི་སྒེར་གཉིས་ལྷན། beneficial both to the individual and the society རང་གིས་ལས་འགན་ཧུར་ཐག་བསྒྲུབ་ན་སྤྱི་སྒེར་གཉིས་ཀར་ཞལ་འདེབས་རེད། If one performs one's duty sincerely, it is a contribution to both oneself and one's society.

སྤྲོ་སེམས་འཁོལ་བ། to bubble with joy ཁྱེད་རང་འདིར་གར་ཕེབས་པར་སྤྲོ་སེམས་རབ་ཏུ་འཁོལ་བའི་ངང་ནས་ཕྱགས་རྗེ་ཆེ་ཞུ་གི་ཡོད། We are very pleased with your visit here and would like to thank you whole-heartedly for the same.

ཕ་ཚན་དན་གྱི་སྡོང་པོ་ལ། བུ་ཆུ་ཤུང་གི་འོམ་བུ། Lit.: His father was like a sandalwood but he is like a hollow bamboo/ Sense implied: opposite of "like father, like son"

ཕ་ཤུལ་བུས་འཛིན། a son following one's father's tradition/to take the responsibility of one's father དེ་རིང་གི་གཞོན་ནུ་ཚོས་རང་གི་རིག་གཞུང་ལ་སྲུང་བརྩོན་གནང་སྟེ་ཕ་ཤུལ་བུས་འཛིན་བྱེད་པ་རེད། The youths of today take the responsibility of their fathers by preserving their culture and tradition.

ཕ་གཏམ་བུར་འཛགས། father's words imprinted on their sons ཕ་བཞད་བུ་ཉན་བྱེད་ན་ཕ་གཏམ་བུར་འཛགས་ཡོང་། If a son listens to his father, his words will be imprinted on him.

ཕ་སྦྱག་པས་བུ་སྦྱག་རྒྱུ་མེད། A bad father does not mean a bad son.

ཕ་སྤུན་དགྲ་རུ་སོང་ཡང་རུས་པ་གསེར། Although brothers become enemies, their lineage is gold (pure). This proverb is spoken to emphasise the importance of heritage and lineage.

ཕ་སྤུན་ལ་རྒུ། respecting blood relationship ཕ་སྤུན་གྱི་ལ་རྒྱར་བརྩི་བ་ལ་རབས་ཀྱི་དགས་ཡིན། It is a sign of good manner to regard and respect one's blood relationship.

ཕ་རབས་བུ་རབས། ཕ་ཚོ་བུ་རབས། generations ཕ་ཚོ་བུ་རབས་ནས་བདག་པའི་རང་གི་ལུང་པར། བསྟན་དགྲ་རྒྱ་དམར་གྱིས་བདག་བཟུང་བྱས་ཏེ། ཆ་མེད་རྒྱས་མེད་གཞན་གྱི་ལུང་པར་མི་འདོད་བཞིན་དུ་ཡུལ་གྱར་དུ་འགྲོ་བ་འདི་ལ། ལེགས་པར་བཤགས་ན་སྟོན་གྱི་ལས་ཚབས་པོ་ཆེ་ཁོ་ནའི་འབྲས་དང་ཡིན་པར་གདོན་མི་ཟ། It is undoubtedly the result of our bad karma to have been exiled from our native land which has been ours for many generations due to the colonialism of Communist China.

ཕག་ཉན་སློག་འཕད། to listen and speak in a hidden manner

ཕན་གྲོགས་རོགས་རམ། benefit and help སྨན་པས་ནད་པར་ཕན་གྲོགས་རོགས་རམ་བྱེད་པ་རེད། Doctors help and benefit patients.

ཕན་མེད་གནོད་འགྱུར། to harm instead of benefit གླེན་པོའི་རྒྱབ་སྐྱོར་དེ་སྐབས་རེ་ཕན་མེད་གནོད་འགྱུར་ཆགས་པ་ཡོད། The support of stupid persons sometimes brings more harm than benefit.

ཕན་ཚུན་འགྲན་བསྡུར། competition ཉེད་མོ་ཕན་ཚུན་འགྲན་བསྡུར་སྤྲས་ལྟ་མོ་བལྟ་མཁན་མང་པོ་ཡོད། There are many spectators to watch the competing sportsman in games.

ཕན་ཚུན་གཉིས་ཕན། mutual benefit གཞན་ལ་སློབ་སྟོང་བསླབ་པ་ནི་ཕན་ཚུན་གཉིས་ཕན་གྱི་བྱ་བ་ཞིག་རེད། To teach others is a mutually beneficial job.

ཕན་ཚུན་དགའ་སྡང་། mutual respect ཆོས་ལུགས་ཆང་མ་ལ་ཕན་ཚུན་དགའ་སྡང་སྡང་དགོས། One should cultivate mutual respect to all religions.

ཕན་ཚུན་བཟོད་སྒོམ། being patient to each other ང་རང་ཚོ་ཕན་ཚུན་ བཟོད་སྒོམ་གནང་རྒྱུ་དེ་ཞེ་དྲག་གལ་ཆེན་པོ་འདུག It is very important for us to cultivate mutual patience for each other.

ཕར་དཀྲུག་ཚུར་དཀྲུག to create dissension མི་ངན་དེས་ལུང་པ་ཆང་མ་ཕར་ དཀྲུག་ཚུར་དཀྲུག་བཟོས་སོང་། That evil person created dissension throughout the country.

ཕར་ཁག་ཚུར་དགི། to blame one another ཕར་ཁག་ཚུར་དགི་བྱས་པར་སྐྱོ་བས་ ཡོད། We regret putting blame on one another.

ཕར་འདྲེས་ཚུར་འདྲེས། mingle ས་མཚམས་ཁག་གི་མི་རྣམས་རྒྱལ་ཁབ་གཉིས་ཀྱི་ དབར་ཕར་འདྲེས་ཚུར་འདྲེས་ཞེ་དྲག་བྱེད་པ་རེད། The people of two neighbouring countries living at the border areas often mingle with one another.

ཕར་རྒྱུགས་ཚུར་རྒྱུགས། to run here and there ཚོང་ཡག་པའི་སྐབས་སུ་ཚོང་ པ་རྣམས་ཅ་ལག་བཏོན་དུ་ཕར་རྒྱུགས་ཚུར་རྒྱུགས་བྱེད་པ་རེད། During good business the businessmen run here and there to acquire supplies.

ཕར་རྒོལ་སྲིད་བྱུས། offensive strategy དང་པོ་ཉིད་ནས་མེད་པར་བཟོ་འདོད་ན་ ཕར་རྒོལ་སྲིད་བྱུས་བསྐྱར་དགོས། Right from the beginning if one wants to destroy someone, apply the offensive strategy.

ཕར་འགྲོ་བཙུ་དང་ཚུར་འགྲོ་སྟོང་། to have many travellers/coming in and going out in hundreds ནག་ཚུ་ཁའི་ཚོམ་ར་ན་ཚོང་པ་ཕར་འགྲོ་ བཙུ་དང་ཚུར་འགྲོ་སྟོང་རེད། There are hundreeds of travellers coming in and going out at the Nagchukha Business Centre/market.

ཕར་བལྟ་ཚུར་བལྟ། looking everywhere རྐུན་མ་ནང་བཞིན་ཕར་བལྟ་ཚུར་
བལྟ་མང་པོ་མ་བྱེད། Don't look everywhere like a thief.

ཕར་འཐབ་ཚུར་འཐབ། to fight with one another ཁྱི་གཉིས་རུས་པའི་ཆེད་
དུ་ཕར་འཐབ་ཚུར་འཐབ་བྱེད་ཀྱི་འདུག Two dogs are fighting one another
for a bone.

ཕར་སྤྲོད་ཚུར་ལེན། crediting and debiting དངུལ་ཁང་ལ་ཕར་སྤྲོད་ཚུར་ལེན་
བྱས་རྗེས་སྒོར་དུག་ཅུ་མ་གཏོགས་ལྷག་མི་འདུག After crediting and
debiting in the bank, only Rs.60.00 is left as balance.

ཕར་འབུར་ཚུར་འབུར། Lit.: sticking towards here and there/
Sense implied: flattering or leaning towards here and
there བོད་མི་བླུན་ཅུང་འགའ་ཤས་ཀྱིས་སྐབས་རེ་རྒྱ་མི་ལ་ཕར་འབུར་སྐབས་རེ་བོད་
མི་ལ་ཚུར་འབུར་བྱེད་ཀྱི་ཡོད་པ་རེད། A few silly Tibetans sometimes
lean towards the Chinese and at other times they lean
towards the Tibetans.

ཕར་བཤད་ཚུར་བཤད། to discuss one another གནས་ཚུལ་འདིའི་སྐོར་ཕར་
བཤད་ཚུར་བཤད་བྱེད་ན་འགྲིག་གི་རེད། It would be alright to discuss one
another about this matter.

ཕུ་རྒྱུགས་མདའ་རྒྱུགས། to run all over the valley དོན་མེད་ཕུ་རྒྱུགས་
མདའ་རྒྱུགས་བྱེད་པ་ནི་དུས་ཚོད་འཕྲོ་བླུག་རེད། It is waste of time to run all
over the valley without any purpose.

ཕུ་ཐག་ཐུང་ཐུང་། short sighted/one who cannot think much for

140

future བསམ་ཚོ་ཕུ་ཐག་ཕུང་ཕུང་བདང་ན་དགེ་གས་ཡུལ་ཆེན་པོ་སྒྲུབ་ཐུབ་ཀྱི་མ་རེད།
If one is short sighted, one cannot fulfll one's big aims.

ཕུ་དུང་ཕུང་ལ་ལག་པ་རིང་བ། Lit.: short sleeves with a long arm/
Sense implied: shortage of funds for a big plan

ཕུ་ཕྲོས་མདའ་ཕྲོས། to flee up and down the valley དཀུན་མ་ཕུ་ཕྲོས་
མདའ་ཕྲོས་སོང་ནས་མཐོང་རྒྱུ་མི་འདུག The thieves having fled up and
down the valley, they are no where to be seen now.

ཕུན་སུམ་ཚོགས་པ། excellent སྣ་ཡུལ་ནི་ཕུན་སུམ་ཚོགས་པའི་ཞིང་ཁམས་ཤིག་རེད།
Heaven is an excellent celestial abode.

ཕུལ་དུ་བྱུང་བ། the best རྩོམ་ཡིག་ཕུལ་དུ་བྱུང་བ་དེ་ལ་གསོལ་རས་ཐོབ། The best
article won the prize.

ཕེར་ཉ་ཚ་པོ། naughty and showy གཞོན་ནུའི་དུས་སུ་ཕེར་ཉ་ཚ་པོ་ཡོང་།
During youthhood, one may be naughty and showy.

པ་ཁྲོ་གའི་ཁོག་པར་མདའ་ཕོང་མདུང་ཤོང་། Lit.: A brave man's heart
has a room for arrows and spears/ Sense implied: A
brave man can bear many difficulties.

ཕོ་དཔའ་ རྟ་མགྱོགས། brave man and fast horse ཁམས་ཀྱི་དུ་པ་དེ་ཕོ་
དཔའ་ལ་རྟ་མགྱོགས་པ་འདུག The horsemen of Kham were very
brave and their horses very swift.

ཕོ་མོ་ཁྱད་མེད། no difference in sex/irrespective of sex དམངས་
གཙོའི་རྒྱལ་ཁབ་ནང་ཕོ་མོ་ཁྱད་མེད་ཀྱི་སྐོ་ནས་ལས་ཀ་འདྲ་མཉམ་བྱེད་པ་རེད། In a
democratic country, people work equally irrespective of sex.

141

ཕོ་རབ་ཁོག་པར་རྟ་བརྒྱ་རྒྱུག་ས་ཡོད། Lit.: A braveman's heart has a space for hundred horses to run through/ Sense implied: A braveman can bear many hardships.

ཕོ་རབ་གཅིག་གི་རློ་ཚུལ་ལས་ཕོ་འབྲིང་གསུམ་གྱི་གྲོས་བསྡུར་དགའ། A discussion with three mediocres would be better than an idea of a wiseman. The proverb is used to emphasise the importance of discussion.

ཕོ་རོག་ཐམས་ཅད་ནག་མཉམ་ཡིན། Lit.: All crows are equally black. Sense implied: All are equally guilty.

ཕོ་རོག་ལ་སྐྲ་དཀར་ནས་སྐྱེ། Lit.: unitl a crow grows white hair/ Sense implied: a time that will never come

ཕོ་ཧྲེང་མོ་ཧྲེང་། single (man or woman) ཕོ་ཧྲེང་མོ་ཧྲེང་གི་སྐབས་སུ་ལས་ཀ་ བྱེད་དུས་སྤྱབས་བདེ་པོ་ཡོད་རེད། When one is single it is very convenient to work.

ཕྱག་བརྟག་དགོངས་དོན། in accordance with a divination ཁོང་གིས་ ཕྱག་རྟགས་དགོངས་དོན་ཞབས་རིམ་ཚང་མ་བསྒྲུབས་སོང་། He performed all the rites in accordance with the divination.

ཕྱག་ལེན་དོན་འཁྱེལ། to implement and materialise or to succeed ཚོགས་འདུར་གྲོས་ཆོད་བཞག་པ་རྣམས་ཕྱག་ལེན་དོན་འཁྱེལ་ཡོང་བའི་ཆེད་ཡིན་པ་རེད། The resolutions put up at the meeting were meant to be implemented or were to materialise the aim.

ཕུར་བ་གྱུ་འདེགས། co-operative effort རང་གི་རྒྱལ་ཁབ་ཀྱི་དོན་དུ་ཆང་མས་

ཕྱར་བ་བླུ་འདེགས་བྱེད་པ་རེད། All people co-operate for their national cause.

ཕྱི་གོས་ཆེན་ཙམ་ཁུག Lit.: to keep ordinary tsampa in a brocade bag/ Sense implied: very showy although one is vey poor

ཕྱི་རྒྱལ་ལམ་ལུགས། foreign or alien custom ཕྱི་རྒྱལ་གྱི་ཆང་ས་བའི་ལམ་ ལུགས་དེ་སྟབས་བདེ་པོ་གཅིག་ཡོད། The foreign marriage custom is convenient.

ཕྱི་དགྲ་ལས་ནང་དགྲ་ཐུབ་པ་དཀའ། An enemy inside is more difficult to subdue than an enemy outside.

ཕྱི་པོ་ཕྱི་པོ། very late བུ་མོ་མཚན་ལ་ཕྱི་པོ་ཕྱི་པོ་འགྲོ་རྒྱུ་ཡོད་པ་མ་རེད། Girls should not go out late at night.

ཕྱི་ཨེ་ལྡུགས་རེ་ནང་གི་ནོར་བུ། Lit.: the outer fence and the inner jewel/ Sense implied: the most precious/everything པ་རྒྱལ་ བ་ཡིད་བཞིན་ནོར་བུ་ནི་བོད་མི་ཐམས་ཅད་ཀྱི་ཕྱི་ཨེ་ལྡུགས་རེ་དང་ནང་གི་ནོར་བུ་དེ་ཨིན། His Holiness the Dalai Lama is the most precious to all Tibetans.

ཕྱི་གསལ་ནང་གསལ། Lit.: transparent/ Sense implied: open secret/known to everyone གནས་ཚུལ་འདི་ཕྱི་གསལ་ནང་གསལ་རེད། This news is known to every one.

ཕྱིན་པའི་རྗེས་དང་དུད་པའི་ཤུལ། Lit.: trace of a walk and an imprint of digging/ a feat whether good or bad

143

ཕྱོགས་ཀུན་ནས། from every direction གངས་སྐྱིད་དུ་ཕྱོགས་ཀུན་ནས་མི་མང་

པོ་བསླེབས་འདུག Many people have come to Gangkyi from
everywhere.

ཕྱོགས་གཞན་ནས། on the other hand ཕྱོགས་གཅིག་ནས་ཆར་པས་དཀའ་ངལ་

བཟོས་ཀྱང་ཕྱོགས་གཞན་ཞིག་ནས་ཕན་ཐོགས་ཆེན་པོ་བྱུང་ཡོད། On the one hand
the rain creates trouble and on the other hand it is very
helpful also.

ཕྱོགས་བཞི་མཚམས་བརྒྱད། Lit.: the four directions and the eight

sub-directions/ Sense implied: from all directions དུས་

འཁོར་དབང་ཆེན་སྐབས་སུ་ཕྱོགས་བཞི་མཚམས་བརྒྱད་ཀྱི་མི་འཛོམས་འདུག At the
Kalacakre Initiation, people gathered from all directions.

ཕྱོགས་ལས་རྣམ་རྒྱལ། Victorious/ victory from all directions སློབ་

དཔོན་ཆོས་གྲགས་ལ་ཕྱོགས་ལས་རྣམ་རྒྱལ་གྱི་དངོས་གྲུབ་ཐོབ། Acharya
Dharmakirti won the accomplishment of victory from all
directions.

ཕྲ་མཐོང་ཆེ་ཤེལ། Lit.: magnifying glass that enlarges small

things/ Sense implied: microscope ཕྲ་མཐོང་ཆེ་ཤེལ་གྱི་འཕྲུལ་ཆས་ལ་

བརྟེན་ནས་ཕྲ་བའི་འབུ་སྲིན་རྣམས་ངོས་འཛིན་བྱེད་ཐུབ། With the help of a
microscopic machine, the invisible insects are identified.

ཕྲ་མ་དཔྱེན་སྦྱོར། slander ཕྲ་མ་དཔྱེན་སྦྱོར་བྱེད་པ་སྡིག་པའི་རྒྱུ། The act of
slander is a cause of non-virtue.

ཕྲག་དོག་མཁྲེགས་བཟུང་། to be deeply in jealous of and stubborn

144

དོན་མེད་ཕྱག་དོག་མཁྲེགས་བཟུང་བྱེད་པ་སྨྱོན་པའི་ལས། It is an act of madness to be deeply jealous of and stubborn to someone without any reason.

ཕྲ་ཞིང་ཕྲ་བ། precise, in every detail གནས་ཚུལ་འདི་སྐོར་ཕྲ་ཞིང་ཕྲ་བ་ང་ལ་ ཤུས་ཡོད། I know in every detail about this matter.

ཕྲ་ལ་ཕུན་བུ། a little bit ཁོང་གིས་ང་ལ་ཕན་ཕྲ་ལ་ཕུན་བུ་ཕོགས་བྱུང་། He helped me a little bit.

ཕྲུ་གུའི་ད་འབོད་ཨ་མ། Lit.: children cry to their parents/ Sense implied: upon whom one is relied/upon whom requests are to be made

འཕུར་འཕུར་བཏང་བ། to rub མིག་འཕུར་འཕུར་མ་གཏོང་། Don't rub your eyes.

འཕྱ་ལད་དམའ་འབེབས། disparage, to say low of somebody གཞན་ལ་འཕྱ་ལད་དམའ་འབེབས་ནམ་ཡང་གཏོང་མི་རུང་། One should never disparage others.

འཕྲལ་ཕུགས་གཉིས་ཀར། temporary and ultimate བསམ་པ་བཟང་པོ་བྱེད་ པ་ནི་འཕྲལ་ཕུགས་གཉིས་ཀར་ཕན་པ་ཡིན། Generating good-heart is beneficial temporarily and ultimately.

འཕྲལ་ཡུན་ལམ་སྟོན། to guide for future བླ་མའི་མདུན་དུ་འཕྲལ་ཡུན་ལམ་ སྟོན་གྱི་བཀའ་སློབ་ཞུ་བར་བཅར། I approached the spiritual teacher for temporary and ultimate guidance.

འཕྱལ་མེལ་སྐྱ་བཙོས། to take it very easy ལས་དོན་གང་འདུ་ཞིག་ཡིན་ར་ ཡང་འཕྱལ་མེལ་སྐྱ་བཙོས་བྱ་རྒྱུ་མེད། One should not take it very easy whatever the kind of work it might be.

146

བ་མོ་དགུར་བཞོ་དགུན་ནས་གསོ། Lit.: to feed cow during winter for summer milk/ Sense implied: to think or prepare in advance

བ་བསད་པ་ལས་བཞོས་པ་དགའ། Lit.: It is better to milk a cow than to kill her/ Sense implied: to make use of something without harming the other/ to think for the long run.

བག་ཡོད་ཚུལ་མཐུན། careful and modest སྤྱི་ཚོགས་ནང་དུ་བག་ཡོད་ཚུལ་ མཐུན་བྱེད་མཁན་ཚོར་བཀུར་སྟི་ཐོབ་པ་རེད། The careful and the modest persons are respected in a society.

བར་གྱི་མི་དང་མཚམས་ཀྱི་རྡོ། Lit.: witness and a rock that marks the boundary/ Sense implied: witness and boundary line དབྱིན་ཇི་ནི་རྒྱ་བོད་དབར་གྱི་བར་གྱི་མི་དང་མཚམས་ཀྱི་རྡོ་དེ་ཡིན་པ་རེད། Britain is a witness like a boundary line between Tibet and China.

བུ་ལོན་གྱིས་ཁྱབ་རྒྱལ། to be in great debt བུ་ལོན་གྱིས་ཁྱབ་རྒྱལ་གྱང་ད་དུང་ བུ་ལོན་ལེན་གྱི་འདུག Although he is in great debt, still he is taking loans.

བུ་ལོན་གྱི་གཏའ་མ། mortgage དངུལ་བུ་ལོན་ལེན་སྐབས་གཏའ་མ་གསེར་འཇོག་ དགོས། To ask for a loan one has to keep gold as mortgage.

ཞེད་མེད་ཆུད་ཟོས། to waste ཁོང་གིས་དུས་ཚོད་ཞེད་མེད་ཆུད་ཟོས་གཏོང་གི་མ་རེད། He will not waste time.

བེད་སྤྱོད་བྱེད་བདེ། convenient to use སྐམ་སྦྱུག་དེ་ཚོ་ཡིག་ཚད་ལ་བེད་སྤྱོད་བྱེད་ བདེ་པོ་ཞེ་དྲག་ཡོད་རེད། Ball point pens are very convenient to use in the examinations.

བོང་བ་གསེར་གཟིགས། Lit.: to consider a donkey worth a gold/ Sense implied: to give great regards to a humble person ཁྱེད་ནས་ང་ལ་བོང་བ་གསེར་གཟིགས་ཀྱི་ཚུལ་དུ་ཆ་འཛིག་གནང་བར་ཐུགས་རྗེ་ཆེ། Thank you very much for your kind consideration (toward me).

བོང་བུ་བཞོན་ནས་བོང་བུ་འཚོལ། Lit.: to search for the donkey one is riding on/ foolishness/ Sense implied: stupidity

བོང་བུའི་ཁ་ནས་གསེར་བསྐྱག་མི་ཡོང་། Lit.: A donkey will never vomit gold./ Sense implied: impossible expectation

བོང་བུས་མ་བགྲོད་ལམ་འཕང་མང་། There are many passes where donkeys have not crossed (sarcastic remark). This proverb is used to point out someone's narrow scholarship.

བོད་རེ་བས་འཕྱང་། རྒྱ་དོགས་པས་འཕྱང་། Tibetans are overly hopeful and the Chinese are overly suspicious. This is used to express that Tibetans are always hopeful and Chinese are always suspicious of something.

བོད་ལྷ་བརྒྱ་བསྒོམས་ནས་ལྷ་གཅིག་མི་འགྲུབ། རྒྱ་ལྷ་གཅིག་བསྒོམས་ནས་ལྷ་ བརྒྱ་འགྲུབ། Indians meditate upon one deity and actualize a hundred deities whereas Tibetans meditate on a hundred deities but do not actualise even one deity.

བྱ་དགའ་གཟེངས་བསྟོད། to honour with award འབྲི་རྩོམ་ལེགས་ཤོས་སུ་ བྱ་དགའ་གཟེངས་བསྟོད་སྐྱལ། The best article was awarded.

བྱ་གོད་ལྟོགས་ཀྱང་རྩྭ་ལྗྡང་མི་ཟ། Lit.: Even if a vulture is starving it will never eat green grass./ Sense implied: to express that one will never do

བྱ་བརྒྱ་འུར་རྡོ་གཅིག་གིས་དེད་པ། Lit.: One hundred birds driven away by one sling shot/ Sense implied: a rule that binds all people

བྱ་ནག་གི་གྲིབ་མ་བྱ་དཀར་ལ་ཕོག Lit.: shadow of black birds falling on white birds/ Sense implied: bad influence

བྱ་ཕོ་མེད་སར་བོང་བུས་ནམ་ཚོད་འཛིན། In the absense of a cock, a donkey would herald the dawn.

བྱ་བ་ཁམས་ཆེན་པོ། a task of serious nature (negative)/ a disastrous work བྱ་བ་སྟྀང་ཁམས་ཆེན་པོ་དེ་འདྲ་མ་བྱེད། ལས་འབྲས་ཕྲ་ལ་ ལས་འབྲས་ཟབ། Don't do such a disastrous work, the karmic result is subtle and profound.

བྱ་ཟིན་ཉ་ཟིན། Lit.: catching birds and fish/ Sense implied: to do something in an unsystemetic way/ to touch many works at a time

བྱི་ལ་གཉིད་ཁུག་ཀྱང་ཙི་ཙི་ཡིད་ལ་འཁོར་འཁོར། Lit.: Even when cat is asleep, it thinks of (catching) rats.

149

བུས་མེད་བུས་འཁྲི། to interfere other's business གཞན་གྱི་ལས་ཀར་བུས་ མེད་བུས་འཁྲི་བུས་ན་ཡག་པོ་མ་རེད། It is not good to interfere in other's work.

བྱེ་མ་ཆུ་སིམ་ལྟ་བུ། Lit.: Like sand absorbing water/ Sense implied: to disappear

བྱེད་མདོག་ཁ་པོ། likely to do/ active or smart མི་ཕ་གི་ལས་ཀ་བྱེད་མདོག་ ཁ་པོ་གཅིག་འདུག That man is likely to do a job.

བྲད་བྲད་ཕུད་ཕུད། to scratch ས་བྲད་བྲད་ཕུད་ཕུད་བཏང་ན་རྨས་ཡང་དྲག་གི་མ་རེད། If wound is scratched, it won't get healed.

བྲན་གཡོག་བརྐུལ་རེད། exploitation of servants དཔོན་ངན་རྣམས་ཀྱིས་བྲན་ གཡོག་ལ་རྐུལ་རེད་བྱེད་པ་རེད། Bad masters exploit their servants.

བྲེལ་བ་ཆུབ་ཆུབ། in a rush and hurry བྲེལ་བ་ཆུབ་ཆུབ་ངང་ལ་ཁྱེད་རང་ཐུག རྒྱུ་བརྗེད་སོང་། Being in rush I forgot to meet you.

བླ་འཁྱེར་དོན་པོར། shocked and losing one's spirit ཕྲུ་གུ་ལ་ཞེད་སྣང་སྦྱང་ ན་བླ་འཁྱེར་དོན་པོར་ཆགས་པའི་ཉེན་ཁ་ཡོད། If you scare children there is a danger of their getting shocked and losing spirit.

བླ་ཆེན་མི་ཆེན། religious and political heads/ dignitaries བོད་དུ་བླ་ ཆེན་དང་མི་ཆེན་རྣམས་མཐུན་པོ་ཡོད་པ་རེད། The religious and political heads were friendly with one another in Tibet.

150

བླ་ན་མེད་པ། supreme/ unsurpassable སངས་རྒྱས་རྣམས་ལ་བླ་ན་མེད་པའི་
ཡོན་ཏན་ཡོད་པ་རེད། Buddhas have unsurpassable knowledge.

བླ་མ་དཀོན་མཆོག honest/ very saintly/ one of the four objects
of refuge/ naive མི་འདི་བླ་མ་དཀོན་མཆོག་གཅིག་ཡོད་པ་རེད། This man
is very saintly, honest and naive.

བླ་མས་ར་བསད་ཆོག་སར་ཉེ་གནས་ཀྱིས་རྒྱ་མ་བཅུང་མི་ཆོག་པ་གང་ཡིན་ནམ།
If a Lama can kill a goat why can't a disciple make
sausage(questioning someone with sarcastic remark).

བླ་སློབ་ཀྱི་དམ་ཚིག the spiritual commitment between a
teacher and his disciple བླ་སློབ་ཀྱི་དམ་ཚིག་ལེགས་པར་བསྲུང་དགོས།
One needs to observe the spiritual commitment between a
teacher and his disciple.

བླང་དོར་ཁ་ཉེན། What is to be cultivated and eliminated, what
is beneficial and detrimental རྣམ་དཔྱོད་ཡོད་ན་བླང་དོར་ཁ་ཉེན་མ་
འཛོལ་བ་གནང་དགོས། If one is wise, one should not make mistake
with regard to what is beneficial and what is detrimental, and
what should be cultivated or eliminated.

བླང་དོར་ལམ་སྟོན། guidance རང་གི་ཕ་མ་དང་དགེ་རྒན་གྱིས་བླང་དོར་ལམ་སྟོན་
གནང་གི་རེད། One's teachers and parents will give guidance.

བླུན་པོ་དྲང་བཀོད། a fool's sincerity བླུན་པོས་དྲང་པོ་བྱེད་ཀྱང་ཕན་ཐོགས་ལས་
གནོད་པ་ཆེ་བ་སྐྱེལ་སྲིད། A fool's sincerity might prove more
detrimental than beneficial.

151

བློ་དཀར་དུང་བདེན། faithful and caring ང་ལ་བློ་དཀར་དུང་བདེན་གྱི་གྲོགས་པོ་ གཅིག་ལས་མེད། I have only one faithful and caring friend.

བློ་དཀར་ཅན་མེད། extrmely good hearted བློ་དཀར་ཅན་མེད་ཀྱི་མི་རྣམས་མི་ ཚེའི་ནང་སྐྱིད་པོ་ཡོང་གི་རེད། Extremely good hearted persons will be happy in their life.

བློ་དཀར་སེམས་དཀར། good and kind hearted བློ་དཀར་སེམས་དཀར་གྱི་ མི་རྣམས་སྐྱིད་པོ་ཡོང་བར་ཤོག May good and kind hearted persons be happy!

བློ་ཁོག་ཆེ་བསྐྱེད། with courage དཀའ་ངལ་གང་དང་འཕྲད་ཀྱང་བློ་ཁོག་ཆེ་བསྐྱེད་ ཀྱི་སྒོ་ནས་ཕྱག་ལས་གནང་དགོས། One needs to perform work with courage, despite all kinds of difficulties.

བློ་ཁ་རྩེ་གཅིག single minded བློ་ཁ་རྩེ་གཅིག་གི་མི་རྣམས་ཀྱི་བསམ་དོན་ལྷུན་ གྱིས་འགྲུབ་ཀྱི་རེད། People with single mindedness will accomplish their aims.

བློ་རྒྱ་ཆེ་ཆུང་། scope of attitude ཐེག་ཆེན་གྱི་ཆོས་དང་ཐེག་དམན་གྱི་ཆོས་རྣམས་ གདུལ་བྱ་བློ་རྒྱ་ཆེ་ཆུང་གི་སྒོ་ནས་གསུངས་ཡོད། Mahayana and Hinayana Buddhism have been taught according to disciple's scope of intellect and attitude.

བློ་གཅིག་སེམས་གཅིག one thought and one mind བཟའ་ཚང་གཉིས་པོ་ དེ་བློ་གཅིག་སེམས་གཅིག་ནང་བཞིན་ཆམ་པོ་འདུག That couple is very close as if they have been one thought and one mind.

152

བློ་གཏད་ཡིད་བཅོལ། to entrust with full faith ནང་པ་ཡིན་ན་དཀོན་མཆོག་ གསུམ་ལ་བློ་གཏད་ཡིད་བཅོལ་གནང་དགོས། If one is a Buddhist one must entrust the triple gem(s) whole heartedly.

བློ་བརྟན་འགྱུར་མེད། firm and unchanging mind/ faithful ང་ལ་བློ་ བརྟན་འགྱུར་མེད་ཀྱི་གྲོགས་པོ་གཅིག་ལས་མེད། I have just one faithful friend.

བློ་ཐག་ཆོད་པོ། decisive/ determined ཐེ་ཚོམ་གྱི་སྐབས་སུ་བློ་ཐག་ཆོད་པོ་ཡོད་ན་ ཡག་པོ་རེད། It is better to be decisive when one has been lingering in doubt.

བློ་ཐག་ཉད་བཅད། resoluteness/ determination/ to be completely determined ཨ་མེ་རི་ཁ་ལ་བློ་ཐག་ཉད་བཅད་ནས་ཡོང་པ་ཡིན། I came to the United States with full resoluteness.

བློ་བདེ་བག་ཕེབས། relaxed and be at ease རྒྱ་གར་ལ་བསླེབ་ན་བློ་བདེ་བག་ ཕེབས་བྱེད་ནས་བསྡད་ཆོག་གི་རེད། We can relax and be at ease when we reach India.

བློ་བདེ་ཞི་སྟོད། peaceful and relaxed ཁྱེད་རང་འདི་རུ་བློ་བདེ་ཞི་སྟོད་བྱེད་ནས་ བཞུགས་ཨ། You can stay here in peace and relax.

བློ་འདས་བརྗོད་བྲལ། inconceivable and inexpressible སྟོང་ཉིད་ཀྱི་དོན་ དེ་མི་ཕལ་པས་བློ་ལས་འདས་པ་དང་བརྗོད་པ་ལས་བྲལ་བ་རེད། The meaning of emptiness is inconceivable and inexpressible to ordinary beings.

བློ་སྲ་ཐུང་བ། mentally short-sighted བློ་སྲ་ཐུང་བའི་མི་ཚོས་མ་འོངས་པའི་དོན་དུ་བསམ་བློ་གཏོང་ཐུབ་ཀྱི་མ་རེད། A mentally short-sighted person cannot think for the future.

བློ་ཕམ་ཡིད་སྐྱོ། sadness and unhappy ཨ་ཁུ་ལགས་གཤེགས་པའི་གནས་ཚུལ་གོ་སྟེ་བློ་ཕམ་ཞེ་དྲག་སྐྱེ་བྱུང་། We were very sad and unhappy to hear the passing away of our paternal uncle.

བློ་བབ་ཡིད་སྨོན། to prefer or like ཁོང་ཚོའི་དགེ་རྒན་ལ་བློ་བབ་ཡིད་སྨོན་བྱུང་། I prefer their teacher to be ours.

བློ་ཁ་རྩེ་གཉིས། two pointed minds/ wavering ཁབ་རྩེ་གཉིས་ཀྱིས་འཚེམ་བུ་མི་ཐེབ། བློ་རྩེ་གཉིས་ཀྱིས་དོན་མི་འགྲུབ། A needle with two points cannot stitch and a mind with two points cannot fulfill aims.

བློ་རྩེ་གཅིག་མཐུན། like minded/ common in ideology བློ་རྩེ་གཅིག་མཐུན་གྱི་མི་རྣམས་མཐུན་པོ་ཡོད་རེད། People with the same ideology are friendly.

བློ་འཛིན་སྐྱོར་སྦྱངས། practising memorization and recitation གྲྭ་པ་ཚོས་ཁ་འདོན་བློ་འཛིན་དང་སྐྱོར་སྦྱངས་ཞེ་དྲག་གནང་གི་རེད། Monks practise a lot in memorization and recitation of prayers.

བློ་ཡངས་ཁོག་གསལ། broad minded and open ང་ཚོའི་སྐུ་ངོ་ནི་བློ་ཁོག་ཡངས་ལ་ཁོག་པ་གསལ་བ་ཞིག་ཡིན། Our boss is open and broad-minded.

བློ་རོགས་གྲོས་རོགས། a friend with whom one seeks advice and

154

wisdom བཀའ་ཤེས་ལགས་ངའི་སློ་རོགས་སྒྲོས་རོགས་ཡིན། Mr. Tashi is my friend with whom I seek advice and wisdom.

སློ་གསལ་ན་གཞོན། young intellectual དེང་སང་བོད་ནས་སློ་གསལ་ན་གཞོན་ མང་པོ་ཡོང་གི་འདུག Many young intellectuals are coming from Tibet these days.

སློ་སེམས་གཅིག་བསྒྲིལ། unity/ integrity བོད་མི་ཚོས་སློ་སེམས་གཅིག་ཏུ་ བསྒྲིལ་ནས་རྒྱ་མི་ལ་ངོ་རྒོལ་བྱས་པ་རེད། Tibetans unitedly fought against the Chinese invasion.

སློ་སེམས་རྩེ་གཅིག concentrated mind/ single minded སློ་སེམས་རྩེ་ གཅིག་གི་ཉམས་ལེན་བྱས་ན་སྒྲུབ་པ་ལག་ཏུ་ལོན་གྱི་རེད། If one practises with a concentrated mind one will achieve the goal of realization.

སློ་གསལ་ལག་བདེ། wise and dexterous ངའི་བུ་ནི་སློ་གསལ་པོ་དང་ལག་པོ་ བདེ་པོ་ཡོད། My son is intellegent and dexterous.

སློ་སྐྱིད་བག་ཕེབས། comfortable/ relaxed and content རྒྱ་གར་དུ་བོད་ མི་རྣམས་སློ་སྐྱིད་བག་ཕེབས་བྱས་ནས་བཞུགས་འདུག Tibetans in India are living comfortably.

དབང་ཤེད་བཙན་གཏམ། a dictatorial command/ to scold harshly སྤྱིན་བདག་ངན་པས་རང་གི་གཡོག་པོ་ལ་རྟག་ཏུ་དབང་ཤེད་བཙན་གཏམ་བྱེད་པ་རེད། Bad masters always dictate and scold their servants.

དབུལ་པོ་དབུལ་རྒྱུང་། very poor/impoverished ཨ་ཕི་རི་ཁ་ནི་རྒྱལ་ཁབ་ དབུལ་པོ་དབུལ་རྒྱུང་ཞིག་རེད། Africa is an impoverished country.

155

དབུལ་ཕྱུག་འཁོད་སྙོམས། to equalize the rich and the poor བོད་ཀྱི་རྒྱལ་པོ་མུ་ནེ་བཙན་པོས་དབུལ་ཕྱུག་འཁོད་སྙོམས་ལན་གསུམ་གནང་སྐྱོང་བ་རེད། Muni Tsanpo, a king of Tibet, distributed the wealth of his subjects three times equally for them.

དབུལ་ཕྱུག་བར་ཁྱད། the gap between the haves and the have-nots རྒྱ་གར་ནང་མི་ཚང་དབུལ་ཕྱུག་དབར་བར་ཁྱད་ཆེན་པོ་ཡོད། There is a vast gap in India between the haves and the have-nots.

དབུལ་ཕོངས་ཉམ་ཐག poverty striken/ poor and down trodden མི་ཚང་ཕྱུག་པོ་དེ་ཚོས་དབུལ་ཕོངས་ཉམ་ཐག་ལ་ཕན་ཐོགས་བྱེད་ན་ག་འདྲ་ཡག་པོ་ཡོད་རེད། How nice it would be if the rich families help the poor families.

དབྱུག་པ་ལེབ་རྡུང་། Lit.: to flatten with a stick/ Sense implied: to suppress equally རྒྱ་མིའི་དམག་མིས་བོད་མི་ཚོར་དབྱུག་པ་ལེབ་རྡུང་གི་མནར་གཅོད་བཏང་བ་རེད། All Tibetans have equally been suppressed by the Chinese army.

དབྱེན་སྐྱོར་དཀྲུགས་ཤིང་། making division by means of divisive talk གྲོགས་པོ་མཐུན་པོ་ཡོད་ན་ཡང་དབྱེན་སྐྱོར་དཀྲུགས་ཤིང་གི་དབང་དུ་སོང་ན་མ་མཐུན་པ་ཆགས་ཉེན་ཡོད། If over-powered by divisive talk there is a danger of even close friends becoming unfriendly.

འབག་གི་འབྱུག་གི something that is not clear/ to whisper ཚོགས་འདུ་འཚོགས་པའི་སྐབས་སུ་བཀའ་མོལ་འབག་གི་འབྱུག་གི་གནང་ན་ཡག་པོ་མི་འདུག It is not good to whisper while the meeting is being held.

འབད་པ་བརྒྱ་ཕྲག hundreds of attempts/ tremendous effort མི་
ལུས་རིན་པོ་ཆེ་དེ་འབད་པ་བརྒྱ་ཕྲག་གི་སྒོ་ནས་དོན་དང་ལྡན་པ་བཟོ་དགོས། We
should make this precious human life meaningful through
tremendous effort.

འབད་འབད་དུང་དུང་། to make effort with difficulty ཕ་མ་ནམས་ཆུང་
ནམས་ཀྱི་རང་གི་ཕྲུ་གུའི་དོན་དུ་འབད་འབད་དུང་དུང་བྱེད་ཀྱི་རེད། The poor
parents make every effort for their children.

འབད་མེད་ལྷུན་གྲུབ། effortlessly and spontaneously སངས་རྒྱས་ཀྱི་
མཛད་པ་འཕྲིན་ལས་ནམས་འབད་མེད་ལྷུན་གྲུབ་ཕ་ཕྲག་རེད། All the activities of
a Buddha are effortless and spontaneous.

འབད་བརྩོན་སློད་མེད། unfailing effort སློབ་སྦྱོང་ལ་འབད་བརྩོན་སློད་མེད་བྱེད་ན་
གྲུབ་འབྲས་ཡག་པོ་ཡོང་གི་རེད། If studied with unfailing effort, there
will be good results.

འབར་རེ་འབུར་རེ། protruding/ bumpy/ uneven ས་ཆ་འབར་རེ་འབུར་
རེ་སྟེང་དུ་ཁང་པ་རྒྱག་རྒྱ་ལས་སྐ་པོ་མ་རེད། It is not easy to construct a
house on a bumpy land.

འབོལ་ལེ་འབོལ་ལེ། soft and spongy གདན་འབོལ་ལེ་འབོལ་ལེ་སྟེང་དུ་གཉིད་
ཁུག་སྐ་བ་ཡོད། It is easier to sleep on soft and spongy
mattresses.

འབུ་ཆེས་ཆུང་ཟོས། Lit.: big worms eating small ones/ Sense
implied: exploitation/imperialism འཛམ་གླིང་ནང་རྒྱལ་ཁབ་ཆེ་བ་མང་
པོས་རྒྱལ་ཁབ་ཆུང་བ་ནམས་ལ་འབུ་ཆེས་ཆུང་ཟོས་བྱེད་ཀྱི་ཡོད་པ་རེད། Many big
nations of the world exploit the smaller ones, just as big
worms eating the smaller ones.

འབུ་གསོད་པར་སྟ་རེ་འཕྱར་བ། Lit.: brandishing an axe to kill an insect/ Sense implied: unnecessary torture ཉམ་ཆུང་ལ་བདང་བ་ནི་འབུ་གསོད་པར་སྟ་རེ་འཕྱར་པ་རང་རེད། Beating the poor and down trodden is to brandish an axe to kill an insect.

འབུ་གསོད་པར་སྟ་རེ་འཕྱར་མི་དགོས། There is no need to brandish an axe in order to kill an insect.

འབེན་མེད་མདའ་འཕེན། to shoot arrows without a target དམིགས་ཡུལ་མེད་པར་ལས་ཀ་བྱེད་པ་ནི་འབེན་མེད་པར་མདའ་འཕེན་པ་དང་གཅིག་པ་རེད། The work without aim is same as shooting without a target.

འབེལ་འབེལ་ལྱག་ལྱག in abundance ཕྱི་ཟླ་དགུ་པ་ལ་མ་ན་ལི་རུ་ཀུ་ཤུ་འབེལ་འབེལ་ལྱག་ལྱག་ཡོད་པ་རེད། Apples are abundant in Manali in September.

འབོར་ཁོབ་ཆེ་པོ། boastful ཕྱི་རྒྱལ་ནས་ཡོང་བའི་ཚོང་པ་དེ་ཚོ་འབོར་ཁོབ་ཆེ་པོ་ཞི་དྲག་འདུག The businessman coming from abroad countries are very boastful.

འབྲས་བུ་གཡུར་དུ་ཟ་བ། rich harvest དལོ་ཆར་པ་མང་པོ་བབ་ཅང་སྟོན་ཐོག་གཡུར་དུ་ཟ་བ་ཡོང་གི་རེད། This year it rained heavily therefore there will be a rich harvest.

འབྲས་བུ་སྨིན་པ་ས་ལ་ལྷུང་བ། ripe fruit falling on the ground འབྲས་བུ་སྨིན་པ་ས་ལ་ལྷུང་བ་རྣམས་བྱ་ཕྱུར་ཟ་གི་རེད། The ripe fruit fallen on the ground will be eaten by birds.

འབྲུ་དོན་འགལ་མེད། to stick to the points of resolution/ without violating the words (agreement) གཞུང་གི་ལས་བྱེད་རྣམས་གཞུང་ ཁྲིམས་འབྲུ་དོན་འགལ་མེད་བསྲུང་དགོས། Government officials need to observe the rules of the goverment strictly.

འབྲུ་ཕུན་གྱིས་ཆུ་རགས་བརྒྱབ་པ། to build a dam out of grain husks ཕྱི་ལོ་ ༡༩༥༩ ལོར་བོད་ཀྱི་ཆབ་སྲིད་ཀྱི་གནས་སྟངས་ནི་འབྲུ་ཕུན་གྱིས་ཆུ་རགས་བརྒྱབ་ པ་ནང་བཞིན་ཆགས་ཡོད། In 1959, the political condition of Tibet was like that of a dam built with grain husk.

འབྲུག་མགོ་སྦྲུལ་མཇུག Lit.: a dragon's head with the tail of a snake/ Sense implied: great beginning and poor end བོད་ པའི་ལས་ཀ་མང་ཆེ་བ་འབྲུག་མགོ་སྦྲུལ་མཇུག་ལྟ་བུ་མཐོང་གི་འདུག I see most of the Tibetan works great in the beginning and poor at the end.

འཕོང་བསད་པས་མ་ཚད་ང་མའི་དར་ལྕོག Lit.: not only did he kill a wild deer but he made a flag with its tail/ Sense implied: to be extremely disrespectful ཁོས་ཀྱུ་མ་བཀུས་པས་མ་ཚད་ད་དུང་ངོམ་ གྱི་འདུག འདི་ནི་འཕོང་བསད་པ་མ་ཟད་ང་མའི་དར་ལྕོག་བཟུགས་པ་རང་རེད། Not only did he boast of it which is just like not only killing a wild deer but making a flag out of its tail.

སྦལ་པ་རྒྱ་མཚོའི་གཏིང་ནས་དུ་བ། ལྷའི་དབང་པོའི་སྙན་ལ་མི་གསན། Lit.: The frog's croak from the bottom of an ocean is not heard by the king of gods/ Sense implied: An officer in the high post cannot understand the problems of down trodden

ཐབ་རོད་གྱིལ་གྱིལ། Lit.: rolling laugh/ Sense implied: to roar with laughter ཇག་དཔོན་དེ་ཐབ་རོད་གྱིལ་གྱིལ་གད་མོ་ཤོར་སོང་། The chief of the bandits roared with laughter.

སྦལ་པ་མཐོང་དུས་སྦྱུང་མོ་སངས་རྒྱས་རེད། Lit.: compared to frogs a tadpole is a Buddha/ Sense implied: comparatively he is as innocent as a Buddha.

སྦུག་སྦུབ་དོག་པོ། packed/ no room ང་ཚོའི་འཛིན་གྲ་སྦུག་སྦུབ་དོག་པོ་ཞེ་དྲག་འདུག Our class is fully packed.

སྦུད་པ་ཉིར་སྒྲ་ཆེ་ཡང་ལག་པའི་འོག Although the bellows roar loudly, they are under the control of the hand.

སྦྱང་བཙོན་གཏིང་ཟབ། thorough training ཁོང་གིས་དགོན་པ་ནས་དཔེ་ཆ་སྦྱང་བཙོན་གཏིང་ཟབ་པ་གནང་བ་རེད། He did thorough study of the religious texts from the monastery.

སྦྱོར་དངོས་རྗེས་གསུམ། the three: the preparation, the actual session and the conclusion ངས་སེམས་བསྐྱེད་ཀྱི་སྦྱོར་དངོས་རྗེས་གསུམ་སློབ་སྦྱོང་བྱས་པ་ཡིན། I studied the preparation, actual session and conclusion of the generation of boddhicitta.

སྦྱོར་ཤེས་ན་དུག་ཀྱང་སྨན་ལ་འགྲོ If one knows pharmocology even poisons can be used as medicine.

སྦྲུལ་མདུད་སྦྲུལ་བཤིག Lit.: the coiled up snake unwinds itself/

Sense implied: The dispute must be settled within the parties.

སྦྲུལ་བཙིར་ན་ཡན་ལག་ Lit.: If you squeeze a snake you will see its hand./ Sense implied: If you interogate a person you will see his true nature.

མ་བསྐུལ་དང་རང་ཤུགས། དང་དུ་ལེན་པ། voluntary/ taken up without being asked for བྱང་ཆུབ་སེམས་པ་རྣམས་ཀྱིས་མ་བསྐུལ་དང་རང་ཤུགས་ཐོག་གཞན་དོན་བྱེད་པ་རེད། Boddhisattvas work for others' benefit without being asked for.

མ་བསྐུལ་རང་མོས། self-motivated/ without being asked but with interest སློབ་ཕྲུག་ཡག་པོ་ཚོས་མ་བསྐུལ་རང་མོས་ཐོག་སློབ་སྦྱོང་གནང་གི་རེད། Good students do their study without having to be exhorted.

མ་གོ་མ་ཐོས་མེད་པ། to everyone's knowledge/ There is no room for complaining, "I haven't heard" དགེ་རྒན་ཆེན་མོས་གསལ་བསྒྲགས་མ་གོ་མ་ཐོས་མེད་པ་གནང་སོང་། The Headmaster made the announcement to everyone's knowledge.

མ་གྲོས་བསམ་པ་གཅིག་མཐུན། unanimous / coscensus without having discussion སྲིད་འཛིན་གསར་པ་དེ་ལ་ཡུལ་མི་ཚང་མས་མ་གྲོས་བསམ་པ་གཅིག་མཐུན་གྱི་སྣེ་ནས་དགའ་བསུ་ཞུས་པ་རེད། The new president was unanimously welcomed by all the citizens without discussion.

མ་དགའ་ཞེ་འཛིན། bearing a grudge ཕན་ཚུན་མ་དགའ་ཞེ་འཛིན་བྱེད་པ་སྡུག་བསྔལ་གྱི་རྒྱུ་རེད། To bear a grudge against one another is a cause of suffering.

162

མ་དགའ་ལྷ་གསོལ། treating someone like god though you don't like him ཞིང་བྲན་ལམ་ལུགས་ཀྱི་སྐབས་སུ་སྡིན་བདག་ངན་པ་ཚོ་ལ་འབངས་མི་མེར་རྣམས་ཀྱིས་མ་དགའ་ལྷ་སོལ་བྱེད་པ་རེད། During feudalism the bad feudal lords were treated like gods by their subjects although they did not like them.

མ་འགྲིགས་མ་འཐུས། lacking somewhere/ short coming/ opposite of quite O.K. ལས་ཀ་འདི་ཡི་ཆེད་དུ་ཁོང་མ་འགྲིགས་མ་ཐུས་པ་གང་ཡང་མི་འདུག He is quite O.K. for this work.

མ་འགྲོ་རང་འགྲོ no choice but to go ད་ལོ་ང་བོད་དུ་ཕ་མ་ཕྲག་ཏུ་མ་འགྲོ་རང་འགྲོ་ཡིན། This year I have no choice but to go to Tibet to see my parents.

མ་འགྲིགས་རང་འགྲིགས། had to be satisfied with ཟླ་བ་ལ་སྒྱ་ཆ་སྟོར་མོ་ཆིག་སྟོང་ཐམ་པ་དེ་མ་འགྲིགས་རང་འགྲིགས་རང་རེད། One has to be satisfied with a monthly salary of one thousand rupees.

མ་བསྒྲིགས་ལྷུན་གྲུབ། spontaneously accomplished without prearrangement དགས་དང་མཚན་མ་བཟང་པོ་འདི་རྣམས་མ་བསྒྲིགས་ལྷུན་གྲུབ་བྱུང་སོང་། All these good signs arose spontaneously without prearrangement.

མ་ཏུ་རང་ཏུ། no choice but to weep བུ་མོ་འདི་ལ་དཀའ་ངལ་མང་པོ་འཕྲད་དེ་མ་ཏུ་རང་ཏུ་རང་ཆགས་སོང་། She faced many probems which made her breakdown and weep helplessly.

མ་འཛིན་འཛིན་མདོག   claiming capable of doing something
although not/false claim   མ་འཛིན་འཛིན་མདོག་གནང་ན་ཡག་པོ་མ་རེད།
It is not good to make a false claim as if one can do it.

མ་བརྗེད་སྙིང་བཅངས།   not to forget but to keep in the heart/to
keep in mind   འཛིན་གྲྭའི་ནང་ལ་བསླབས་པ་རྣམས་མ་བརྗེད་སྙིང་བཅངས་གནང་
དགོས།   One should keep in mind what is taught in the class.

མ་ཉན་རང་ཉན།   no choice but to listen   མ་འདོད་ན་ཡང་དཔོན་པོའི་བཀའ་ལ་
མ་ཉན་རང་ཉན་རེད།   One has to listen to the leader's order even if
one does not want to.

མ་ཉེས་ཁ་གཡོགས།   to blame   རང་གི་ནོར་འཁྲུལ་གཞན་ལ་མ་ཉེས་ཁ་གཡོགས་བྱེད་ན་
སྡིག་པ་ཆེན་པོ་རེད།   It is a big negavity to blame others for one's
own mistake.

མ་གཏོར་རང་གཏོར།   no choice but to demolish   མའོ་ཚེ་ཏུང་གི་བཀའ་
ལ་བརྟེན་ནས་ལྷ་ཁང་མང་པོ་མ་གཏོར་རང་གཏོར་ཆགས་པ་རེད།   They had to
demolish many temples at the order of Mr. Mao.

མ་རྟོགས་ལོག་རྟོག   what is not understood and wrong
conception   མ་རྟོགས་ལོག་རྟོག་གཅོད་པ་ལ་སྟོང་པ་ཉིད་བསྒོམ་དགོས་པ་ཡིན།
To dispel wrong understanding and to understand that
which is not understood, one needs to meditate on emptiness.

མ་དག་རྒྱུན་འཛམས།   wrong usages that have been coming
through the ages   དམིགས་བསལ་དོ་སྲུང་མ་བྱེད་ན་ཉིན་མ་དག་རྒྱུན་འཛམས་ལ་

དག་བཅོས་བྱེད་རྒྱུ་ཁག་པོ་རེད། It is difficult to correct the wrong usages that have been coming through the ages unless special attention is given to them.

མ་བདག་བདག་བཟུང་། false claim of ownership རྒྱ་མིས་བོད་དེ་མ་བདག་བདག་བཟུང་བྱས་པ་རེད། China seized Tibet and made false claim of her ownership.

མ་ནག་ནག་ལ་བུ་དཀར་དཀར་སྐྱེས། Lit.: A black mother giving birth to a white son./ Sense implied: A non-virtuous mother gives birth to a virtuous son.

མ་གཞི་དངོས་གནས་བྱས་ན། actually/ in reality མ་གཞི་དངོས་གནས་བྱེད་ན་ང་གྲྭ་པ་བྱེད་རྒྱུ་རེད། Actually, I was supposed to become a monk.

མ་ལངས་རང་ལང་། no choice but to wake up སང་ཉིན་ང་སྔ་པོ་མ་ལང་རང་ལང་ཡིན། Tomorrow I have to wake up early in the morning.

མ་ཎི་བགྲང་བགྲང་། Lit.: as often as Mani (a mantra) is recited/ Sense implied: continuously, many and repetitions དགེ་ལགས་ཀྱིས་ང་ཚོ་ལ་བཀའ་བཀོན་མ་ཎི་བགྲང་བགྲང་གནང་བྱུང་། Our teacher scolded us continuously like reciting mani.

མ་ཎི་རང་གིས་མི་འདོན་ན་ཕྲེང་བ་གཞན་ལ་སྤྲོད། If one doesn't recite mani mantra, pass the rosary to others.

མ་བོས་མགྲོན་པོ། uninvited guest དེ་རིང་ང་ཁྱེད་རང་གི་མ་བོས་པའི་མགྲོན་པོ་ཡིན། Today I am your uninvited guest.

མ་བྱན་མར་ཁུའི་རྒྱ་མཚོ། ཤི་ན་དམྱལ་བའི་གཏིང་དོ། Lit.: The cook is in the ocean of liquified butter, but if he dies, he will like an anchor, go to the depths of hell./ Sense implied: A monastic cook who steals will go to hell after his death.

མ་བྱས་རང་བྱས། མ་བྱས་ཀ་མེད། had no choice but to do it ད་ལོང་བོད་རི་གཞོན་ནུའི་ཚོགས་གཙོ་མ་བྱས་ཀ་མེད་ཐུག་སོང་། I had to be the president of the Tibetan Youth Congress this year.

མ་བྱེད་མ་བལྟ། Lit.: to advise not to do and not to look/ Sense implied: restriction དེང་སང་ཕ་མ་ཚོས་མ་བྱེད་མ་བལྟ་གཆོག་བཤད་ཀྱང་ཕྲུ་གུ་ཚོས་ཉན་གྱི་མི་འདུག These days children do not listen to their parents inspite of their parents giving them advice.

མ་མྱོང་དགུ་མྱོང་། to experience all kinds of troubles རྒྱ་མིའི་ལོག་དུ་བོད་མི་ཚོས་མ་མྱོང་དགུ་མྱོང་མྱངས་ཡོད། Tibetans have suffered all kinds of troubles under the Chinese regime.

མ་མྱོང་རང་མྱོང་། no choice but to bear it སློབ་སྦྱོང་ཡག་པོ་མ་གནང་ན་དཀའ་ངལ་དེ་མ་མྱོང་རང་མྱོང་རང་རེད། If you do not study properly, there is no choice but to bear the problems.

མ་རྩའི་རོགས་རམ། capital loan (help) ཁྱེད་རང་ཚོང་བཀྱོན་ན་མ་རྩའི་རོགས་རམ་དངུལ་ཁང་ནས་ལེན་ཆོག་གི་རེད། If you do business, you can take a capital loan from the bank.

མ་ཟ་རང་ཟ། to be compelled to eat or taking a bribe/ he had to eat since he was hungry གྲོད་ཁོག་ལྟོགས་ནས་ཁ་ལག་གང་འདུ་བྱུང་

166

ཡང་མ་ཟ་རང་ཟ་རེད། When hungry one has to eat whatever kind of food may be available.

མ་འོངས་སྟོན་གཟིགས། to foresee the future/ to see beforehand འཐྲུལ་བ་ཡིད་བཞིན་ནོར་བུའི་མ་འོངས་སྟོན་གཟིགས་ཀྱི་བཀའ་སློབ་ལ་ང་ཚོ་ཚང་མས་དོ་ སྣང་བྱེད་དེ་སློབ་སྦྱོང་བྱེད་དགོས། All of us should study with interest His Holiness the Dalai Lama's speeches foretelling the future.

མ་འོངས་ལུང་བསྟན། future prediction ནང་པ་ཚོས་སངས་རྒྱས་བཅོམ་ལྡན་ འདས་ཀྱི་མ་འོངས་ལུང་བསྟན་ལ་ཡིད་ཆེས་བྱེད་པ་རེད། Buddhists believe the future prediction of Lord Buddha.

མ་ཡིན་ཡིན་མདོག མ་ཡིན་ཡིན་ཆུལ། to pretend to be what you are not དཔོན་པོ་མ་ཡིན་ཡིན་མདོག་བྱེད་ན་ཉིན་གཅིག་ཏུ་གོ་གི་རེད། One day it will be known if one pretends to be an officer though one is not. བོད་པ་མ་ཡིན་ཡིན་ཆུལ་བྱེད་ནས་ཕན་ཐོགས་གང་ཡོང་། What is the use of pretending to be a Tibetan when one is not.

མ་རབས་ཟ་འཁལ། extremely immodest མ་རབས་ཟ་འཁལ་གྱི་ལས་ཀ་ལ་ནམ་ ཡང་སེམས་འགུགས་སྤྲ་མི་རུང་། One should never encourage extremely immodest work.

མ་རབས་ཐབས་སྤུག to be immodest and evil རྒྱ་མིས་དགོན་པ་གཏོར་ བའི་མ་རབས་ཐབས་སྤུག་གི་ལས་ཀ་དེ་འདྲུ་བྱས་ཡོད། The Chinese indulged in the immodest and evil destruction of monasteries.

མ་རབས་མགོ་བསྐོར། indecent and to deceive ཁྱེད་རང་མ་རབས་མགོ་ བསྐོར་ཤ་སྟག་གི་དཀྱིལ་ལ་བསྡད་ན་ཡ་རབས་ཆགས་ཐབས་མེད། You cannot become decent if you are always surrounded by indecent and deceitful people.

མ་རུངས་ཁོག་བཅངས། ulterior motive མ་རུངས་ཁོག་བཅངས་ཀྱི་ཐོག་ནས་ལས་ཀ་བྱེད་ན་སྐྱིད་པོ་ཡོང་གི་མ་རེད། One cannot be happy if one works with an ulterior motive.

མ་ལན་མ་འགྱོད་པ། no guilt/no regret/ no repentance ལྷག་བསམ་རྣམ་དག་གི་ཐོག་ནས་ལས་ཀ་བྱེད་ན་མ་ལན་མ་འགྱོད་པ་ཡོང་གི་རེད། If you work sincerely, you will have nothing to repent.

མ་ལུས་ཀུན་འདུས། gathered everything without missing ཡོན་ཏན་མ་ལུས་ཀུན་འདུས་བྱུང་བའི་གདམས་ངག་ནི་བླ་མ་བསྟེན་རྒྱུ་དེ་ཡིན། To cultivate one's teacher is an instruction for gathering knowledge without missing any.

མ་ལུས་ཀུན་ཚང་། all/ complete/ without any missing ཁོང་གི་དེབ་མ་ལུས་ཀུན་ཚང་ངས་ཕྱིར་སློག་བྱས་པ་ཡིན། I returned all his books without missing any.

མ་ཤེས་རྨོངས་པ། ignorance མ་ཤེས་རྨོངས་པ་ལ་བརྟེན་ནས་ང་ཚོ་འཁོར་བར་འཁོར་བ་རེད། We are in this cycle of existence due to ignorance.

མ་ཤེས་ཤེས་མདོག pretending to know what one does not ཨིན་ཇི་མ་ཤེས་ཤེས་མདོག་བྱེད་ན་དཀའ་ངལ་འཕྲད་ཡོང་། You might face difficulties if you pretend to know English (when you do not).

མ་བསླབས་རང་བསླབས། no way but to learn or teach བོད་པ་ཚོ་ལ་

དེང་སང་ཨིན་ཇི་མ་བསླབས་རང་བསླབས་རེད། These days Tibetans have no choice but to learn English.

མ་གསང་རྡུང་གཏུམ། an open and honest statement དེང་སང་ཁ་གསང་རྡུང་གཏུམ་བཤད་ན་ཡང་གཟབ་གཟབ་གནང་དགོས། These days one should be careful even though one speaks openly and honestly.

མ་བསམ་དགུ་བསམ། to think about everything/ over-thinking མ་བསམ་དགུ་བསམ་བྱེད་ན་སྨྱོ་བའི་ཉེན་ཁ་ཡོད། If you think of everything, there is a danger of becoming mad.

མག་གི་མུག་གི murmer འཛིན་གྲྭའི་ནང་ལ་མག་གི་མུག་གི་མ་བྱེད། Do not murmer in the class.

མང་ཉུང་སྙོམས་པོ། a moderate number དེང་སང་དངུལ་ཁང་ལ་ཡང་དངུལ་མང་ཉུང་སྙོམས་པོ་ཞིག་ལས་མི་འདུག These days even the bank has only moderate amount of cash.

མང་ཐག་ཆོད། exceedingly many/ a good number of ངས་གྲོགས་པོ་ཉམ་ཆུང་དེའི་དོན་དུ་དངུལ་ཁང་ལ་དངུལ་མང་ཐག་ཆོད་བཞག་ཡོད། I have kept a large amount of money in the bank for my simple friend.

མང་དུ་མང་དུ། more and more དབྱར་ཁ་ར་རས་ས་ལ་ལ་ཕྱི་རྒྱལ་བ་མང་དུ་མང་དུ་འགྲོ་གི་འདུག More and more westerners come to Dharamsala during the summer.

མང་ཉེ་ཉུང་གིས་མི་བཟེན། minority cannot challenge the majority

མང་སྟོབ་ཆུང་གིས་མི་བརྟེན་པའི་དཔེ་བཞིན་ནམ་ཆུང་གིས་སྟོབས་ལྡན་རྒྱགས་ཁ་གི་མ་རེད།
The weak cannot challenge the strong just as the minority cannot challenge the majority.

མང་འཕྲི་ཉུང་སྣོན། Lit.: deducting from the larger and adding it to the lesser/ Sense implied: to balance དཔལ་འབྱོར་མང་བ་ནས་ འཕྲི་བ་དང་ཉུང་བ་ལ་སྣན་ན་ཚང་མ་དཔལ་འབྱོར་འཁོད་སྙོམས་པོ་ཡོང་གི་རེད། There will be a balance in the economy if one deducts from the rich and adds to the poor.

མང་མོས་འདེམས་བསྐོ། elected by the majority བཀྲ་ཤིས་ལགས་ང་ཚོའི་ ཚོགས་གཙོར་མང་མོས་འདེམས་བསྐོ་བྱུང་སོང་། Mr. Tashi was elected as our president by the majority.

མན་ངག་ཁ་རྒྱན་མ་བྱེད་དོན་ལ་སྦྱོས། Don't take quintessential instruction as an adornment but ponder upon its meaning.

མར་དཀྱིལ་ནས་སྐྲ་བཏོན་པ། Lit.: pulling a hair from butter/ to be singled out ཆུང་དུས་སློབ་སྦྱོང་ཡག་པོ་མ་གནང་ན་ཆེན་པོ་ཆགས་དུས་སྤྱི་ཚོགས་ ནང་དུ་མར་དཀྱིལ་ནས་སྐྲ་བཏོན་པ་ནང་བཞིན་ཆགས་ཀྱི་རེད། If you do not study well when you are young, you will feel singled out later in the society.

མར་མེ་སྤྲམ་ཟད། བྱ་གཤུན་སྒྲོ་ཟད། Lit.: a lamp with exhausted butter/a bird with wornout feathers/ Sense implied: a sign of old age/a sign of ending.

མར་ཚམ་ད་ག just a little away from here འདི་ནས་མར་ཚམ་ད་ག་བོད་པའི་

ཟ་ཁང་ཡོད་རེད། There is a Tibetan hotel just a little down from here.

མི་དཀར་ཞྭ་ནག Lit.: a white man with a black hat/ Sense implied: to accuse an innocent མི་དཀར་པོ་ལ་ཞྭ་ནག་པོ་གཡོག་ན་ ཁ་མཆུ་འབོགས་མ་ལེན་པ་དང་གཅིག་པ་རེད། Accusing the innocent is like inviting a case against oneself/getting involved in legal case.

མི་དཀར་ལ་ཞྭ་ནག་དང་ཏ་དཀར་ལ་སྲབ་ནག Lit.: A black hat for a white man and a black rein for a white horse/ Sense implied: to blame an innocent

མི་རྐྱང་ཏ་རྐྱང་། a man and a horse དེ་རིང་ང་ཚོའི་གྲོང་གསེབ་ལ་བོད་ནས་མི་ རྐྱང་ཏ་རྐྱང་ཞིག་བསླེབས་སོང་། Today a man and a horse came to our village from Tibet.

མི་ཁ་གཏམ་ངན། infamy/curse ལས་ཀ་གང་བྱས་ཀྱང་མི་ཁ་གཏམ་ངན་མི་ཡོང་བ་ གནང་དགོས། Whatever work we do we should see that no bad reputation comes to us.

མི་ཁོམ་མི་ལྷུག་ས། no time to do སང་ཉིན་ང་བོད་དུ་འགྲོ་རྒྱར་ཁོམ་པ་མི་འདུག I have no time to go to Tibet tomorrow.

མི་གོ་བ་ཅན་ལ་ཚིག་གཅིག དྲ་འགྲོ་བ་ཅན་ལ་ལྕག་གཅིག A word for a man of understanding and a whip for a horse that gallops well.

མི་དགའ་རང་སྐྱིད། happiness for oneself and others མི་གཞན་དག

171

དགའ་པོ་བཟོ་ཐུབ་ན་རང་ཉིད་སྐྱིད་པོ་ཡོང་གི་རེད། You will be happy if you can make other people happy.

མི་འགྲོ་ཆེད་གཉེར། to depute people with purpose བོད་ཀྱི་དཔེ་མཛོད་ཁང་ནས་རྒྱལ་སྤྱིའི་བོད་ཀྱི་སྐད་ཡིག་བགྲོ་གླེང་ཚོགས་འདུ་ཞིང་ས་གཉིས་པར་ང་ཉིད་མི་འགྲོ་ཆེད་གཉེར་བཏང་གནང་སོང་། I was sent on deputation by the LTWA to attend the International Seminar on Tibetan Language.

མི་རྒས་ཡུལ་དྲན་བྱ་རྒས་ཤིང་། When people get older they remember their native country and when birds get older they remember their nest (wood)./ Sense implied: feeling homesick

མི་བརྒྱ་ཁ་གཅིག Lit.: a hundred people with one voice/ Sense implied: unanimous དགྲ་པོ་ལ་རྒོལ་དུས་མི་བརྒྱ་ཁ་གཅིག་དེ་འདུ་དགོས་པ་ཡིན། When fighting against an enemy, unanimity is required.

མི་བརྒྱ་སེམས་གཅིག Lit.: a hundred people with one mind/ Sense implied: unity ཡུལ་ལ་བདེ་སྐྱིད་ཡོད་དུས་ཡུལ་མི་ཚང་མ་མི་བརྒྱ་སེམས་གཅིག་ལྟ་བུ་ཡོད། When the country is peaceful and happy all the countrymen live like a hundred people with one mind.

མི་ངན་ཁ་མཐུན། collaboration among evils/accomplice མི་ངན་ཁ་མཐུན་ན་ཡུལ་ལ་བདེ་སྐྱིད་མི་ཡོང་། There won't be peace and happiness in a country if evils collaborate with each other.

མི་ངན་བརྟེན་སྐོར། relying on an evil person/ to be under the influence of an evil person མི་ངན་བརྟེན་ན་སྐྱོད་ངན་ཤེས་ཡོང་། If you rely on an evil person you will know indecent things.

172

མི་གཅིག་ལག་གཅིག Lit.: one man and one hand/ Sense implied: single handed ང་མི་གཅིག་ལག་གཅིག་གིས་ལས་ཀ་གང་ཡང་བྱེད་ཐུབ་ཀྱི་མ་རེད། I cannot do anything single handedly.

མི་ཆ་ཞན་པ། lesser and poor human resource ང་ཚོའི་ཁྱིམ་ཚང་ལ་ད་ལོ་མི་ཆ་ཞན་པོ་སོང་ཙང་ཞིང་ལས་བྱེད་རྒྱུ་ཁག་པོ་རེད། It is difficult for us to do farming this year as we have very few persons in our family.

མི་ཉམས་གོང་འཕེལ། ཉམས་པ་སོར་ཆུད། to preserve, promote and restore ཨ་མྱེས་རྨ་ཆེན་བོད་ཀྱི་རིག་གཞུང་ཞིབ་འཇུག་ཁང་གི་དམིགས་ཡུལ་ནི་བོད་ཀྱི་རིག་གནས་མི་ཉམས་གོང་འཕེལ་དང་ཉམས་པ་སོར་ཆུད། དེ་བཞིན་རིག་གནས་གསར་པ་བོད་སྐད་དུ་བསྒྱུར་རྒྱ་བཅས་ཡིན་པ་རེད། The aims and objectives of Amnye Machen Institute are to preserve, promote and restore Tibetan literature and to translate new literature into Tibetan.

མི་ཉམས་རྒྱུན་འཛིན། preservation དགོན་པ་ཁག་ཏུ་མ་སོང་བ་བརྒྱུད་པའི་ཕྱག་ལེན་མི་ཉམས་རྒྱུན་འཛིན་གནང་གི་ཡོད་རེད། The traditional practices are very well preserved in the monasteries.

མི་ཉམས་ཡུན་གནས། preservation for a long time རིག་གཞུང་མི་ཉམས་ཡུན་གནས་བྱུང་བ་ལ་གཞུང་གི་རྒྱབ་སྐྱོར་དགོས་པ་ཡིན། Government support is needed for the long term preservation of Tibetan Culture.

མི་ཉེ་མི་རྒྱང་། neither too close nor too far ལུང་པའི་རྒྱལ་པོ་དང་མི་ཉེ་མི་རྒྱང་བ་གནང་གལ་ཆེ། It is important neither to be too close nor remain too far from a king of the country.

མི་གཉིས་བར་ནས་རྫ་ཆག Lit.: an earthen pot broken between two people/ Sense implied: too many cooks spoil the broth.

མི་བསྟོད་དགུ་བསྟོད། to praise too much ཕྱུ་གུ་ཆུང་ཆུང་ལ་མི་བསྟོད་དགུ་བསྟོད་བྱེད་རྒྱུ་མེད། One should not praise children too much.

མི་ཐོག་ནས་མི་ཐོག from generation to generation རྒྱ་གར་གཞུང་ནས་མི་ཐོག་ནས་མི་ཐོག་བར་བོད་པ་ལ་རོགས་པ་བྱེད་ཐུབ་ཀྱི་མ་རེད། The government of India cannot help the Tibetans from generations to generations.

མི་མཐུན་ནང་འཐབ། disharmony/ fight among themselves རྒྱལ་ཁབ་ཕན་ཚུན་མི་མཐུན་ནང་འཐབ་བྱུང་ན་དམག་ཆེན་ལང་བའི་ཉེན་ཁ་ཡོད། If there is a fight between the countries, there is a danger of war of breaking out.

མི་བདེན་བདེན་ཆ་ལུ། to tell something that is not true as if it is true རྒྱ་མིས་མ་བདེན་བདེན་ཆ་ལུ་བཤད་དེ་འཛམ་གླིང་མགོ་བསྐོར་ཐེབས་ཀྱི་མ་རེད། China cannot deceive the world by stating or declaring false statements as if they were true.

མི་དྲག་གྲལ་རིམ། the noble class མི་དྲག་གྲལ་རིམས་ཀྱི་ཁྱིམ་ཚང་མང་ཆེ་བ་ཕྱུག་པོ་རེད། Most of the noble class families are rich.

མི་དྲན་དགུ་དྲན། to think wildly/ to think too much མི་ཚེ་ཐུང་ཐུང་གཅིག་གི་དོན་དུ་མི་དྲན་དགུ་དྲན་ག་རེ་བྱེད་རྒྱུ་ཡོད་རེད། What is there to think too much about for this short life ?

174

མི་བདེན་བརྫུན་སྒྲིག   to lie/ false མི་བདེན་བརྫུན་སྒྲིག་གི་གཏམ་ཁ་འདད་ལ་ང་ཚོས་ ཡིད་ཆེས་བྱེད་ཀྱི་མ་རེད། We will not trust a false statement.

མི་རྡུང་རང་དུས། to beat others and cry oneself མི་བྲབ་ཆུང་ཚོས་མི་རྡུང་ རང་དུས་བྱེད་ཀྱི་རེད། Silly people beat others and cry themselves.

མི་ནག་མེད་ལ་ནག་དང་རྡོ་ཟུར་མེད་ལ་ཟུར།   to blame an innocent person and to say a stone has an edge when it does not./ Sense implied: false accusation

མི་ནུབ་ཡུན་གནས།   to flourish for a long time without degeration སངས་རྒྱས་ཀྱི་བསྟན་པ་མི་ནུབ་ཡུན་གནས་ཡོང་བ་ལ་དགེ་འདུན་གྱི་ ཚུལ་ཁྲིམས་ཚུལ་བཞིན་བསྲུང་དགོས་པ་ཡིན། The monk community should observe their discipline very strictly so that Buddha's teaching may flourish for a long time without degeneration.

མི་ཕར་བསད་སྟོང་ཆུར་ལེན།   to take thousands in addition to killing a person ཇག་པས་མི་ཕར་བསད་པས་མ་ཚད་སྟོང་ཆུར་ལེན་པ་རེད། The bandits not only killed the person but also claimed thousands in addition.

མི་ཕུང་རང་བརྔགས། to ruin others and oneself མི་ངན་གྱི་ཁ་ལ་ཉན་ན་མི་ ཕུང་རང་བརྔགས་ཡོང་གི་རེད། If one listens to evil persons one will ruin oneself and others.

མི་བབ་ཚོད་ཟིས།   to take advantage of/ to ignore ལུང་པའི་དཔོན་པོས་ མི་བབ་ཚོད་ཟིས་བྱེད་ན་ཡུལ་མི་ཚོས་རོ་རྒོལ་བྱེད་ཀྱི་རེད། If the leader of a country takes advantage of a subject the people will revolt against him.

175

མི་བུད་ཁྲིམ་སྐྱོང་། exiled ཕྱི་ལོ་ ༡༩༥༩ ལོར་བོད་མི་སྐྱོང་ཕྱག་མང་པོ་མི་བུད་ཁྲིམ་སྐྱོང་ཆགས་པ་རེད། Thousands of Tibetans were exiled in 1959.

མི་འབོར་ཆེ་ཆུང་། size of population མི་འབོར་ཆེ་ཆུང་ཚང་མའི་ནང་ལ་མི་སྣ་ཚོགས་ཡོང་གི་རེད། In all the different sizes of population we find various types of people.

མི་བྱེད་ཀ་མེད། to have no choice but to do ལས་ཀ་འདི་ཁོང་གིས་མི་བྱེད་ཀ་མེད་རེད། He has to do this work.

མི་བྱེད་དགུ་བྱེད། to do all sorts of things (negative) རྒྱ་མིའི་གྱི་དམག་མི་ཚོས་མི་བྱེད་དགུ་བྱེད་ཆང་མ་བྱེད་པ་རེད། Chiness Indian soldiers do all sorts of things.

མི་མང་ཁ་མང་དེ་དུག་ཡིན། མི་མང་ལག་མང་དེ་གསེར་ཡིན། The mouths of people are poison but their hands are gold.

མི་མང་ལྷེ་མང་། the more people, the more criticisms ཆབ་སྲིད་ཀྱི་དཔོན་པོ་ཚོས་མི་མང་གི་ལྷེ་མང་ལ་བཟོད་པ་བྱེད་པ་རེད། The political leaders are patient with public criticism.

མི་མང་འདུ་ཚོགས། public gathering མི་མང་འདུ་ཚོགས་ཀྱི་དབུས་སུ་ཚོགས་གཙོས་གསུང་བཤད་གནང་སོང་། The president addressed the public gathering.

མི་མེད་ལུང་སྟོང་། a deserted place མི་མེད་ལུང་སྟོང་ཡིན་ན་མཚམས་བསྲུངས་ལ་ཡག་པོ་ཞེ་དྲག་ཡོད་རེད། A deserted place is very good for retreat.

མེས་སློན་རང་སྐྱེད། to feel happy and inspirational to others སློབ་

སྦྱོང་ཡག་པོ་བྱེད་ན་མེས་སློན་རང་སྐྱེད་ཡོང་གི་རེད། If you study hard, you will be happy and inspire others to be like you.

མི་ཚེ་སློང་ཟད། to waste one's life གཞུང་དུས་ནས་ནོར་དང་རིག་པ་གང་རུང་ལ་མ་བསླབས་ན་མི་ཚེ་སློང་ཟད་དུ་འགྲོ་བའི་ཉེན་ཁ་ཡོད་རེད། If one does not either amass wealth or study from young age there is a danger of wasting one's life.

མི་ཚེ་དོན་ལྡན། to have a purposeful life/ meaningful life ངའི་

བསམ་ཚུལ་ལ་ནང་བཞིན་བྱེད་ན་ཚོས་དང་མ་འཕྲད་ན་མི་ཚེ་དོན་དང་ལྡན་པ་ཁག་པོ་རེད། In my opinion, it is difficult to have a meaningful life if one does not encounter Dharma.

མི་ཚེ་ལས་གཏམ་ཚེ་རིང་། name lasts longer than one's life གཏམ་

དན་ལ་འཛེམས་དགོས་པ་ཡིན། མི་ཚེ་ལས་གཏམ་ཚེ་རིང་བ་ཡོང་། One should care for one's reputation as name lasts longer than one's life.

མི་ཚོགས་མང་ཉུང་། the size of a population མི་ཚོགས་མང་ཉུང་ལ་དཔག་

པའི་རོགས་རམ་བྱེད་ཀྱི་ཡིན། We will help according to the size of the population.

མི་འཛོམས་དགུ་འཛོམས། to have gathered everything ཟ་ཁང་ཕ་གིའི་

ནང་ལ་འགྲུལ་པ་མི་འཛོམས་དགུ་འཛོམས་བྱེད་ཀྱི་རེད། All sorts of travellers gather in that hotel.

མི་འོས་མི་འཚམ་པ། unsuitable/ unfit/ not deserving/ unqualified

ཕྲུ་གུ་ལ་མི་འོས་མི་མཚམ་པའི་ལས་ཀ་ཞེ་དྲག་མ་སྐུལ། Do not make children do things which are unfit for them.

177

མི་རིགས་ཁྱད་འཛིན། racial or ethnic discrimination འཇར་མན་གྱི་མི་རིགས་ཁྱད་འཛིན་གྱི་སྣ་བས་དམག་ཆེན་གཉིས་པ་འབོད་པ་རེད། The racial discrimination of Germans invited the II World War.

མི་རུང་ཉམ་ཚོད། an inappropriate and shameless argument བདེན་པ་མེད་པ་ལ་ད་དུང་མི་རུང་ཉམ་ཚོད་བྱེད་ན་སུས་ཉན་གྱི་རེད། Who will listen to a shameless argument when there is no truth in it.

མོ་རེ་ངོ་རེ། each and everyone/ individually ངས་ཁྱེད་རང་ཚོ་མི་རེ་ངོ་རེ་ལ་བཀའ་མོལ་ཞུ་ཐུབ་ཀྱི་མ་རེད། I cannot speak to everyone of you.

མི་ལས་དགུ་ལས། to do all sorts of work/ to do too much work རང་གི་ཕྲུ་གུའི་དོན་དུ་ཕ་མ་ཚོས་མི་ལས་དགུ་ལས་བྱེད་ཀྱི་རེད། The parents do all sorts of work for the benefit of their children.

མི་ཤི་ཁྱིམ་སྟོང་། Lit.: death and extinction of a family/ Sense implied: total extinction ད་ལོ་ཁོ་ལ་མི་ཤི་ཁྱིམ་སྟོང་བྱུང་སོང་། This year he had to face the extinction of his family through death.

མི་ཤེས་ཤེས་མདོག pretend to know something although one does not/ མི་ཤེས་ཤེས་མདོག་ནམ་ཡང་གཏང་མི་རུང་། One should never pretend to know something when one does not.

མི་བཤད་དགུ་བཤད། speaking about everything སྐད་ཆ་མི་བཤད་དགུ་བཤད་བྱེད་ན་གཞན་གྱིས་ཡིད་ཆེས་བྱེད་ཀྱི་མ་རེད། If you talk too much people will not trust you.

མི་ཤུགས་ཆུ་ཤུགས། the power of man and the power of

wealth ཨ་མེ་རི་ཁ་ལ་དེང་སང་མི་ཤུགས་དང་རྒྱུ་ཤུགས་གཉིས་ཀ་ཡོད་པ་རེད།
Today the United States has both human and material resources.

མི་ཡི་རོགས་རམ། to help with human resource དེང་སང་ས་ཆ་གང་ས་
ག་ལ་རྒྱུ་ཡི་རོགས་རམ་ལས་མི་ཡི་རོགས་རམ་དཀོན་པ་ཡོད། Today human resource help is more scarce everywhere than material help.

མི་ཤེས་དགུ་ཤེས། to know everything འཛི་གློགས་པོ་དོན་གྲུབ་ལགས་ཀྱིས་
ཀམ་པྱུ་ཏར་སྐོར་མི་ཤེས་དགུ་ཤེས་ཆང་མ་ཤེས་ཀྱི་འདུག My friend Dhondup knows everything about the computer.

མི་སར་རང་སྡོད། to sit oneself at other's place གཞན་ལ་སྐྱོན་བརྗོད་བྱེད་
དུས་མི་སར་རང་སྡོད་བྱེད་ནས་སྐྱོན་བརྗོད་བྱེད་ན་སྐྱོན་བརྗོད་རྣམ་དག་ཡོང་བ་ཡིན། If you think of yourself as the person you are criticising, then the criticism will be very honest and constructive.

མི་སེམས་མི་གཅིག་སོ་སོའི་གདོང་དང་འདྲ། People do not have the same mind, just as they do not have the same face.

མི་བསད་ཁྲག་སྐྱོར། killing humans and causing bloodshed གཅོད་
ཉ་ཕྲག་ཀྱང་མི་བསད་ཁྲག་སྐྱོར་གྱི་ལས་ཀ་མི་བྱེད་ཐག་གཅོད་ཡིན། I am determined not to indulge in killing humans and causing bloodshed regardless of how desperate the situation may be.

མི་བསམ་དགུ་བསམ། to think of all sorts of things མི་ལ་དཀའ་ངལ་
འཕྲད་དུས་མི་བསམ་དགུ་བསམ་བྱེད་ཀྱི་རེད། People think of all sorts of things when they face problems.

179

མིག་རྒྱང་ཐུང་ཐུང་། near-sightedness ཁྱེད་རང་ལ་མིག་རྒྱང་ཐུང་ཐུང་གི་དཀའ་ངལ་ཡོད་ན་སྨྱན་ཤེལ་མཆོད་དགོས། You should wear glasses if you have a problem with near sightedness.

མིག་རྒྱང་རིང་པོ། far-sighted people རྒྱལ་ཁབ་ཀྱི་དབུ་འཁྲིད་ཚོ་མིག་རྒྱང་རིང་པོ་ཞེ་དྲག་ཡོད་རེད། The leaders of nations are far-sighted people.

མིག་སློབ་ངན་འགྲན། imitate bad examples འགྲན་སེམས་ཅན་གྱི་སྤྱི་ཚོགས་སུ་མིག་སློབ་ངན་འགྲན་མང་པོ་བྱེད་པ་རེད། In a competative society, many imitate bad examples.

མིག་སློབ་ཡར་འགྲན། imitating good examples ཡར་རབས་ཅན་གྱི་སྤྱི་ཚོགས་སུ་མིག་སློབ་ཡར་འགྲན་བྱེད་པ་རེད། In a civilized society, people imitate good examples.

མིག་སློབ་རིམ་ལེན། to gradually adopt (someone's habit) སྤྱི་ཚོགས་ནང་ལ་ཕོ་སྦྲག་ཉེད་ཡག་གི་མིག་སློབ་རིམ་ལེན་བྱུང་ན་ཡག་པ་མ་རེད། It is not good to adopt gambling gradually in the society.

མིག་མཐོང་རྣ་ཐོས། Lit.: to see with the eyes and to hear with the ears/ Sense implied: real གནས་ཚུལ་འདི་བདེན་པ་རེད། ངས་མིག་གིས་མཐོང་བྱུང་། རྣ་བས་ཐོས་བྱུང་། This is true news. I have seen it with my own eyes and heard it with my own ears.

མིག་མཐོང་གཟུགས་གྲུབ། Lit.: very visible/ Sense implied: very obvious ཁོང་མཁས་པ་ཆེན་པོ་ཞིག་ཡིན་པ་མིག་མཐོང་གཟུགས་སུ་གྲུབ་པ་རེད། It is very visible/obvious that he is a great scholar.

མིག་མཐོང་ལག་ཟིན། Lit.: to see with the eye and to hold with the hand/ Sense implied: evident to all/ caught red handed དལོ་དངུལ་ཁང་ལ་རྐུན་མ་གཉིས་མིག་མཐོང་ལག་ཟིན་བྱུང་བ་རེད། Two thieves were caught red-handed this year in a bank.

མིག་འདྲིས་རྣར་འཛགས། Lit.: to have your eyes used to and your ears familiar with/ Sense implied: to have learned a lesson thoroughly. གཞུང་གསར་པ་སྦྱངས་དུས་མིག་མ་འདྲིས་པ་དང་རྣ་བར་མ་འཛགས་པའི་དཀའ་ངལ་ཞེ་དྲག་ཡོད་རེད། It is very difficult to have one's eyes and ears accustomed to a new text when studying.

མིག་ལྔན་གཡང་མཆོངས། Lit.: to jump off the cliff with open eyes/ Sense implied: to make mistakes knowingly ཆང་གི་ཉེས་དམིགས་ཤེས་བཞིན་དུ་ཆང་འཐུང་བ་ནི་མིག་ལྔན་གཡང་མཆོང་བྱེད་པ་དང་ཁྱད་པར་མེད། To drink chang even after knowing its effect is same as leaping off the cliff with open eyes.

མིག་ན་ལག་བཟོས། Lit.: the eye pain is made by the hand/ Sense implied: oneself is responsible for the harm ཁྱེད་རང་གི་དཀའ་ངལ་དེ་ཁྱེད་རང་གིས་བཟོས་པ་རེད། དཔེར་ན་མིག་ན་བ་ལག་པས་བཟོས་པ་བཞིན། You are responsible for your problems just as your hand is responsible for causing eye-pain.

མིག་ནང་གི་གྲ་མ་དང་ཤ་ནང་གི་ཚེར་མ། Lit.: grit in the eye and a thorn in the flesh/ Sense implied: very troublesome and disliked ང་ཚོའི་རྒྱུད་ཀྱི་གཏི་མུག་མ་རིག་པ་འདི་ནི་འཁོར་བ་ལས་ཐར་པ་ལ་མིག་ནང་གི་གྲ་མ་དང་ཤ་ནང་གི་ཚེར་མ་ནང་བཞིན་རེད། Ignorance is just like a grit in the eye and a thorn in the flesh, for us seeking liberation from this cyclic-existence.

མིག་ནང་གི་ཚེར་མ། Lit.: like a thorn in one's eye/ Sense implied: to dislike somebody རྒྱ་ནག་གཞུང་གི་མིག་ལ་བོད་ཀྱི་གཞོན་ནུ་ལྷན་ཚོགས་ འདི་ཚེར་མ་ལྟ་བུ་ཆགས་ཡོད། The Tibetan Youth Congress has become like a thorn in the eye of Chinese Government.

མིག་སྨན་མིག་ཐོག Lit.: an eye lotion soothes the eye/ Sense implied: to use property for what it is meant ཁྱེད་རང་གི་ཞལ་ འདེབས་དེ་ངས་མིག་སྨན་མིག་ཐོག་བརྒྱི་གི་ཡིན། I shall dedicate your donation towards that for which it is meant.

མིག་ལ་མིག་ལན་དང་སོ་ལ་སོ་ལན། Lit.: an eye for an eye and a tooth for a tooth/Sense implied: revenge.

མིང་དོན་མཆུངས་པ། the work in accordance with one's title/ to accord one's deed with one's name ལས་དོན་གང་དང་གང་ཡིན་ ཡང་མིང་དོན་མཆུངས་པ་བྱུ་དགོས་པ་རེད། Whatever the type of work it may be, one should be performing it worth its name.

མིང་ཡོད་དོན་ཡོད། to have both name and purpose གཞན་ཕན་བྱེད་ མཁན་ཚོ་ལ་མིང་ཡོད་པ་མ་ཟད་དོན་ཡང་ཡོད་པ་རེད། Those who work for the welfare of others have not only name and purpose too.

མིའི་རི་མོ་ནང་དང་སྟག་གི་རི་མོ་ཕྱི་ལ་ཡོད། The true picture of a man is within; the stripe of a tiger is on the outside.

མུ་གེའི་ཁ་ལ་ཟླ་ལྷག Lit.: In addition to famine, there is an extra month./ Sense implied: The extra month has prolonged starvation during famine.

མུ་མཐའ་མེད་པ། limitless/ endless/ boundless འཁོར་བ་མུ་མཐའ་མེད་པའི་ ནང་དུ་ད་བར་ང་ཚོ་འཁོར་བ་རེད། We have been wandering in this boundless cyclic existence until now.

མུ་མཐུད་རྒྱུན་འཁྱོངས། to continue ལས་འགུལ་འདི་མུ་མཐུད་རྒྱུན་འཁྱོངས་བྱེད་པ་ ལ་ཁྱེད་རང་གི་རོགས་རམ་དགོས་ཡོད། We need your help to continue this project.

མུན་འཐོམས་ཐལ་བསྐྱོད། follow blindly རང་གིས་མི་ཤེས་ན་གཞན་ལ་བཀའ་ འདྲི་ཞུ་དགོས། མུན་འཐོམས་ཐལ་བསྐྱོད་བྱེད་ན་འགྲིགས་ཐབས་མེད། When one does not know, one should ask. It is not alright to follow.

མུན་ནག་སྤྲ་མྱུལ། groping in the dark གློག་མེད་ན་མཚན་མོ་མུན་ནག་སྤྲ་ མྱུལ་བྱེད་ན་ཡང་ཅ་ལག་བརྙེད་ཀྱི་མ་རེད། You won't find things at night even by groping when there is no light.

མུན་ནག་འདོམས་འཇལ། to measure darkness by armspan མི་ ཤེས་ཤེས་མ་དོག་བྱེད་པ་ནི་མུན་ནག་འདོམས་འཇལ་དང་མ་ཚུངས་པ་ཡི་ན། Pretending to know something although one does not, is same as to measure the darkness by armspan.

མུན་མུན་ཐོམ་ཐོམ། dark and dull/ inactive ཁོང་རང་བསྙུན་ནས་མུན་མུན་ཐོམ་ ཐོམ་ཆགས་འདུག Since he has fallen ill, he has become dull and inactive.

མེ་ཁ་ཁ་དུ་བ་སོ་སོ། Lit.: fire and smoke are distinct/ Sense implied: Though friendly still different གྲོགས་པོ་གཉིས་མཐུན་པོ་ ཡོད་ཀྱང་དངུལ་གྱི་རྩ་ལ་མེ་ཁ་ཁ་དང་དུ་བ་སོ་སོ་རེད། Although the two friends are friendly, yet their accounts are different.

མེ་ཁབ་རྩེ་ཙམ་གྱིས་རི་བོ་བསྲེགས། Lit.: A needle point fire can burn mountain/ Sense implied: A spark neglected burns the mountain ཚག་སྟ་ག་ས་ག་ལ་མ་གཡུག་མེ་ཁབ་རྩེ་ཙམ་གྱིས་རི་བོ་བསྲེགས་པའི་ དཔེ་ཡོད། Don't throw match sticks everywhere. There is a saying that a needle point can burn a mountain.

མེ་ལྕེ་གནམ་འབར། flaring up flame in the sky བོད་ཀྱི་རིག་གནས་ཕྱོགས་ ཐམས་ཅད་དུ་མེ་ལྕེ་གནམ་ལ་འབར་བ་ནང་བཞིན་དར་གྱི་ཡོད་རེད། The Tibetan studies flourish in all the directions just like the flaring up flame in the sky.

མེ་ཏོག་ཆུང་ཡང་ལྷ་རྫས། Lit.: However small a flower is, it's still an offering to god/ Sense implied: The gift however small it may be, it is still a token of gratitude.

མེ་འཆིན་མཚམས་འཇོག cease-fire/ to make a cease-fire དེང་སང་རྒྱ་ དཀར་ནག་དབར་མེ་འཆིན་མཚམས་འཇོག་གི་དུས་ཚོད་རེད། At present there is cease-fire between India and China.

མེ་འབར་བའི་སྐྱང་ལ་ཤིང་བའགས་པ། Lit.: adding fuel to the fire/ Sense implied: to excite people or instigate མཐུན་པོ་མེད་པའི་ སྐྱང་ལ་ཚིག་རྩུབ་བའད་པ་ནི་མེ་འབར་བའི་སྐྱང་ལ་ཤིང་བའགས་པ་ནང་བཞིན་རེད། To abuse somebody on top of being unfriendly is just like

184

adding fuel to the fire.

མེ་རང་ཞི་དུད་དུ་བ་རང་ཡལ། Lit.: let the fire cease and the smoke fade away/ Sense implied: to calm/ pacify on its own གནས་ཚུལ་འདི་མེ་རང་ཞི་དུད་དུ་བ་རང་ཡལ་བཏུག་ན་ལེགས། It is good to let this news subside on its own.

མེད་དུ་མི་རུང་བ། indispensable རང་སང་མི་ལ་གཏམ་བརྗོད་རང་དབང་མེད་དུ་མི་རུང་བ་ཡིན། Freedom of expression is indispensable to people these days.

མེས་ཚིག་མེར་གཏུགས། Lit.: to be exposed to fire when burnt by fire/ Sense implied: to respond with similar treatment འདོད་ཆགས་ཀྱིས་ང་ཚོ་འཁོར་བར་འཁྲིད་པ་རེད་ལ། སྔགས་གཞུང་ནས་འདོད་ཆགས་ ཀྱིས་འཁོར་བ་ལས་ཐར་ནས་པའི་ཐབས་དེ་ནི་མེས་ཚིག་མེར་གཏུགས་རང་རེད། The attachment has led us to this cyclic existance. In Tantric text, there is a method of using attachment to liberate us from cyclic existance. This is like exposing fire when burnt by fire.

ཞས་མཐུན་ཐག་གཅོད། bilateral decision/ an agreement རྒྱ་གར་ལ་སློབ་ཕྲུག་གཏོང་རྒྱར་མོས་མཐུན་ཐག་གཅོད་བྱུང་སོང་། A mutual decision was taken to send students to India.

ཞ་མཐུན་ཞལ་བཞེས། acceptance རྒྱ་གར་གཞུང་ནས་ང་ཚོའི་འདོད་སྦྱལ་ལ་ མོས་མཐུན་ཞལ་བཞེས་གནང་སོང་། The government of India gave acceptance to our recommendation.

པག་དཔོན་མང་ན་དམག་དུས་ཉེས། too many commanders spoil the strategy/ too many cooks spoil the broth

185

དམར་འབེབས་བརྐྱས་དམོད། to humiliate and defame/ to criticise དག་པར་དམར་འབེབས་བརྐྱས་དམོད་བྱེད་ན་བཟོད་ཐུབ་ཀྱི་མ་རེད། One cannot bear humiliations and insult for all the time.

དམར་ཆལ་དགུ་ཆལ། Lit.: covered with red-blood/ Sense implied: badly wounded ཁ་སང་རྒྱག་རེ་ཕོར་ནས་ངའི་གྲོགས་པོ་དམར་ཆལ་དགུ་ཆལ་བཏང་ཤག Yesterday my friend was badly wounded in his fight.

དམིགས་བཀར་རོགས་རམ། specific/special aid བོད་གཞུང་ནས་མི་མང་ནས་ཐབ་ལ་ལོ་ལྟར་དམིགས་བཀར་རོགས་རམ་གནང་གི་ཡོད་རེད། Every year the Tibetan government provides specific aid to the poor and destitute.

དམིགས་ཡུལ་གཙོ་བཟུང་། to aim primarily for one's goal ལས་འགུལ་གང་འདྲ་ཞིག་ཡིན་ན་ཡང་དམིགས་ཡུལ་གཙོ་བཟུང་ཐོག་ལས་ཀ་བྱེད་རྒྱ་གལ་ཆེན་པོ་རེད། Whatever work it may be, it is important to work focussed on the main goal.

དམིགས་བསལ་ཐུགས་སྣང་། to pay special attention ཁོང་གིས་མི་མང་ཉམ་ཐག་ལ་དམིགས་བསལ་ཐུགས་སྣང་གནང་གི་འདུག He gives special attention to the poor people.

དམིགས་བསལ་མཐུན་རྐྱེན། special facilities དགོན་པ་རྣམས་ལ་བོད་གཞུང་ནས་དམིགས་བསལ་མཐུན་རྐྱེན་ཡག་པོ་གནང་གི་ཡོད། The Tibetan government provides special facilities to the monasteries.

དམིགས་བསལ་གཞིན་སྐུལ། special request བོད་གཞུང་གི་དམིགས་བསལ་

གཞིན་སྐུལ་ལ་བརྟེན་ནས་རྒྱ་གར་གཞུང་གིས་བོད་པའི་སློབ་གྲྭ་རྣམས་བཙུགས་པ་རེད། The Indian government opened many Tibetan schools at the special request of the Tibetan government.

ཁྱི་ལ་ཁན་ན་ཁྱི་ཚིལ་ཡིན་ཡང་བྱུག If it helps to cure the sore even if it's dog's fat, apply it.

སྔ་གཞི་སྲ་བརྟན། strong foundation ཁང་པའི་སྔ་གཞི་སྲ་བརྟན་མིན་ན་ཐོག་ བརྩིགས་བརྒྱབ་ཐུབ་ཀྱི་མ་རེད། If the house's foundation is not strong one cannot build the upper stories.

ཕྱོགས་ཞེན་ཕྱོགས་འཛིན། blind loyalty/ prejudiced/ regionalism དམངས་གཙོའི་རྒྱལ་ཁབ་ནང་ལ་ཕྱོགས་ཞེན་ཕྱོགས་འཛིན་གྱི་ཉེན་ཁ་ཆེ་ཤོས་ཡོད། The biggest danger of blind loyalty or prejudiced regionalism is found in a democratic nation.

སྨན་བཅོས་འཕྲོད་བསྟེན། medical care and health ལས་བྱེད་ཚོ་ལ་སྨན་བཅོས་ མཐུན་རྐྱེན་ཆེད་ཟླ་རེར་སྒོར་བརྒྱ་རེ་ཡོད། The members of staff have one hundred rupees per month as a medical allowance.

སྨན་ལན་དུག་འཇལ། to give poison in response to medicine སྨན་ ལན་དུག་འཇལ་ནི་ཉིན་ལན་ལོག་འཇལ་རེད། If you give poison in response to medicine, it is an ugly reaction.

སྤྱོ་བཅོས་བབ་བཅོལ། crazy/ eccentric རྒྱལ་སྲས་ཡིན་ན་ཡང་སྤྱོ་བཅོལ་བབ་ བཅོལ་ཞེ་དྲག་བྱེད་ན་གཞན་གྱིས་རྩིས་ཀྱི་མ་རེད། If you act eccentrically people will not have regard for you even if you are a prince.

ཙ

ཙག་གེ་ཙིག་གེ། miscellaneous/ odds and ends ལོ་གསར་སྐབས་ཙག་གེ་ཙིག་གེ་ལ་འགྲོ་གྲོན་ཞེ་དྲག་འགྲོ་གི་འདུག Buying those miscellaneous things during Losar is costly.

ཙན་དན་གྱི་གོ་ཡོག་དང་གོས་ཆེན་གྱི་ཐབ་ཕྱིས། Lit.: to use sandalwood as a fire-iron and brocade as dustcloths./ Sense implied: extravagance

ཙོག་གེ་ཙོག་གེ། to squat (like a rabbit) སྲིན་བདག་གི་མདུན་དུ་འདོགས་ཁྱི་དེ་ཙོག་གེ་ཙོག་གེ་བསྡད་འདུག The watch dog is squatting in front of its master.

གཙང་སྦྲ་འཕྲོད་བསྟེན། health and hygienes གཙང་སྦྲ་འཕྲོད་བསྟེན་ལ་དོ་སྣང་བྱེད་རྒྱུ་དེ་གཞུང་སྒེར་གཉིས་ཀའི་ལས་འགན་རེད། It is the duty of both the government and the individuals to take care of health and hygiene.

གཙང་མ་གཙང་རྐྱང་། perfectly clean/ immaculate རི་མཐོ་པོའི་ས་ཆ་གཙང་མ་གཙང་རྐྱང་རེད། All the areas of the high mountain are perfectly clean.

གཙོ་གལ་ཆེ་བ། of prime importance གཞོན་ནུའི་དུས་སུ་ཤེས་ཡོན་གཙོ་གལ་ཤིན་ཏུ་ཆེ་བ་ཡིན། Education is of prime importance at a young age.

བཙན་གནོན་བཀོད་སྐྱིག oppressive command/ to be under duress རྒྱ་མིའི་བཙན་གནོན་བཀོད་སྐྱིག་འོག་བོད་པ་ཚོ་ཚུད་པ་རེད། The Tibetans have been kept under control through the oppressive command of Chinese authority.

བཙན་པོ་དབང་ཡོད། by force ངའི་དེབ་དེ་ཁོང་གིས་བཙན་པོ་དབང་ཡོད་བྱེད་ནས་འཕྲོགས་སོང་། He seized my books by force.

བཙན་པོའི་ཁ་ནོན་དང་ནམ་རྒྱུན་གི་རྒྱབ་རྟུ One who supports the poor and rises against the oppressive authority. ཤེས་ཡོན་སླུན་པའི་མི་དངོས་གནས་ཡིན་ན་བཙན་པོའི་ཁ་ནོན་དང་ནམ་རྒྱུན་གི་རྒྱབ་རྟུ་བྱེད་དགོས། If one is really educated, one should support the poor and rise against the oppressive authority.

བཙན་པོའི་གཉའ་ཞིང་དང་ནམ་རྒྱུན་གི་ཕ་མ། One who yokes the tyrannical and be parents for the poor དམར་ཕོག་གི་མགོ་འཛིན་དེ་ཚོ་བཙན་པོའི་གཉའ་ཞིང་དང་ནམ་རྒྱུན་གི་ཕ་མ་ཡིན་པའི་ཁུལ་རེད། The Communist leaders are supposed to be the ones who yoke the tyrannical and are parents for the poor and down-trodden.

བཙོག་གཏམ་རྒྱང་རྒྱང་། to talk of only dirty things/ romantic ཁོང་ནི་རབ་བྱུང་ཡིན་ན་ཡང་བཙོག་གཏམ་རྒྱང་རྒྱང་བཤད་ཀྱི་འདུག Inspite of being a monk he always speaks about romanticism.

རྩྭ་ཁའི་ཟིལ་པ། dew drops on blades of grass ནང་ཆོས་སུ་ཆོས་ཐམས་ཅད་རྩྭ་ཁའི་ཟིལ་པ་ལྟ་བུར་དཔེར་འཛིན་བྱེད་ཀྱི་ཡོད། In Buddhism all phenomena are viewed as dew drops on blades of grass.

རྩ་མེད་གཏོང་དག completely rid of/ finish གྲུབ་མཐའ་གཅིག་ལ་རྒྱབ་རྟེན་ ཆད་མ་ཡོད་ན་རྩ་མེད་གཏོང་དག་བཟོ་ཐུབ་ཀྱི་མ་རེད། If a tenet has a sound and reasonable backing, one cannot destroy it completely.

ཞད་གཅོད་ཞིབ་བཤེར། thorough investigation ཞད་གཅོད་ཞིབ་བཤེར་བྱེད་ན་ རྒྱལ་ཁབ་གཞན་གྱི་སོ་པ་སུ་ཡིན་མིན་གསལ་པོ་ཤེས་ཀྱི་རེད། If a thorough investigation is carried out then it will be clear who is a traitor (spying for other nations).

རྩུབ་རལ་རྩུབ་ནག completely worn out/ torn to pieces/ unserviceable འགྲེམས་སྟོན་ཁང་གི་ཅ་ལག་མང་ཆེ་བ་རྩུབ་རལ་རྩུབ་ནག་ཆུང་ ཆུང་རེད། Most of the things in the museum are completely worn-out.

རྩི་ཤིང་ལོ་ཏོག plants and crops ང་ཚོར་རྩི་ཤིང་ལོ་ཏོག་ལ་བརྟེན་ནས་འཚོ་བའི་ རླུང་དང་ཟས་ཐོབ་ཀྱི་ཡོད། We get oxygen from plants and crops for our survival.

རྩིབ་མ་ཚུང་ཚུང་། ribs coming out ཤ་སྐམས་པོ་ཆགས་དུས་རྩིབ་མ་ཚུང་ཚུང་མཐོང་ གི་འདུག When one becomes thin, we see their ribs coming out.

རྩིས་བརྒྱབ་པ། to calculate/ to do accounts of ལམ་འགྲོན་རྩིས་བརྒྱབ་པའི་ རྗེས་སུ་སྒོར་མོ་བརྒྱ་ལྷག་འདུག When we calculated the travelling expenses one hundred rupees was the remainder.

རྩིས་མེད་རྡོག་རོལ། to ignore and insult རྒྱལ་པོའི་བཀའ་ན་དེ་ཡང་དག་པ་ཞིག་ མིན་ན་ཡང་རྩིས་མེད་རྡོག་རོལ་བྱེད་ཐུབ་ཀྱི་མ་རེད། One cannot ignore and insult the king's order even if it is not right.

རྩིས་མེད་སྤྱང་ཅུང་། to disregard and neglect རང་གི་རིག་གཞུང་ལ་རྩིས་
མེད་སྤྱང་ཅུང་བྱེད་ན་རང་མགོ་རང་གིས་བསྐོར་བ་རེད། One is deceiving oneself if one neglects or disregards one's culture.

རྩིས་སྤྲོད་རྩིས་ལེན། to settle accounts/to handed-over the responsibilities ལས་བྱེད་འཕོ་འགྱུར་སྐབས་སུ་རྩིས་སྤྲོད་རྩིས་ལེན་གཙང་མ་
བྱེད་རྒྱུ་ཞེ་དྲག་གནད་འགགས་ཆེན་པོ་རེད། It is very important to settle or handed-over the accounts clearly whenever there is a transfer of staff.

རྩེ་གཅིག་གུས་གཅིག to be single minded/ devoted སྔགས་ལམ་ལ་
གཞུག་དུས་རང་གི་བླ་མ་ལ་རྩེ་གཅིག་གུས་གཅིག་དད་པ་བྱེད་དགོས། When one enters into Tantric practices one must trust one's teacher single mindedly.

རྩོད་སྒྲུབ་རིག་པ། dialectics/ polemic study རྩོད་སྒྲུབ་རིག་པ་སྒྲུབ་བ་རྣམས་
རིགས་པ་ཁོ་ན་ལ་མ་གཏོགས་ལུང་ལ་མི་བརྟེན་པ་རེད། The dialecticians do not rely on scriptural quotations but reasonings only.

རྩོད་རྙོག་འཕྲོ་ཅན། an unresolved dispute ཁོང་རྩོད་རྙོག་འཕྲོ་ཅན་དེ་ཡི་ནང་
དུ་ཚུད་ཡོད། He is involved in the unresolved dispute.

རྩོད་པ་གྱེན་ལོག counter productive རྩོད་པ་རྒྱག་སྟངས་ལག་པོ་མ་ཤེས་
ན་རྩོད་པ་གྱེན་ལོག་ཡོང་ཉེན་ཡོད། There is a danger for the debate to turn into counter productive, if one does not know the proper way of debating.

རྩོད་པས་བརྟར་ཤ། to analyse through debate ཆོས་ཀྱི་དཀའ་གནད་རྣམས་

ཆོད་པས་བརྡར་ཤ་གཏོད་པ་ཨིན། The difficult and vital points in dharma are analysed through debates.

བཅུ་སྐྱངས་ལྟ་སྐྱངས། how a person is regarded or viewed མི་ཡག་ རྱག་དེ་སོ་སོའི་ཉིས་སྐྱངས་དང་ལྟ་སྐྱངས་ལ་རག་ལུས་པ་རེད། The goodness and badness of a person depends upon how one regards and views that person.

བཙོན་འགྲུས་གོ་ལོག wrong effort or perseverance མི་དགེ་བའི་ལས་ ལ་དཀའ་བ་སྤྱད་པ་ནི་བཙོན་འགྲུས་གོ་ལོག་རེད། To strive for non-virtues is a wrong effort or enthusiastic perseverance.

ཆ་ག་ཚི་གི། ཆ་གི་ཚི་གི་བྱེད་པ། ཆ་ག་ཚི་གི་ཆ་པོ། restless, excited and nervous མི་ཁ་ཤས་རང་བཞིན་གྱིས་བརྟན་པོ་དང་མི་ཁ་ཤས་རང་བཞིན་གྱིས་ཆ་གི་ ཚི་གི་ཆ་པོ་ཡོད་རེད། Some people are very stable while others are very restless and nervous by nature.

ཆ་འཇམ་གཉིས་ཀ both strict and gentle means/ སློབ་སྟོང་སྤྲད་དུས་ཆ་ འཇམ་གཉིས་ཀ་བྱེད་དགོས་པ་ཡིན། While giving education one needs to apply both strict and gentle means.

ཆ་ནན་སྙིད་གསུམ། the strict, emphatic and forceful སྔོན་གྱི་རྒྱལ་པོ་ རྣམས་ཀྱི་བཀའ་རྣམས་ཆ་ནན་སྙིད་གསུམ་ཤ་སྟག་ཡོད་རེད། All the orders of the ancient kings were very strict, emphatic and forceful.

ཆ་ཆ་ཉུར་ཉུར། vigorous ངལ་རྩོལ་མི་མང་རྣམས་ཀྱིས་རྒྱ་ཚོད་མང་པོ་ཆ་ཆ་ཉུར་ ཉུར་དཀའ་ལས་བརྒྱབས་སོང་། The labourers vigorously worked hard for many hours.

ཆང་འཛོམས་གོ་བསྒྲུར། congregation for discussion/ assembled for discussion ལས་བྱེད་ཆང་འཛོམས་ཐོག་ཕྲ་ཚའི་སྐོར་གོ་བསྒྲུར་བྱེད་དགོས། It is necessary to discuss salary when all the members of the staff are assembled.

ཆང་ལ་མ་ཆང་། sometimes complete and sometimes incomplete/ shortage དེབ་རོ་ཡག་ལ་དདུལ་ཆང་ལ་མ་ཆང་ཕུང་སོ་ན་ངས་

གཡར་གོ I will lend you money if there is a shortage of money for buying books.

ཚད་ལྡན་ཚུལ་མཐུན། qualified as well as modest དགེ་སློང་ཚད་ལྡན་ཚུལ་མཐུན་ཡིན་ན་ཁྱིས་སོ་བཏབ་ཐུབ་ཀྱི་མ་རེད། If one is a qualified as well as a modest Bhikshu, dogs' cannot bite one (it is said).

ཚད་ཆད་བསྡུར་བསྡུར། compete/challange ཨི་རག་གིས་དམག་ཤུགས་ཐོག་ཨ་མེ་རི་ཁ་ལ་ཚད་ཚད་བསྡུར་བསྡུར་བྱེད་པ་རེད། Iraq challanged the USA in military strength.

ཚད་ལྱོངས་ཆ་འཇོག recognition སློབ་གྲྭ་ཕན་ཚུན་ལག་ཁྱེར་ལ་ཚད་ལྱོངས་དང་ཆ་འཇོག་བྱེད་པ་རེད། Schools recognize each others' certificates.

ཚད་གཞི་ཆ་བགོས། proper distribution སློར་མོ་དེ་ཚོ་ཉན་ཁོག་རྣམས་ལ་ཚད་གཞི་ཆ་བགོས་བྱེད་དེ་གནང་རོགས་གནང་། Please, distribute this money properly among the elderly people.

ཚབ་བི་ཆུབ་བི། hasty, hurry གུང་སེང་དེ་ཚབ་བི་ཆུབ་བི་དང་ལ་ཙོགས་སོང་། The holiday was completed in haste.

ཚར་དུ་དངར་བ། coming one after another in succession འཛམ་བུ་གླིང་འདི་ཡི་སྟེང་དུ་སྐྱེས་བུ་ཆེན་པོ་ཚར་དུ་དངར་བ་རིམས་པར་བྱོན་པའི་དང་ནས་ཆེས་མ་ཆོག ཏུ་གྱུར་པ་ཞིག་ནི་ཡཀྱལ་བ་རིན་པོ་ཆེ་རེད། Of the great men who have come in succession to this world, His Holiness the Dalai Lama is one of the greatest.

ཚར་ཚར་བར་དུ། མ་ཚར་བར་དུ། until completion གསུང་ཚོས་མ་ཚར་བར་དུ་

ང་རྡོ་རྗེ་གདན་ལ་བསྡད་ཀྱི་ཡིན། I will stay at Bodhgaya until the completion of the teaching.

ཚིག་སྐམ་སྐྱོང་བའད། empty and dry words དཔོན་པོའི་ཚིག་སྐམ་སྐྱོང་བའད་ལ་མང་ཚོགས་ཀྱིས་མགོ་འཕོར་མི་རུང་། The general populace should not get deceived by empty and dry words of their leaders.

ཚིག་ཁྲུན་གཙང་བཅད། clear cut settlement ཁ་མཚུ་འདི་དེ་རིང་ཚིག་ཁྲུན་གཙང་བཅད་བཟོ་གི་རེད། There will be a clear cut settlement of the case today.

ཚིག་ངན་ཟུར་མདའ་འཕེན་པ། insulting hint/cynical rebuke རྒྱལ་ཁབ་ཕན་ཚུན་མཐུན་པོ་མེད་ན་ཚིག་ངན་ཟུར་མདའ་འཕེན་རེས་བྱེད་པ་རེད། When the nations are not friendly, they pass cynical rebukes to one another.

ཚིག་ཉུང་དོན་ཚང་། a fewer words with complete sense འབྲི་རྩོམ་ཡག་པོ་ཡིན་ན་ཚིག་ཉུང་ལ་དོན་ཚང་བ་དགོས། A good composition should have few words with complete meaning.

ཚིག་སྙན་དོན་བཟང་། elegant expression with good meaning དགེ་འདུན་ཚོས་འཕེལ་གྱི་རྩོམ་རྣམས་ཚིག་སྙན་ལ་དོན་བཟང་བ་ཡོད། Mr. Gedun Chophel's compositions are elegant in expression and contain good meaning.

ཚིག་ཐོག་དོན་འཁེལ། to implement the words/very practical རྒྱལ་ཁབ་ཕར་ཚུར་ཆིངས་ཡིག་བཞག་པ་ཚིག་ཐོག་དོན་ལ་འཁེལ་བའི་ཆེད་དུ་ཡིན། The purpose of making a treaty between nations is to implement their words.

ཚིག་པ་ཟ་བ། ཁོང་ཁྲོ་ཟ་བ། to get angry ཚིག་པ་ཟ་ན་བཟོད་པ་བསྐྱོམས། Be patient if you are getting angry.

ཚུལ་མཐུན་སྐྱོམས་ཆུང་། ethical and modest སྟོན་པའི་ཉན་ཐོས་རྣམས་ཚུལ་མཐུན་སྐྱོམས་ཆུང་དགོས་པ་ཡིན། The disciples of a Buddha should be ethical and modest.

ཚུལ་མཐུན་ལུགས་མཐུན། ethical and traditional སྤྱི་ཚོགས་ཀྱི་ནང་དུ་ཚུལ་མཐུན་ལུགས་མཐུན་གནས་ཐུབ་ན་གཞན་ལ་ཕན་ཐོགས་མང་བ་བྱེད་ཐུབ་ཀྱི་རེད། If you can live in society ethically and traditionally, you can work better for others.

ཚུལ་སྟོད་ཀུན་མཐུན། modest and in accordance with the tradition རང་ཉིད་ཡ་རབས་ཤིག་བྱེད་འདོད་ན་ཡ་རབས་རྣམས་ཀྱི་ཚུལ་སྟོད་ཀུན་དང་མཐུན་པ་གནང་དགོས། If you wish to be decent you must behave modestly and in accordance with traditional rules of decency.

ཚུལ་མིན་སྤྱོད་པ། immoral behaviour དགེ་རྒན་གྱིས་ཚུལ་མིན་སྤྱོད་པ་གནང་ན་དགེ་ཕྲུག་གིས་ལོས་བྱེད། Of course the students will behave immorally when the teachers themselves behave that way.

ཚེ་གང་གཏན་འདུན། life-partner རང་གི་ཁམས་དང་མཐུན་པའི་ཚེ་གང་གཏན་འདུན་བཙལ་དགོས། One needs to search a life-partner that suits one's personality.

ཚེ་གཅིག་ལུས་གཅིག in one life-time རྗེ་བཙུན་མི་ལ་ཚེ་གཅིག་ལུས་གཅིག་ལ་སངས་རྒྱས་ཀྱི་གོ་འཕང་ཐོབ་པ་རེད། Jetsun Mila achieved the state of Buddhahood in one life span.

ཚེ་རབས་ནས་ཚེ་རབས། from life after life དཀོན་མཆོག་གསུམ་ནི་ཚེ་རབས་ནས་ཚེ་རབས་བར་འགྲོ་བ་ཡོངས་ཀྱི་མགོན་རེད། The Triple-Gems are the protectors of all sentient beings from life after life.

ཚེ་སྟོག་ཆུད་ཟོས། a waste of life ནོར་ཁོ་ནའི་དོན་དུ་མི་ཚེ་བཏང་ན་ཚེ་སྟོག་ཆུད་ཟོས་བཏང་བ་དང་ཁྱད་པར་མེད། There is no difference between wasting a life and spending one's life only for amassing riches.

ཚེགས་ཆེན་དོན་ཆུང་། greatly difficult but of little benefit ལག་རྩལ་ནི་ཚེགས་ཆེ་ལ་དོན་ཆུང་བ་ཡིན། Manual work is very difficult but of little benefit.

ཚེར་མ་རྣོ་ཡང་བྲག་རི་འབིགས་མི་ཐུབ། No matter how sharp the thorn may be it cannot pierce rock.

ཚོང་དུས་གཉིག་ལ་སྟེ་ཐང་གཉིས་མི་ཡོང་། One cannot do business at two business seasons at a time.

ཚོང་དང་འཐབ་མོ་གར་ཡོང་མི་ཤེས། One never knows where business and fights will take place/ Sense implied: uncertainty

ཚོད་དཔག་ཆུང་དྲགས། underestimate མི་ལ་ཚོད་དཔག་ཆུང་དྲགས་ན་མཐོངས་ཆུང་ཆགས་འགྲོ་གི་རེད། It becomes an insult if you underestimate a person.

ཚོད་དཔག་ཆེ་དྲགས་ན། over-estimate གང་ཡང་མི་ཤེས་པའི་བྱིས་པ་ལ་མཁྱེན་ཡོན་ཅན་དུ་འཛིན་པ་ནི་ཚོད་དཔག་ཆེ་དྲགས་པའི་སྐྱོན་ཡིན། Considering a child to be a great scholar is a fallacy of over-estimation.

ཚད་མེད། ཤི་མ་ཤི། ཁ་མེད་སྣ་མེད། limitless/ too much རིག་པ་མེད་ན་སྦོབ་
སྦོང་ཤི་མ་ཤི་བྱས་ཀྱང་ཤེས་ཀྱི་མ་རེད། Without intelligence even if one
studies hard will not learn anything.

མཆན་སྙན་གྲགས་བརྗིད། fame and eminance མཁས་དབང་ནམ་མཁའི་ནོར་བུ་ནི་
མཆན་སྙན་གྲགས་བརྗིད་དང་ལྡན་པ་ཞིག་རེད། Professor Namkhay Norbu is
a famous and eminent scholar.

མཆན་མཐོངས་ལ་རྒྱུ། name and reputation བོད་རྒྱལ་ཁབ་ཀྱི་མཆན་མཐོངས་
ལ་རྒྱར་ང་ཚོ་ཚང་མས་བརྩི་དགོས་པ་ཡིན། All of us should respect the
name and reputation of the Tibetan nation.

མཚམས་མཚམས། at times/ sometimes ཆར་དུས་སྐབས་ལ་མཚམས་མཚམས་
ཉིན་གུང་བར་གཉིད་ལོག་གི་ཡོད། During rainy season sometimes I
sleep until noon.

མཛེར་སྡུག་ལང་ཚོ། beauty and youthfulness མཛེར་སྡུག་ལང་ཚོ་ལྡན་པའི་
སྐབས་སུ་ངེས་འབྱུང་རྣམ་དག་སྐྱེ་བ་ཤིན་ཏུ་དཀའ། It is extremely difficult to
generate pure renunciation when one is young and beautiful.

འཚང་ཁ་ཤིག་ཤིག rush/crowded/ squashed together རྒྱ་གར་ནང་དུ་
ས་ཆ་གན་ཚུན་འགྲུལ་བགྲོད་དུས་འཚང་ཁ་ཤིག་ཤིག་ཡོད་ཡོད་པ་རེད། There is
always a rush in India whenever one travels from one place
to another.

འཚོ་ཐེན་འདུ་འགོད། to earn one's living ཁྱིམ་ཚང་གཅིག་ལ་ཕྲུ་གུ་མང་པོ་ཡོད་
ན་འཚོ་ཐེན་འདུ་འགོད་བྱེད་རྒྱུར་དཀའ་ངལ་ཞེ་དྲག་ཡོད་རེད། It is difficult to
earn a living if a family has many children.

འཚོ་ཐབས་ཕྱུ་ཆུགས། steady/ reliable/ a confirmed and good livelihood འཚོ་ཐབས་ཕྱུ་ཆུགས་ཡོང་བར་བྱེད་པ་ལ་ཚོང་རྒྱག་དགོས་བསམ་གྱི་འདུག I am thinking of undertaking a business to have a steady and good livelihood.

ཚིག་རྩུབ་ངག་འཁྱལ། harsh words and idle gossip ཚིག་རྩུབ་ངག་འཁྱལ་ནི་མི་དགེ་བའི་ནང་ཚན་ཞིག་རེད། Using harsh words and idle gossiping are in the list of ten non-virtues.

ཚིག་རོ་ཚོ་མེད། senseless words ཚིག་རོ་ཚོ་མེད་ལ་བདག་པོ་བརྒྱབ་ན་རང་ཉིད་མ་སྐྱིད་པ་ཡོང་གི་རེད། If you harbour senseless words it will make you unhappy.

ཚིག་རོ་རྙོག་བའད། useless verbiage/ hackneyed language ཚོགས་འདུར་ཚིག་རོ་རྙོག་བའད་མང་པོ་གཏང་ན་ཚོགས་གཙོས་ངེས་པར་བཀག་འགོག་གནང་གི་རེད། If one uses hackneyed language in the meeting, definitely the chairman will certainly stop one from speaking.

ཚིག་ལན་ཚིག་རྒྱག Lit.: a word for a word/ Sense implied: to disobey རང་གི་དགེ་རྒན་ལ་ཚིག་ལན་ཚིག་རྒྱག་ནས་ཡང་བྱེད་མི་རུང་། One should never disobey one's teachers.

ཇ་རེ་ཛོ་རེ། ཇ་རེ་ཛོ་རེ་ཚོ་པོ། ཇ་རེ་ཛོ་རེ་བྱེད་པ། keeping things topsy turvy/ wearing clothes untidily/ a mess of things སོ་སོའི་ ཁྱིམ་ཚང་དག་ཏུ་ཇ་རེ་ཛོ་རེ་མ་བཞག Never keep one's home untidy/in a mess.

ཛོད་ཛོ་ད་ཛོད་ལ། aimlessly ངའི་གྲོགས་པོ་ལེ་ལོ་ཅན་དེ་ཛོད་ཛོ་ད་ཛོད་ལ་འཁྱམས་ཀྱི་ འདུག My lazy friend is wandering aimlessly.

མཇའ་མཐུན་གང་ཟབ། profound friendship དུས་རབས་བདུན་པའི་ནང་རྒྱ་བོད་ ཀྱི་འབྲེལ་བ་མཇའ་མཐུན་གང་ཟབ་ཡོད། In the seventh century, Tibet and China had a profound friendly relationship.

མཇའ་བཤེས་གཉེན་མཐུན། friends and relatives མཇའ་མཐུན་གཉེན་བཤེས་ ཡོངས་ལ་བཀྲ་ཤིས་བདེ་ལེགས་ཞུ། Tashi Delek to all friends and relatives.

མཇུབ་སྟོན་བྱེད་གལ། important to point out སྤྱི་པའི་ནོར་ལ་སྐྱེར་གྱིས་ཝེད་ སྟོད་བྱེད་མཁན་ཚོར་མཇུབ་སྟོན་བྱེད་གལ་ཆེ། It is important to point out those who use public property for their personal gain.

མཇུབ་མོ་གར་སྟོན་ཕར། Lit.: wherever he points, that is the east/ Sense implied: very harsh rule སྤྱི་ཚོགས་རྙིང་པའི་ནང་དུ་མཇུབ་མོ་ གར་སྟོན་ཕར་རེད། In the old Tibetan society wherever the finger was pointed at, that was the east.

མཛུབ་མོས་གནམ་འབིགས་མི་ཐུབ། Lit.: a finger cannot pierce the sky/ Sense implied: something that cannot be done

མཛེས་ཆོས་དང་དོད། conscious of one's beauty/ concerned with one's personal appearance ན་ཆུང་དེ་ཚོས་མཛེས་ཆོས་དང་དོད་ཞེ་དྲག་བྱེད་ནས་ཁྲོམ་ལ་འགྲོ་བ་རེད། The young ladies go to market taking great care of their beauty and elegance.

མཛེས་བཞིད་གཉིས་ལྡན། beautiful as well as grand རྒྱལ་པོའི་སྲས་མོ་དེ་ཚོ་མཛེས་བཞིད་གཉིས་ལྡན་ཤ་སྟག་རེད། The princesses are beautiful as well as grand.

མཛེས་སྡུག་ཡིད་འོང་། beautiful and lovely ཁྱོས་པ་ཆང་མ་ལ་རང་གི་ཆུང་མ་མཛེས་སྡུག་ཡིད་འོང་སྣང་གི་ཡོད། To all husbands, their wives appear beautiful and lovely.

མཛེས་མི་མཛེས། Lit.: whether pretty or not མཛེས་མི་མཛེས་བལྟ་མཁན་གྱི་མིག་ལ་རག་ལས་པ་རེད། Beauty lies in the eyes of beholders.

མཛོ་རྒན་ལམ་རྒྱུས། Lit.: an old dzo knows the way better/ Sense implied: to have more experience ང་ཡོན་ཏན་མི་ཆེ་ཡང་མཛོ་རྒན་ལམ་རྒྱུས་ཆེ་བ་ཡིན། Although I am not well-educated, I have more experience like an old dzo.

མཛོད་པ་དོ་ལས། the manager and the staff ཡིག་ཕྲིས་འདི་མཛོད་པ་དོ་ལས་ལ་ཕུལ་རོགས་གནང་། Please hand-over this letter to the manager and the staff.

འཛིན་སྐྱོང་སྤེལ་གསུམ། the three: preservation, promotion and propagation ཆོས་སྤེལ་མཁན་རྣམས་ཀྱི་ལས་འགན་ནི་རང་གི་ཆོས་འཛིན་སྐྱོང་སྤེལ་གསུམ་བྱ་རྒྱུ་དེ་ཡིན། The activities of missionaries are to preserve, promote and propagate their religious beliefs.

འཛིན་གྲྭ་ཚུགས་གྲོལ། the beginning and the end of a class འཛིན་གྲྭ་ཚུགས་གྲོལ་སྐབས་སུ་དྲིལ་དིང་བརྡུང་བ་རེད། The bell rings at the beginning and the end of a class.

འཛུགས་བསྐྲུན་ཡར་རྒྱས། development བཟོ་གྲྭ་འཛུགས་བསྐྲུན་བསྐྲུན་ཡར་རྒྱས་ཀྱི་ཆེད་དུ་སྒོར་མོ་འབུམ་ལྔ་ཞལ་འདེབས་བྱུང་བ་རེད། Five hundred thousand rupees were received in donation for the development of a factory.

འཛུམ་དམུལ་དམུལ། to smile འཛུམ་དམུལ་དམུལ་བྱེད་མཁན་ཚང་མ་ལ་དགའ་དགོས་དོན་མེད། There is no need to feel happy with all those who smile.

འཛུལ་གཞུག་གང་ཐུབ། to strive for admission or recruitment དོང་རང་དམག་མིར་འཛུལ་གཞུག་གང་ཐུབ་བྱས་ཀྱང་ཚུད་མ་སོང་། Though he strove hard to enter in the army, he could not get admission.

འཛེམ་མེད་བག་མེད། heedless/ careless ཡུལ་ཁྲིམས་ལ་འཛེམས་མེད་བག་མེད་བྱེད་ན་མ་རབས་ཀྱི་སྤྱོད་པ་རེད། It is uncivilized to be careless about a country's laws.

འཛེམས་འཛེམས་ཐོག་ཐོག to be careful ར་བཟི་བའི་རྗེས་སུ་འཛེམས་འཛེམས་ཐོག་ཐོག་བྱེད་རྒྱུ་ཆང་མ་བཟི་ད་འགྲོ་གི་རེད། One forgets to be careful after getting drunk.

རྫབ་ཆེན་ཨ་ར་དཀར་པོ། ring leader or very naughty (jokingly expressed) རྫབ་ཆེན་ཨ་ར་དཀར་པོ་དེ་ག་བ་ཕྱིན་སོང་། Where did the very naughty guy go ?

རྗིག་རྗིག་རྔམ་རྔམ། domineering and wrathful ཆོས་སྐྱོང་སྲུང་མ་རྣམས་དག་ཏུ་རྗིག་རྗིག་རྔམ་རྔམ་བཞུགས་པ་རེད། The Dharma protectors always stay in a domineering and wrathful position.

རྫུན་སྤངས་བདེན་འཛིན། abandon lying and upholding the truth རང་ཉིད་ཆོས་པ་བྱེད་འདོད་ན་རྫུན་སྤངས་བདེན་འཛིན་གནང་དགོས་པ་ཨིན། If one wishes to become a practitioner, one needs to abandon lying and uphold the truth.

ཝ་སྟོར་མས་སེང་གེ་ལ་འགྲན་པ། Lit.: a coward fox challenging a lion ཝ་སྟོར་མས་སེང་གེ་ལ་འགྲན་པ་ནི་སྤྱུག་དགགས་ཤིག་ཡིན་པ་ཐག་ཆོད། It must be a bad omen for a cowardly fox to challenge a lion.

ཤྲལ་ལེ་ཤྲལ་ལེ། clear and distinct རིམ་པས་གནས་ཚུལ་ཤྲལ་ལེ་ཤྲལ་ལེར་ཆགས་ཡོང་། Gradually, the news will be clear and distinct.

ཞུ་དཔེ་ལྷམ་ལ་འགེབས་པ། Lit.: taking a shoe as an example to make a hat/ Sense implied: wrong model

ཞབས་ཏོག་བསྙེན་བཀུར། service and respect བོད་མི་ཚོས་དགེ་འདུན་ལ་ཞབས་ ཏོག་བསྙེན་བཀུར་གང་དྲག་ཞུ་བ་རེད། Tibetans offer service and respect as best they can to the spiritual communities.

ཞབས་འཁྱིང་སེར་སྐྱ། lay and monk retinues པཎ་ཆེན་རིན་པོ་ཆེ་ལ་ཞབས་ འཁྱིང་སེར་སྐྱ་སྟོང་ཕྲག་མང་པོ་ཡོད། Panchen Rinpoche had thousands of lay and monk retinues.

ཞལ་འདེབས་བསྡུ་འབུལ། collecting and offering donations མི་ཁ་ཤས་ ཀྱིས་ཕྱུག་པོ་རྣས་ཞལ་འདེབས་བསྡུས་ཏེ་ཉམ་ཆུང་ལ་སྤྲོད་པ་རེད། Some people collect donations from the rich and offer these to the poor and down-trodden.

ཞལ་ལ་པད་མ་འདབ་བརྒྱད། ཐུགས་ལ་འཚེར་མ་སྡོང་བུ། His mouth is like an eight petalled lotus and his mind a thorny plant

ཞལ་རས་ངག་པོ། frowning face/ angry looking ཁོང་ཞལ་རས་ངག་པོ་ ཡོད་ན་ཡང་ཐུགས་སེམས་བཟང་པོ་ཡོད་རེད། Though he has a frowning face he has a good heart.

ཞལ་རས་མཛུམ་མདངས། smiling face ཁོང་གིས་ང་ལ་ཁ་མང་ཞལ་རས་མཛུམ་

205

མ་དངས་བསྟུན་གནང་བྱུང་། Yesterday, he smiled at me.

ཞི་རྒྱས་དབང་དྲག peace, increase, power and wrath གསང་སྔགས་ལ་ ཐབས་ཀྱི་སྒོ་ནས་དབྱེ་ན་ཞི་རྒྱས་དབང་དྲག་བཅས་ཡོད། In terms of methods, secret mantra can be classified into peace, increase, power and wrath.

ཞི་དུལ་བག་ཡོད། peaceful, humble and modest ཞི་དུལ་བག་ཡོད་རྣམས་ དགེ་བའི་བཤེས་གཉེན་གྱི་མཚན་ཉིད་ཡིན། Being peaceful, humble and modest are the features of a spiritual guide.

ཞི་བདེ་ཡ་རབས། peaceful, happy and civilized རྒྱ་མི་མ་བསླེབས་པའི་ གོང་དུ་བོད་དེ་ཞི་བདེ་ཡ་རབས་ཀྱི་རྒྱལ་ཁབ་གཅིག་རེད། Tibet was a peaceful, happy and civilized nation before Chinese came in.

ཞི་བདེ་སྲུང་སྐྱོབས། for the security and peace ཡུལ་མི་ཞི་བདེ་སྲུང་སྐྱོབས་ ཀྱི་ཆེད་དུ་དམག་མི་ཉར་དགོས་པ་རེད། It is essential to keep an army for the security and peace of a country.

ཞི་བདེ་སྟིང་འཇགས། calm and peaceful ཡུལ་མི་རྣམས་མཐུན་པོ་ཡོད་ན་ཡུལ་ ལ་ཞི་བདེ་སྟིང་འཇགས་ལས་ཀྱིས་ཡོང་། If the people in a country are harmonious, naturally there will be calm and peace in a country.

ཞི་དྲག་གཉིས་འཛོམས། both peaceful and wrathful ནང་པའི་གཞུང་དུ་ ཞི་དྲག་གཉིས་འཛོམས་ཀྱི་ཐབས་ལམ་གསུངས་ཡོད། In Buddhist treatises, both peaceful and wrathful means are explained.

ཞི་མི་གཉིད་ལ་ཕོར་ཡང་བསམ་རྒྱུ་ཙི་ཙོ། Even when cat has fallen asleep it still thinks of mice.

ཞིང་ནགས་ཕྱུགས་གསུམ། The three : farming, forestry and the animal husbandry རྒྱལ་ཁབ་ཡར་རྒྱས་ཡག་པོ་ཡོང་བ་ལ་ཞིང་ནགས་ཕྱུགས་གསུམ་ངེས་པར་ཡར་རྒྱས་གཏོང་དགོས་པ་རེད། For the development of a country, it is absolutely necessary to improve the techniques of farming, forestry and animal husbandary.

ཞིང་པ་འཕྲོས་ཞན། poor peasant རྒྱ་གར་གྱི་ཞིང་པ་མང་ཆེ་བ་འཕྲོས་ཞན་པོ་རེད། Most of the Indian farmers are poor.

ཞིང་བྲན་ལམ་ལུགས། feudal system ཞིང་བྲན་ལམ་ལུགས་དེ་མཐའ་གཅིག་ཏུ་སྐྱོ་ཚག་མ་རེད། The system of feudalism is not bad in all respects.

ཞིང་བྲན་ཞིང་བདག feudal serfs and feudal lords ཞིང་བྲན་དང་ཞིང་བདག་ཆམ་པོ་ཡོད་ན་སྐྱིད་པོ་ཡོད་རེད། There is happiness when feudal serfs and feudal lords are in good terms.

ཞིང་རྨོས་འཕུལ་འཁོར། Lit.: machines for ploughing land/ Sense implied: tractors དེང་སང་བོད་པའི་གཞིས་ཆགས་སུ་ཡང་ཞིང་རྨོས་འཕུལ་འཁོར་བེད་སྤྱོད་བྱེད་པ་རེད། Tractors are used in Tibetan settlements also these days.

ཞིང་ལས་གླ་སྩོག hired for farming ཞིང་ལས་གླ་སྩོག་གི་ཆེད་དུ་མི་བཅོ་ལྔ་མ་དགས་ཡོད། I have hired fifteen people for farming.

ཞིམ་ཐག་ཆོད། very tasty ཆང་ཞིམ་ཐག་ཆོད་དུ་བྱུང་སོང་། The beer was very good.

207

བཞུ་མར་འཚོལ་བར་བཞུ་མར་དགོས། You need a lamp to look for another lamp.

ལུས་མེད་སྙིང་སྟོབས། undaunted courage བྱ་བ་གལ་ཆེན་པོ་སྒྲུབ་པ་ལ་ལུས་མེད་ཀྱི་སྙིང་སྟོབས་དང་ལྡན་པ་དགོས་པ་ཡིན། It is necessary to have undaunted courage to achieve a big task.

ཞེ་ཁོན་ཞེ་འཛིན། hatred/animosity ང་ཚོ་ཚང་མ་ཞེ་ཁོན་སྡང་འཛིན་གྱི་དབང་དུ་མ་སོང་ན་བདེ་སྐྱིད་ལས་ཀྱིས་ཡོང་། If all of us are not over-powered by hatred and animosity, there will be happiness automatically.

ཞེ་ཌང་དུག་ཆུ་འཁོལ་མ། enmity like boiling liquid poison དགྲ་བོགས་ལ་ཞེ་ཌང་དུག་ཆུ་ལྟར་འཁོལ་ན་ཁང་རང་ཉིད་ལ་གནོད་པ་ལས་དགྲ་ལ་མི་གནོད། Though one shows enmity like liquid poison toward the enemy, it does not harm the enemy but in turn it harms oneself.

ཞེ་ནག་ཁོག་བཅངས། to hold evil thoughts in one's heart ༉རྒྱལ་བ་རིན་པོ་ཆེ་ནས་དབང་ལུས་པའི་རྗེས་སུ་ངས་ཞེ་ནག་ཁོག་བཅངས་ཁྱོན་ནས་བྱས་མ་མྱོང་། I never hold evil thoughts in my heart since I received an empowerment from His Holiness the Dalai Lama.

ཞེ་ནག་སྟོར་ཆུབ། cruel thoughts and deeds ཆོས་པ་ཡིན་ན་ཞེ་ནག་སྟོར་ཆུབ་སྟོང་དགོས། If one is a practitioner, one should abandon cruel thoughts and deeds.

ཞེ་མིན་ལོག་པ། nausea མོ་ཊའི་ནང་ལ་འགྲོ་དུས་ཞེ་མིན་ལོག་གི་འདུག When I travel in an automobile, I get nausea.

208

ཞེ་བསུན་ཐློ་ཐམ། feels inconvenienced and disappointed རང་གི་

དགེ་ཕྲུག་གིས་སློམ་པ་ཕུལ་ན་དགེ་རྒན་ལ་ཞེ་བསུན་དང་ཐློ་ཐམ་ལས་ཀྱིས་ཡོང་བ་ཡིན།
When a disciple gives back his vows, the spiritual master feels inconvenienced and disappointed.

ཞི་སློད་དང་རིང་། relaxed and easy going བརྩོན་འགྲུས་སུ་མཐུད་གནང་རྒྱབ་ན་

ཞི་སློད་དང་རིང་ཡིན་ན་ཡང་དོན་ཆེན་སྒྲུབ་ཐུབ་ཀྱི་རེད། One can accomplish a great purpose with continual diligence even if one is a relaxed and easy-going person.

ཞེན་ལོག་སྟང་མིག་སྟོན་པ། to feel disgusted and show angry eyes ཁ་སང་ནས་རྒན་ལགས་ཀྱིས་ང་ལ་ཞེན་ལོག་སྟང་མིག་སྟོན་གནང་གི་འདུག
From yesterday onward the teacher felt disgusted with me and shows his angry eyes.

ཞོགས་སྔ་ལངས་དང་དགོངས་ཕྱི་ཉལ། early to rise and early to bed

མནའ་མ་གསར་པ་ཚོས་ཞོགས་སྔ་ལངས་དང་དགོངས་ཕྱི་ཉལ་བྱེད་པ་རེད། New brides are early to rise and early to bed.

ཟོར་སློད་འགྲོ་སོང་། miscellaneous expense ཕྱི་རྒྱལ་དུ་ཟོར་སློད་འགྲོ་སོང་ལ་

ཡང་སློར་མོ་སློང་ཕྲག་མང་པོ་འགྲོ་གི་རེད། Abroad, miscellaneous expenses are very high too.

གཞན་སློན་བསྒྲགས་འདོན། to expose others' faults གཞན་གྱི་སློན་བསྒྲགས་

འདོན་བྱེད་པས་རང་ཉིད་ལ་ཕན་ཐོགས་གང་ཡང་མེད། It serves no purpose to oneself to expose others' faults.

གཞན་རྟེན་མི་འཛོག not dependent/ perfect ཁོང་རང་གཞན་རྟེན་མི་འཛོག

པའི་མཁས་པ་ཆེན་པོ་རེད། He is a great scholar who need not depend on others.

གཞན་འགྲན་མ་མཆིས་པ། an outstanding/incomparable སངས་རྒྱས་ བཙོམ་ལྡན་འདས་ནི་གཞན་འགྲན་མ་མཆིས་པའི་སྟོན་པ་ཡང་དག་པ་ཞིག་རེད། Buddha Shakyaminin is a great outstanding perfect teacher.

གཞན་བདེ་རང་སྐྱིད། one's own and others' happiness ཆོས་མཐུན་གྱི་བྱ་ བ་བྱེད་ན་གཞན་བདེ་རང་སྐྱིད་ཡོང་གི་རེད། If one's activities are in conformity with the dharma, there will be happiness for one's self and others.

གཞན་སྡུག་བསྔལ་བ་ལ་སྙིང་ཚིམ་པ། to feel happy over others' suffering གཞན་སྡུག་བསྔལ་བ་ལ་སྙིང་རྗེ་སྐྱེ་དགོས་པ་ལས་སྙིང་ཚིམ་བྱ་མི་རུང་། One ought to feel compassionate but not happiness at others' suffering.

གཞན་དོན་ཁུར་བླངས། to take the responsibilities for others' welfare གཞན་དོན་ཁུར་བླངས་པ་ནི་བྱང་ཆུབ་སེམས་དཔའ་རྣམས་ཀྱི་དམ་ཚིག་རེད། It is the commitment of Boddhisattvas to take the responsibility for others' welfare.

གཞན་ཚོད་འཛིན་ཁྱེར། to dispute and be partial to others ཆབ་སྲིད་ཀྱི་ དབུ་ཁྲིད་ནང་ཁུལ་མ་མཐུན་པ་ཡོད་ན་སྤྱི་ཚོགས་ནང་གཞན་ཚོད་འཛིན་ཁྱེར་ཡོང་གི་རེད། If relations among the political leaders are strained, there will be dispute and partiality in the society.

གཞན་ཟེར་རྗེས་འབྲངས། to follow what others say ཡག་ཉེས་གང་ཡིན་ ཡང་བརྟག་དཔྱད་བྱེད་དགོས་པ་ལས་གཞན་ཟེར་རྗེས་འབྲངས་བྱ་མི་རུང་། It's not right to follow simply at what others say, one should examine whether it is good or bad.

གཞལ་དུ་མེད་པ། immeasurable/ that cannot be repaid/ inconceivable སྟོན་པའི་གཞལ་དུ་མེད་པའི་སྐུ་དྲིན་ལ་བརྟེན་ནས་འཛིག་རྟེན་དུ་དམ་ཆོས་དར། Due to the inconceivable kindness of Buddha, His teaching is flourishing in this world.

གཞི་མེད་སྐུར་འདེབས། baseless under-estimation or insult གཞན་ལ་གཞི་མེད་སྐུར་འདེབས་བྱེད་པ་ནི་རང་ཉིད་དམྱལ་བར་འགྲོ་བའི་རྒྱུ། To disparage others with baseless under-estimation or insult is a cause for one's going to hell.

གཞི་མེད་སྒྲོ་འདོགས། baseless over-estimation ཡོན་ཏན་མེད་པ་ལ་ཡོན་ཏན་ཡོད་པར་སྨྲ་བ་ནི་གཞི་མེད་སྒྲོ་འདོགས་རེད། It is a baseless over-estimation to praise somebody for having good knowledge when he/she has not.

གཞི་མེད་གཞི་བཟོ། to make a base out of baseless སློབ་གྲྭ་ཡར་རྒྱས་གཏོང་རྒྱ་ལས་གཞི་མེད་གཞི་བཟོ་བྱེད་རྒྱུ་དཀའ་ངལ་ཆེ་བ་ཡོད། It is more difficult to start something from nothing campared to improving an already existing school.

གཞིས་བྱེས་མཉམ་འཛོམས། the reunion of the exiled and the native གཞིས་བྱེས་བོད་མི་མཉམ་འཛོམས་བྱུང་བའི་ཉི་མ་མྱུར་དུ་འཁར་བའི་རེ་བ་ཡོད། We hope the day of the reunion of the Tibetans inside Tibet and those in exile will come very soon.

གཞི་རྩ་ལེགས་ཚུགས། a well established base/ strong foundation

དཀ་བཙན་བྱོལ་བོད་གཞུང་གི་གནས་སྟངས་གཞི་རྩ་ལེགས་ཚུགས་ཆགས་ཡོད། At present the foundation of the Tibetan government in exile has become well established.

གཞི་རྩའི་ཐོབ་ཐང་། fundamental rights རྒྱ་གར་གྱི་རྩ་ཁྲིམས་སུ་གཞི་རྩའི་ཐོབ་ཐང་བདུན་བཀོད་ཡོད། Seven fundamental rights are mentioned in the Indian Constitution.

གཞི་རྩའི་གནས་སྟངས། the basic condition དེང་སང་བོད་དུ་གཞི་རྩའི་གནས་སྟངས་ཡག་པོ་ཡོད་ཅེས་ཁྱབ་བསྒྲགས་བྱེད་པ་རེད། It is announced that the basic conditions in Tibet are quite good today.

གཞུང་ལམ་ལེགས་བཟོ། to strengthen the main path/ the construction of high ways བོད་མི་རྣམས་ཀྱིས་ཧི་མ་ཆལ་མངའ་སྡེའི་གཞུང་ལམ་ལེགས་པར་བཟོས་པ་རེད། The Tibetans constructed well the high-ways in Himachal Pradesh.

གཞུང་སེམས་འགྱུར་མེད། unwavering patriotism or love toward the government གཞུང་སེམས་འགྱུར་མེད་རྣམས་ལ་རྒྱལ་གཅེས་པ་ལུ་བ་རེད། People with unwavering patriotism are called nationalists.

གཞུང་སེམས་དྲང་པོ། sincere loyalty/ faith in one's government གཞུང་སེམས་དྲང་པོ་ཡོད་ན་དགྲ་བོས་མགོ་བསྐོར་གཏོང་ཐུབ་ཀྱི་མ་རེད། If one has a firm and sincere loyalty to one's government, one cannot be deceived by the enemies.

གཞུང་སེམས་རྣམ་དག pure loyalty སློབ་ཕྲུག་རྣམས་ལ་གཞུང་སེམས་རྣམ་དག་དགོས་པའི་བཀའ་སློབ་གནང་གལ་ཆེ། It is very important to advise the students to develop pure loyalty to one's government.

གཞོན་པའི་ཤེད་ལས་རྒད་པོའི་བྱུས་ཟབ། An old man's wisdom is better than a young man's might

བཞུགས་དང་མ་བཞུགས། whether to stay or not ཁོང་ད་ལྟ་ལྷ་ས་ལ་ བཞུགས་དང་མ་བཞུགས་ཤེས་ཀྱི་མེད། I don't know whether he stays in Lhasa or not at present.

བཞུགས་མོལ་ཚོགས་འདུ། plenary session བཞུགས་མོལ་ཚོགས་འདུའི་ཚོགས་ གཙོ་སུ་རེད། Who is the chairman of the plenary session ?

ཟ་མཁས་འཛུང་མཁས། to eat and drink frugally/ wise living

ཟ་མཁས་འཛུང་མཁས་བྱེད་ན་ཟ་ཡུན་འཛུང་ཡུན་རིང་བ་ཡོང་། If you eat and drink frugally, your food and drink will last long.

ཟ་རྒྱུ་འཕྱང་རྒྱུ་མང་ན་དགའ། ལབ་རྒྱུ་སྐྱིང་རྒྱུ་ཉུང་ན་དགའ། It is better to have more food and drinks, and fewer complaints.

ཟ་རྒྱུ་མེད་པ་ལས་བཤད་རྒྱུ་མེད་པ་དགའ། It is better to go without food than to be the source of others' gossip.

ཟ་བའི་ཁ་ཡོད་ན་ཡང་འགྲོ་བའི་མིད་པ་མི་འདུག Lit.: Even though one may have a mouth for eating, one does not have a throat for it to pass through./ Sense implied: Wanting something yet not being able to have it

ཟ་ཚོད་རང་གིས་མ་བྱེད་ན་ཕུས་མོ་ཡན་ཆད་གྲོད་ཁོག་ཡིན། Lit.: If one does not limit one's eating, the belly is upto the knees/ Sense implied: over-eating is self-destruction

ཟ་ཡ་འཛུང་ཡ། things for eating and drinking གཟུགས་པོ་བཟང་པོ་ཡོང་བ་ལ་ཟ་ཡ་འཛུང་ཡ་ཤིན་ཏུ་གལ་ཆེན་པོ་རེད། For a healthy body, it is very important to have proper things for eating and drinking.

ཟབ་དོན་གནད་གྲོལ། unfolding or the discovering the profound

214

and essential meaning རྒྱུ་མཚན་མནར་དགག་ལ་བརྟེན་ནས་ཟབ་དོན་གནད་གྲོལ་ ཐུབ་ཀྱི་རེད། One can discover the profound and essential meaning with the help of a teacher's instruction.

ཟམ་མ་ཆད་པ། uninterruptedly/ continuously སྟོན་པ་ནས་ད་བར་འདུལ་ བའི་ཉམས་ལེན་ཟམ་མ་ཆད་པ་བཞུགས་ཡོད། The practice of moral discipline has been uninterruptedly carried out from the teacher, Shakya Muni, to the present day.

ཟམ་མི་ཟིམ་མེ། to feel lazy/ inactive དགའ་ལས་མང་པོ་ཁལ་ན་ཟམ་མི་ཟིམ་མེ་ ཆག་གི་རེད། If one is very tired one feels lazy.

ཟས་གོས་དཔལ་འབྱོར། food, clothes and wealth ཟས་གོས་དཔལ་འབྱོར་ ཕུན་སུམ་ཚོགས་པ་ཡོད་དུས་ཆོས་བྱེད་ཐུབ་ན་ཙེ་ག་རེད། It is best to practise dharma when one has prosperity, an abundance in food, clothing and wealth.

ཟས་ངན་ལུས་ཀྱི་དགྲ། མི་ངན་ཡུལ་གྱི་དགྲ། Bad food is body's enemy and an evil man is country's enemy.

ཟས་ལ་ཟ་མཁས་བྱེད་ན་ཟ་རྒྱུ་ཀྱུན་མི་ཆད། གོས་ལ་གྱོན་མཁས་བྱེད་ན་གོན་ཀྱུ་ ཀྱུན་མི་ཆད། If one is frugal in eating, there will be no shortage of food and if one is frugal in wearing, there will not be shortage in clothing.

ཟས་ནོར་ལོངས་སྤྱོད། Lit.: food, wealth and property/ Sense implied: prosperity ཨ་མི་རི་ཁ་ནི་ཟས་ནོར་ལོངས་སྤྱོད་འཛོམས་པའི་རྒྱལ་ཁབ་ གཅིག་རེད། America is a very prosperous country (with abundance of food, wealth and property).

ཟེ་ལིང་གུ་ལིང་། hustle and bustle རྒྱལ་ས་ཟེ་ལིང་གུ་ལིང་འདིའི་འདུའི་ནང་ལ་ སེམས་ལ་ཞི་བ་ཐོབ་རྒྱུ་ཁག་པོ་རེད། It is difficult to get peace for the mind like this which is full of hustle and bustle.

ཟིན་མ་ཟིན། just about ཆུ་ཚོད་དགུ་པ་ཟིན་མི་ཟིན་ལ་འཛིན་གྲྭ་ཡོད་རེད། There is a class at just about 9 o'clock.

ཟུར་བལྟས་ལེབ་མཐོང་། Lit.: seeing or looking through the edge or corners, one can see the whole thing/ Sense implied: indication is enough གནས་ཚུལ་འདིའི་སྐོར་གསུང་དགོས་ཀྱི་མ་རེད། ཟུར་ བལྟས་ལེབ་མཐོང་རེད། There is no need to tell anything about this information. An indication is enough.

ཟུར་འཕྲོས་ཐུང་ཟད། a small disgression from the topic དེབ་འདིའི་ནང་ ལ་བོད་ཀྱི་སྐོར་ཟུར་འཕྲོས་ཐུང་ཟད་ཅིག་བྲིས་འདུག Tibet is discussed in a small disgression in that book.

ཟུར་ཟ་སྐྱོན་བརྗོད། sarcastic and critical/ cynical criticism རྒྱ་ནག་ གཞུང་གིས་རྒྱ་གར་དུ་ཡོད་པའི་བཙན་བྱོལ་གཞུང་ལ་རྟག་ཏུ་ཟུར་ཟ་སྐྱོན་བརྗོད་བྱེད་ཀྱི་ཡོད། The Chinese government always sarcastically criticizes the Tibetan government-in-exile in India.

ཟེར་རྒྱུ་བུ་མོ་ལ་ཟེར། འཕོག་རྒྱུ་མནའ་མ་ལ་ཕོག to scold one's daughter but hurts the bride.

རྩ་ཕོའམ་ལོ་ཐོ། almanac ལོ་ཐོའི་ནང་ལ་ད་ལོ་ཆར་པ་མང་པོ་བབ་ཀྱི་ཡོད་པ་བཤད་ འདུག In the almanac, it is said that there will be heavy rainfall this year.

216

ཟགས་གྲབས་ཟགས་གྲབས། about to fall/ ready to fall ཤིང་སྟོང་ནས་

ཤིང་ཏོག་ས་ལ་ཟགས་གྲབས་ཟགས་གྲབས་བྱེད་ཀྱི་འདུག The fruits are about
to fall from the tree.

གཟབ་གཟབ་ནན་ཏན། careful/ cautious/ emphasis སྐོམ་བཀྱིན་དུས་གཟབ་

ཟབ་ནན་ཏན་མ་བྱེད་ན་འབྲོགས་ཤོན་གྱི་མ་རེད། If one is not careful in
meditation, it won't be fruitful.

གཟབ་གཟབ་ཤིག་ཤིག very cautious རྒྱ་བལ་གྱི་ས་མཚམས་ལ་བསླེབས་དུས་

གཟབ་གཟབ་ཤིག་ཤིག་བྱེད་དགོས། One should be very cautious when
one reaches the Indo-Nepal border.

གཞི་བཟིད་ཁོག་སྟོང་། empty vessel sounds much

གཟིག་ལྤགས་གྱོན་པའི་བོང་བུ། Lit.: a donkey wearing a tiger's
skin/ Sense implied: artificial/ not real/masquerade

གཟིག་ཚང་སྟོ་འགྱམ་རྒྱ་བའི་ཕག་ཚག Lit.: a musk deer hopping
near a leopard's lair/ Sense implied: a cowardly fellow
pretending to be bold

གཟུགས་མེད་གྲིབ་ཆགས། Lit.: a shadow without a form/ Sense
implied: baseless blame གཟུགས་མེད་ལ་གྲིབ་ཆགས་བཤད་པ་ནི་བརྙས་
བཅོས་ཡིན་པ་རེད། It is an insult to complain about a shadow
without a form.

གཟུགས་མེད་གྲིབ་བཟོ། to create a form where there is no form/

གཟུགས་མེད་ན་གྲིབ་བཙོ་འོང་དོན་མེད། If there is no form there is no cause for a shadow.

གཟུར་གནས་དང་ལྡན། honest and impartial གཟུར་གནས་དང་ལྡན་གྱི་ལས་ཀ་བྱེད་ན་སུས་ཀྱང་སྐྱོན་བརྗོད་བྱེད་ཀྱི་མ་རེད། No one will criticize if one works honestly and impartially.

བཟང་ངན་འགྱུར་ལྷོག Lit.: interchangeability of good and bad/ Sense implied: ups and downs མི་ཚེའི་ནང་ལ་སྐྱིད་སྡུག་བཟང་ངན་འགྱུར་ལྷོག་སྣ་ཚོགས་འོང་གི་རེད། There will be ups and downs in one's life.

བཟང་དུ་བཟང་དུ། getting better and better ཆོས་བྱེད་ན་སེམས་བཟང་དུ་བཟང་དུ་འགྲོ་གི་རེད། If one practises dharma, one's mind gets better and better.

བཟང་པོའི་ཞོར་ལ་ཇ་ཆང་དང་ངན་པའི་ཞོར་ལ་རྒྱག་དུང་། In the company of good people, tea and chang are served and in the company of bad people, one gets a beating.

བཟང་བྱས་ངན་མཆོན། to do good for someone and to feel bad in return བསམ་བློ་མེད་མཁན་མི་ལ་ཡར་བཟང་བྱས་ཀྱང་ཚུར་ངན་དུ་མཆོན། Even though you do good to mindless/thoughtless people, they feel as if you have done bad to them.

བཟང་བྱས་ངན་ལན། to respond negatively for the good done བཟང་བྱས་ངན་ལན་བྱེད་པ་ནི་སྐྱེས་བུ་ངན་པའི་རྟགས་རེད། To respond negatively for the good done is a sign of bad person.

བཟང་མི་བཟང་། whether good or bad མི་མ་འཛིན་ན་སེམས་བཟང་མི་བཟང་ མི་ཤེས། Without interaction one will not know whether or not a person has good mind.

བཟང་ཞན་ཁྱད་པར། the gap between good and bad སྐྱེས་བུ་དམ་པ་དང་ངན་པའི་དབར་བཟང་ཞན་ཁྱད་པར་གནམ་ས་ཡོད། There is a vast difference between sublime and evil people.

བཟང་ལེན་ངན་དོར། to abandon bad and to adopt good སློབ་གྲྭ་ལ་སློད་ལམ་བཟང་ལེན་ངན་དོར་སློབ་གནང་གི་ཡོད། In schools one is taught to abandon bad actions and to adopt good behaviour.

བཟང་པོར་བཟང་ལན་དང་ངན་པར་ངན་ལན། to respond positively for the good done and negatively for the bad done འཛིན་སྐྱོང་མཁས་པ་དེ་ཚོས་བཟང་པོར་བཟང་ལན་དང་ངན་པར་ངན་ལན་བྱེད་ཐུབ་པ་རེད། The able and wise administrator can respond positively for the good done and negatively for the bad done.

ཕོ་བཟས་ནས་མི་ཕུང་ཉལ་ནས་ཕུང་། A man is ruined by sleeping, not by eating.

བཟས་བཟས་ཀྱིས་ཁ་རྩོགས། ཕྱིན་ཕྱིན་གྱིས་ལམ་འདྲང་། By eating too much your mouth has gotten used to eating and by walking continuously you become familiar for climbing up the hills.

བཟི་འཐོམ་འཐོམ། groggy ལོ་གསར་ལ་ཆང་མང་པོ་འཐུང་ཚང་བཟི་འཐོམ་འཐོམ་ཆགས་བྱུང་། I became groggy during the new-year celebration from drinking too much.

བཟི་བོའི་སྐྱིང་གཏམ་ཁ་ལ་བབ། A drunken person brings his secrets to the lips of his mouth.

བཟོ་སྐྲུས་གཉིས་ལྡན། good both in quality and make ཉེ་དོང་ནས་བཟོས་པའི་ཅ་ལག་དེ་ཆོ་བཟོ་སྐྲུས་གཉིས་ལྡན་ཕ་སྤུག་ཡོད། The things that are made in Japan are good both in terms of quality and make.

བཟོ་ཞིང་འབྲོག་གསུམ། agriculture, nomadic and industry ལུང་པའི་བཟོ་ཞིང་འབྲོག་གསུམ་ཡར་རྒྱས་བཏང་ན་ལུང་པ་ཡར་རྒྱས་འགྲོ་གི་རེད། There will be development in a country if there is an improvement in agriculture, industry and nomadic life.

བཟོ་ལས་ཐོན་སྐྱེད། industrial product ཡར་རྒྱས་ཕྱིན་པའི་བཟོ་ལས་ཚང་མར་བཟོ་ལས་ཐོན་སྐྱེད་ཕྱག་ཕྱག་བྱུང་ཡོད། All the developed countries have excellent factory production.

བཟོད་ཐབས་བྲལ་བ། unbearable/ རྒྱ་མིས་བོད་པར་བཟོད་ཐབས་བྲལ་བའི་མནར་གཅོད་བཏང་བ་རེད། The Chinese have exploited the Tibetans unbearably.

ཨ་ཆད་ཨུ་ཕྱུག total desperation ཨ་ཆད་ཨུ་ཕྱུག་མ་ཆགས་བར་གཞན་ལ་རོགས་
རམ་ཞུ་གི་མིན། I shall not seek others' help until I am in total desperation.

ཨ་རེ་ཨུ་རེ། scatter-brained མི་ཨ་རེ་ཨུ་རེ་ཚོས་ལས་ཀ་མཇུག་བསྐྱལ་གྱི་མ་རེད།
The scatter-brained persons will not complete their work.

ཨན་ནེ་འོན་ནེ། inattentive སློབ་ཕྱུག་ཨན་ནེ་འོན་ནེ་དེ་ཚོས་དགེ་ཉན་གྱིས་སློབ་དུས་
ཡག་པོ་ཉན་གྱི་མ་རེད། The inattentive students do not listen well to the teacher during the teaching.

ཨུ་ཕྱུག་ཐབས་ཟད། desperate and helpless ཨུ་ཕྱུག་ཐབས་ཟད་བྱུང་ན་མི་ཡིས་
གང་ཡང་བྱེད་སྲིད་ཀྱི་རེད། A person may do anything when he is desperate and helpless.

ཨུ་ཕྱུག་ཁྱི་ཉན་གྱུང་ལ་མ་ཚོངས། Lit.: A desperate dog jumps at the walls/ Sense implied: helpless

ཨུར་ཨུར་དིང་དིང་། noise/ uproar མི་མང་ཨུར་སྐྲ་དིང་དིང་རྒྱག་ཡོང་གི་འདུག
The mob is running towards me in uproar.

ཨུར་གཏམ་དགྲོག་ཁྲིན། disrupting rumours མཁས་པ་རྣམས་ཨུར་གཏམ་
དགྲོག་ཁྲིན་གྱི་གཞན་དབང་དུ་མི་འགྲོ་བ་རེད། Wise people are not over-powered by disrupting rumours.

ཉུར་ཚ་པོ། an exaggerator ཉུར་ཚ་པོ་དེ་འདྲ་མ་བྱེད། Don't be such an exaggerator.

ཉུར་ཉུར་ཉིལ་ཉིལ། with a bang, uproar ཁོང་ཚོ་ཁ་སང་མཚན་ཁང་ཉུར་ཉུར་ ཉིལ་ཉིལ་བསྡད་སོང་། They spent the whole night yesterday in an uproar.

ཨོ་རྒྱུ་གཅིག་འདྲེས། Lit.: like the mixing of water with milk/ Sense implied: very friendly ང་ཚོ་གྲོགས་པོ་གཉིས་ཨོ་རྒྱུ་གཅིག་འདྲེས་ ནང་བཞིན་ཆམ་པོ་ཡོད། We two friends are very friendly, hard to be separated like milk in the water.

འོད་ཆེམ་ཆེམ། glaring/ glittering འོད་ཆེམ་ཆེམ་མེར་པོ་ཐམས་ཅད་གསེར་མ་རེད། All that glitters is not gold.

འོད་ཟེར་སྟོང་ལྡན། having thousands of rays of light ཤར་ཕྱོགས་རི་ བོའི་རྩེ་ནས་འོད་ཟེར་སྟོང་ལྡན་ཉི་མ་བྱུང་། The sun with thousands of rays of light rises from the top of the eastern hill.

འོས་པའི་འགན། a deserving responsibility མི་སུ་ཡིན་ནའང་འོས་པའི་ འགན་སྤྲད་ན་ངེས་པར་བྱེད་ཀྱི་རེད། Anyone who is given a deserving job will definitely accept the responsibility.

འོས་བབས་སུ་རུང་། whoever is deserving/ appropriate སློབ་ཕྲུག་འོས་ པ་སུ་རུང་ལ་ཉན་བདག་བསྐོ་གཞག་གནང་རོགས་གནང་། Please appoint a deserving student as prefect.

འོས་ཤིང་མཚམས་པ། fitting and appropriate ཁོང་དགེ་ཉན་གནང་བ་དེ་འོས་ ཤིང་མཚམས་པ་ཞིག་བྱུང་འདུག It is very fitting and appropriate for him to become a teacher.

222

ཁ །

ལ་ཁའི་ཉི་མ། Lit.: the setting sun/ Sense implied: old age ཕོ་གནས་ དུས་ལ་ཁའི་ཉི་མ་དང་མཚུངས་པ་ཡིན། Growing old is like the setting sun.

ལ་ཁའི་ཉི་མ་དང་རྒྱུ་ཁའི་གྲིབ་གསོ། Lit.: the setting sun and the fading shadow/ Sense implied: to have become aged ཆོས་ ཀྱི་ཉམས་ལེན་གཅིག་པུས་ལ་ཁའི་ཉི་མ་དང་རྒྱུ་ཁའི་གྲིབ་གསོ་སྐྱབས་སུ་ཕན་གྱི་རེད། Only religious practice can help when one becomes old.

ལ་དགུ་ལུང་དགུ Lit.: nine passes and nine valleys/ Sense implied: distant མར་པ་ཆོས་ཀྱི་བློ་གྲོས་ཀྱིས་ལ་དགུ་ལུང་དགུ་བརྒྱབས་ཏེ་རྒྱ་ གར་དུ་ཕེབས་པ་རེད། The translator Marpa Chokyi Lodoe visited India by crossing nine mountains and nine valleys.

ལ་བརྒལ་ལུང་བརྒལ། Lit.: to cross mountains and valleys/ Sense implied: distant and difficult travel རྒྱ་གར་གྱི་བྱང་ཕྱོགས་ ནས་ལ་ལུང་མང་པོ་བརྒལ་ན་བོད་དུ་བསླེབ་ཀྱི་རེད། If you cross many mountains and valleys toward the north of India, you will reach Tibet.

ལ་རེ་བརྒྱབ་ན་ཐུར་རེ། Lit.: over every mountain pass there is a slope/ Sense implied: after every difficult time there is a good time ང་ཚོའི་མི་ཚེའི་ནང་ལ་ལ་རེའི་བརྒྱབ་ན་ཐུར་རེ་ཟེར་བར་དུ་ཡོང་གི་ རེད། There will be good time after every difficult time in our life.

ལག་མགོ་རིང་ལ་ཕུ་དུང་ཐུང་། Lit.: long arm with short sleeves/ Sense implied: man of ideas but having financial problems ལག་མགོ་རིང་ལ་ཕུ་དུང་ཐུང་དགོས་ནས་ལས་ཀ་བྱེད་ཡག་མི་འདུག I cannot do any work because of financial problems.

ལག་རྗེས། ཕྱག་རྗེས། Lit.: hand print/ Sense implied: legacy/ feat ཐོན་མི་སམ་བྷོ་ཊས་ཡི་གེའི་སྲོལ་བཏོད་དེ་ལག་རྗེས་མཛད་དུ་བྱུང་བ་ཞིག་བཞག་ཡོད། Thonmi Sambhota is credited for leaving behind the legacy of Tibetan writing system.

ལག་རྡུམ་བྲག་འཛེགས། Lit.: to climb a rock with a maimed hand/ Sense implied: a fool's attempt ཐོས་པ་མེད་པའི་སྒོམ་པ་དེ། ལག་རྡུམ་བྲག་ལ་འཛེགས་པ་འདྲ། A meditation done without hearing teachings is just like a handicapped person climbing a rock.

ལག་པ་དམ་པོ། ཕྱག་དམ་པོ། Lit.: tight hand or fist/ Sense implied: stingy/miser/ opposite of spendthrift ང་ཚོའི་སྦྱིན་བདག་ལག་པ་དམ་པོ་ཞེ་དྲག་ཡོད་རེད། Our master is very stingy.

ལག་པ་ཚ་དུས་སྐམ་པ་དྲན། Lit.: remembering a pincer only when one's hand is burnt/ Sense implied: to think only when it is high time to do something ཡིག་ཚད་སྐབས་གཅིག་ཕུར་སློབ་སྦྱོང་ཧུར་དག་གནང་བ་ནི་ལག་པ་ཚ་དུས་སྐམ་པ་དྲན་པ་དང་གཅིག་པ་རེད། Studying hard during the examinations only is like burning one's hand and then remembering the use of a tong.

ལག་པ་ཡ་གཅིག་གི་བརྡོག་པ། Lit.: clapping with one hand/ Sense implied: impossibility ལག་པ་གཅིག་གིས་བརྡོག་པ་བརྒྱབ་ཐུབ་ཡག་ཡོད་མ་རེད། It is not possible to clap with one hand.

ལག་པ་འདངས་པོ། Lit.: liberal hand/ Sense implied: generous/spendthrift/extravagant ལག་པ་འདངས་པོ་མེད་ན་མི་འབོར་གྱི་མ་རེད། If one is not generous, people will not come to one.

ལག་པར་ཤ་ཡོད་ན་ནམ་མཁར་བྱ་འཕིར། Lit.: If one has a piece of meat in the hand, the birds will hover in the sky/ Sense implied: If one has knowledge and wealth, others will gather around him.

ལག་ལེན་འགེལ་འོས། deserving to put into practice ལག་ལེན་འགེལ་འོས་པའི་རིགས་རྣམས་དེས་པར་དུ་ལག་ལེན་འགེལ་དགོས། One should put into practice those things that deserve implementation.

ལག་ལེན་ཅི་ནུས། to practice as much as we can གྲོས་ཆོད་བཞག་པ་རྣམས་ལག་ལེན་དུ་ཅི་ནུས་འགེལ་གྱི་ཡིན། We will implement the resolutions passed as much as we can.

ལག་ལེན་འགེལ་སྟངས། ways of putting into practice རིག་པ་མེད་ན་ལག་ལེན་འགེལ་སྟངས་ཀྱང་ཤེས་ཀྱི་མ་རེད། If one is not intelligent, one will not know the ways of implemention.

ལག་ལེན་འཛོལ་མེད། flawless practice ཉམས་མྱོང་མེད་ན་ལག་ལེན་འཛོལ་མེད་ཁག་པོ་རེད། It is difficult to have flawless practice if you do not have experience.

ལག་ཤེས་སྣ་ཚོགས། various crafts ཁོང་ལག་ཤེས་སྣ་ཚོགས་ལ་མཁས་པ་རེད། He is skilfull in various handicrafts.

ལང་ང་ལིང་ངེ། swaying/ hanging ག་ཁང་ནང་ལ་ཤ་ལང་ང་ལིང་ངེ་གནས་ལ་ བཀལ་འདུག Meats are hanging from the roof in the butchers' shop.

ལང་ལང་པ། while standing ང་ཆུ་ཚོད་ལྔ་པ་ནས་ལང་ལང་པ་ཡིན། I have been awake since 5 O'clock.

ལན་དགུ་ཆད་ཀྱང་ལན་དགུ་མཐུད། ལན་དགུ་ཆད་མཐུད། Lit.: to join nine times even if something is broken nine times/ Sense implied: to try again and again བྱ་བ་ཆེན་པོ་ཞིག་བསྒྲུབ་པར་ལན་དགུ་ ཆད་ཀྱང་ལན་དགུ་མཐུད་དགོས་རེད། One has to try again and agian for the accomplishment of a great task.

ལབ་སྐྱེང་མེད་པ། without any controversy or complaint ལས་ཀ་ ལབ་སྐྱེང་མེད་པར་མཇུག་བསྒྲིལ་རྒྱུ་ཞེ་དྲག་གལ་ཆེན་པོ་རེད། It is very important to complete a work without any complaint.

ལབ་རྒྱ་ཕ་གསོད་མཁན་གྱི་བུ་ལའང་ཡོད། Lit.: A son who killed his father has his reasons to state / Sense implied: justifying one's wrong doings.

ལམ་ནོར་སློག་ཤེས། Knowing how to retreat when one is on the wrong path/ Sense implied: to know how to confess ལམ་ནོར་སློག་ཤེས་ན་གྲུང་པོ་རེད། To avoid wrong path is wise.

ལམ་ནོར་ན་བསྐོར་ས་ཡོད། ཁ་ནོར་ན་བསྐོར་ས་མེད། Lit.: If one loses one's way, one can retreat, but if one says something wrong, it cannot be revoked./ Sense implied: This shows the seriousness of the situation when the wrong information has been conveyed.

226

ལམ་སེང་ལམ་སེང་། fast/quickly/ immediately བོད་ཡིག་ལམ་སེང་ལམ་
སེང་ཤེས་རྒྱ་ཁག་པོ་རེད། It is difficult to learn Tibetan fast.

ལས་ངན་པ་རང་གིས་མ་བྱས་ན། འཇིགས་དགོས་པ་གཤིན་རྗེའི་ཁྲིམས་ར་མིན།
Lit.: If one has not committed negavities one need not fear even the court of Yama, the lord of death./ Sense implied: There is nothing to be afraid of.

ལས་འབྲས་དཔང་འཕེར། Lit.: To stand the test of the law of karma./ Sense implied: honest སོ་སོའི་ལས་ཀ་ལས་འབྲས་དཔང་
འཕེར་བྱེད་ན་ཞེ་དྲག་ཡག་པོ་རེད། It is very good to perform one's duty that stands the test of the law of Karma (honestly).

ལས་འབྲས་བསླུ་མེད། the infallability of karma ནང་པ་ཚོས་ལས་འབྲས་
བསླུ་མེད་ལ་ཡིད་ཆེས་བྱེད་པ་རེད། Buddhists believe in the infallability of karma and its result.

ལས་འཕྲོ་མཇུག་མཐུད། continuation of the remaining work ངས་
ལས་ཀ་འདི་ལོ་རྗེས་མ་ལས་འཕྲོ་མཇུག་མཐུད་བྱེད་ཀྱི་ཡིན། I will continue this work next year.

ལུ་གུ་རྒྱུད་སྦྲེལ། Lit.: sheep following one another in a row./ Sense implied: continuously one after the other དམིགས་
ཡུལ་ངེས་ཅན་ཞིག་བསྒྲུབ་པ་ལ་ཐབས་ཤེས་ལུ་གུ་རྒྱུད་སྦྲེལ་གནང་དགོས་པ་ཡིན། One should strive continuosly for various means in odrer to fulfill one's aims.

ལུག་མགོ་བཀལ་ནས་ཁྱི་ཤ་འཚོང་། Lit.: to hang sheep's head and sell dog's meat/ Sense implied: to play at fraud or to deceive བོད་ཀྱི་ཐོག་ཆུ་མིའི་སྲིད་བྱུས་ནི་ལུག་མགོ་བཀལ་ནས་ཁྱི་ཤ་འཚོང་པ་དང་གཅིག་པ་རེད། The Chinese policy on Tibet is like hanging or showing a sheep's head and selling dog's meat.

ལུག་ཤོར་རྟ་ཐོབ། Lit.: to lose a sheep and obtain a horse/ Sense implied: good bartering/ gain profit རྟ་ཐོབ་ན་ལུག་ཤོར་ཡང་འགྲོད་པ་མེད། It does not matter if you lose a sheep for a horse.

ལུགས་མཐུན་དང་གཞག lawful and honest ལས་ཀ་ལུགས་མཐུན་དང་གཞག་བྱེད་ན་སོ་སོ་ལ་གཏམ་བཟང་ཡོང་གི་རེད། One will get a good reputation if one works honestly and lawfully.

ལུང་ཆུང་ནང་གི་དཔོན་ཆུང་། Lit.: A small leader of a small village/ Sense implied: A big fish in a small pond/ One is trying to be overly bossy in a small village.

ལུང་པ་རེ་ལ་སྐད་ལུགས་རེ། བླ་མ་རེ་ལ་ཆོས་ལུགས་རེ། Every region has its own dialect and every priest has his own religious tradition.

ལུས་དང་གྲིབ་མ་བཞིན། Lit.: like a body and shadow/ Sense implied: inseparable or always together ཆུ་དང་འབྲས་བུ་ལུས་དང་གྲིབ་མ་བཞིན་དུ་བྱུང་བ་ཡིན། Good amd bad deeds are followed by corresponding effects like a shadow following the body.

ལུས་བདེ་ཁམས་དངས། physically and mentally fit/ well and good ང་ལུས་བདེ་ཁམས་དངས་ཡིན། I am fine.

228

ལུས་ལ་ན་ཚ་མེད་པར་གདོང་ལ་ཉེག་པ་འཁོར་དོན་མེད། There is no reason to have dark spots on your face if there is no physical disorder.

ལེགས་ཉེས་རྣམ་དཔྱོད། Lit.: analysis of good and bad/ Sense implied: wisdom for analysis/ intelligence ལེགས་ཉེས་རྣམ་དཔྱོད་ ལྡན་པའི་མི་དང་འགྲོགས་དགོས། One should accompany a man of intelligence.

ལེགས་ཉེས་དབྱེ་འབྱེད། Lit.: to distinguish good from bad/ Sense implied: examine, probe, investigation, distinction, difference འཛིན་སྐྱོང་གི་ངོས་ནས་ལེགས་ཉེས་དབྱེ་འབྱེད་དགོས་པ་ཡིན། There should be a distinction between good and bad from the administrative side.

ལེགས་སྤེལ་ཉེས་འགོག Lit.: to increase goodness and avoid evil/ Sense implied: correction འགན་ཡོད་པའི་མི་རྣམས་ཀྱི་ལས་ཀ་ནི་ ལེགས་སྤེལ་ཉེས་འགོག་བྱ་རྒྱུ་དེ་ཡིན། The duty of responsible people is to promote correct behaviour and stop immoralities in a society.

ལེན་རུང་མ་ལེན་རུང་། whether one accepts or not ཁྱེད་རང་གིས་ལེན་ རུང་མ་ལེན་རུང་འདི་ངོས་ནས་ཕུལ་བ་ཡིན། I offer it to you whether you accept it or not.

ལོ་བརྒྱ་སྨན་དང་འཆི་ཁར་དུག Lit.: To be medicine for a hundred years and become a poison at death/ Sense implied: Very helpful for a very long time and just the reverse at the last moment.

ལོ་ལྟར་རེ་བཞིན། every year ང་ལོ་ལྟར་རེ་བཞིན་རྡོ་རྗེ་གདན་དུ་འགྲོ་གི་ཡོད། Every year I go to Bodhgaya.

ལོ་ནས་ལོ་བསྐྱོད། year after year/ continuously ནང་རྒྱུད་ཀྱི་རྟོགས་པ་དེ་ ལོ་ནས་ལོ་བསྐྱོད་དེ་དཀའ་ལས་བརྒྱབ་ན་ཡང་ལས་སླ་པོར་སྐྱེ་གི་མ་རེད། The inner realization cannot be generated so easily even when you strive for years after years.

ལོ་ཕྱུགས་གཉིས་འཕེལ། Lit.: increasing crops and cattle/ Sense implied: A very good year in which there is good harvest and animal breeding.

ལོ་མས་འབྲས་བསྒྲིབས། Lit.: the leaves covering the fruits/ Sense implied: too much writing spoils the meaning ཚིག་གི་ལོ་ མས་དོན་གྱི་འབྲས་བུ་མ་བསྒྲིབས་པ་དགོས། Do not let too many words obscure the meaning like leaves covering fruits.

ལོང་བས་བསྐལ་ཁུང་ཁམས་གསུམ། Lit.: Even the blind can see the three realms./ Sense implied: Something that is well known to all.

ཤ་སྐམ་རུས་སྐམ། Lit.: skinny and dry bones/ Sense implied: weak and feeble ཁོང་གིས་བོད་ཀྱི་དོན་དུ་ཤ་སྐམ་རུས་སྐམ་མ་ཆགས་བར་དཀའ་ ལས་བགྱིས། He worked hard for the Tibetan cause until he became skinny and skelet.

ཤ་ཁུ་ཤ་ཐིམ། Lit.: letting the soup absorb into meat./ Sense implied: to put into an intended use གཞུང་གི་དངུལ་གཞུང་གི་དོན་ དུ་གཏོང་བ་ནི་ཤ་ཁུ་ཤ་ཐིམ་བྱུང་བ་རེད། Using government money for governmental projects is just like letting the meat soup absorb into meat.

ཤ་ཁྱེར་པགས་ཁྱེར། Lit.: To have taken away meat as well as skin./ Sense implied: to take away everything རྒྱ་མིས་བོད་ནས་ ཤ་ཁྱེར་པགས་ཁྱེར་བྱེད་པ་རེད། The Chinese took away everything from Tibet.

ཤ་ཁྲག་རྒྱུད་པ། blood lineage/ progeny མི་རིགས་གཅིག་པའི་མི་ཚང་མར་ཤ་ ཁྲག་གཅིག་པའི་རྒྱུད་པ་ཡོད། People of one race have the same blood lineage or progeny.

ཤ་རྙིང་དུག་དང་མར་རྙིང་སྨན། Stale meat is poison and rancid butter is medicine.

ཤ་ཐོག་མར་བཞག་ས། Lit.: to add butter to meat/ Sense implied: to give help to those who do not need it ཕྱུག་པོ་ལ་རོགས་རམ་ བྱེད་པ་ནི་ཤ་ཐོག་མར་བཞགས་བྱེད་པའི་དོན་ཨིན། To help the rich man is to add butter to meat.

ཤ་ཤོར་རུས་ཤོར། Lit.: dispersing of flesh and bones/ Sense implied: to destroy completely སེ་ར་དགོན་པའི་གྲྭ་པ་ཚང་མ་ ༡༩༥༩ ལོར་རྒྱ་མིས་ཤ་ཤོར་རུས་ཤོར་དུ་བཏང་བ་རེད། All the monks of Sera Monastery were completely destroyed by the Chinese in 1959.

ཤ་པོའི་ཤེད་དང་དགོ་བོའི་བང་། Lit.: the energy of a stag and the pace of a male antelope/ Sense implied: an example of strength གཞོན་པའི་ཤེད་ནི་ཤ་པོའི་ཤེད་དང་དགོ་བོའི་བང་འདྲ། Youth has the energy of a stag and keeps the pace of a male antelope.

ཤ་ཚ་ཆེ་མདོག་ appearing very affectionate/ pretending to be very affectionate བུ་མོས་ཤ་ཚ་ཆེ་མདོག་ཁ་པོ་བྱེད་ཀྱང་དགའ་རྒྱུ་མེད། There is nothing to feel happy about the seeming affections of a girl.

ཤ་ཚ་རྣམ་དག་ pure love དགེ་རྒན་གྱིས་ཤ་ཚ་རྣམ་དག་ཐོག་ཕྲུ་གུར་བསླབས་ན་ཕན་ ཐོགས་ཆེན་པོ་ཡོད་རེད། It is of great service if teachers teach out of pure love for the children.

ཤ་ཚའི་ཁ་ལ་གཏམ་སྙན་མེད། One cannot expect sweet words from an affectionate person/mouth.

ཁ་ཞེན་དོར་མེད། Lit.: unavoidable love/ Sense implied: sincere loyalty ང་བོད་གཞུང་ལ་ཁ་ཞེན་དོར་མེད་ཡོད། I have sincere loyalty to the Tibetan government.

ཁངས་གཟིངས་མཐོ་པོ། prominent nose ཁངས་གཟིངས་མཐོ་བ་ནི་མཚན་བཟང་ ཞིག་རེད། A prominent nose is a noble size.

ཁར་གཡབ་ནུབ་ཡིབ། Lit.: to hide in the east and west/ Sense implied: to hide everywhere མི་གསོད་མཁན་དེ་ཁར་ནུབ་གང་དུ་གབ་ ཀྱང་ཉི་མ་གཅིག་འཛིན་ཐུབ་ཀྱི་རེད། Wherever the murderer is hiding, east or west, one day he will be caught.

ཁི་ཁར་མ་ཎི་ཚ་ཚ་འདོན། Lit.: to chant the Mani mantra in rush on one's death-bed/ to do something at the last moment ཉེ་ ཁར་མ་ཎི་ཚ་ཚ་འདོན་བྱེད་ཀྱང་ཐབས་ཕོགས་ཆུང་། It is not of much use to recite the Mani mantra in rush on one's death.

ཉི་དུ་རོ་དུ། to weep like anything/to cry to death མི་ངན་གྱི་མདུན་དུ་ ཉི་དུ་རོ་དུ་བྱེད་ཀྱང་ཐབས་ཕོགས་བྱེད་ཀྱི་མ་རེད། Even if you weep like anything for help, evil persons will not care.

ཉི་རུལ་རོ་རུལ། to sleep like a corpse ཁ་སང་མཚན་ལ་ཁོང་རང་ཐེལ་བ་ཞེ་དྲག འདུག དེ་རང་ཞོགས་པ་ཉི་རུལ་རོ་རུལ་བརྒྱབས་འདུག He was very busy last night and this morning he slept like a corpse.

ཉི་འབུར་རོ་འབུར། to settle at one place for a very long time although one does not like it (mainly due to service) བོད་

233

མི་ཚོས་ལས་ཀ་དང་པོ་དེར་ཉི་འབུར་རོ་འབུར་བྱེད་པ་རེད། Tibetans mostly stick to their first job for a very long time.

ཤིག་གི་ལོགས་ནས་རྒྱུས་པའི་རེ་བ། Lit.: Hoping to obtain sinew from a louse/ Sense implied: empty hope དམར་ཤོག་དང་ལ་ཞི་བདེར་རེ་བ་དེ་ཤིག་གི་ལོགས་ནས་རྒྱུས་པའི་རེ་བ་བྱེད་པ་དང་གཅིག་པ་རེད། Expecting peace and happiness in a communist country is same as expecting sinews from a louse.

ཤིག་ལ་བརྒལ་ཀྱང་གོང་བའི་ཕྱི་ནང་། Lit.: even if a louse crosses the neck, it is (still) at the other side of the collar/ Sense implied: one cannot go too far

ཤིག་སེན་ར་སྐོད། Lit.: coming of a louse in between one's nails/ Sense implied: to verify or prove ཁོང་གི་གནས་ཚུལ་དེ་བདེན་པ་ཡིན་པའི་ཤིག་སེན་ར་སྐོད་ཐུབ་སོང་། His information has been verified as truth.

ཤིག་གསོད་པར་སྟ་རེ་འཕྱར་མི་དགོས། Lit.: There is no need to brandish an axe to kill a louse. Sense implied: unnecessary action

ཤིང་སྣ་འདེབས་འཛུགས། planting plants ཁོར་ཡུག་སྲུང་སྐྱོབ་ཀྱི་ཆེད་དུ་ཤིང་སྣ་འདེབས་འཛུགས་བྱེད་པ་རེད། Planting plants is being carried out for the environmental protection.

ཤིང་རྩ་བ་མ་རུལ་ན་ལོ་མ་མི་སྐམ། Lit.: If the root of a tree is not rotten, the leaves won't dry up./ Sense implied: If the root of anything is not spoiled one day it will come up.

234

ཤིང་བཟང་པགས་པའི་འོག་ཏུ་རུལ། Lit.: to let good wood spoil under its bark/ Sense implied: For eg. burying one's knowledge and skills uselessly.

ཤིང་བཟོ་མཁས་ཀྱང་ལྷ་བྲིས་ཡོང་མདོག་མེད། Lit.: A skillful carpenter need not be a good artist/ Sense implied: One need not be skillful in every field.

ཤིང་སོག་ཤིང་ལ་མི་འགོ Lit.: A wooden saw cannot cut wood./ Sense implied: Persons of equal rank cannot control one another.

ཤུགས་མེད་ཤུགས་ངོམ། to boast of strength though one lacks it སྙིང་རྗེ། ཤུགས་མེད་པར་ཤུགས་ངོམ་གྱི་འདུག What a pity ! He boasts of strength he lacks.

ཤེལ་སྒྲོའི་ནང་གི་མོག་མོག Lit.: A momo in a glass show case./ Sense implied: attractive but of no use རྒྱལ་པོའི་སྲས་ལ་འཛིན་སྲངས་མེད་ན་ཤེལ་སྒྲོའི་ནང་གི་མོག་མོག་དང་གཅིག་པ་རེད། If a prince is not able, he would be like a momo in a glass show case.

ཤེས་རིག་བཀྲ་བ། intelligent/ brilliant བོད་མིའི་མཆམས་དུ་བོད་ཕྲུག་ཤེས་རིག་བཀྲ་བ་བཅུ་གཉིས་བཏང་བ་རེད། Sixteen intelligent Tibetan boys were sent to India with the minister, Thonmi Sambota.

ཤེས་རྒྱ་མཐོང་རྒྱ། extent of knowledgeable and observation ཤེས་རྒྱ་མཐོང་རྒྱ་ག་ཚད་ཆེ་ན་ཡང་ལེགས་པ་རེད། It is good if the extent of knowledge and observation is great.

235

ཤེས་ཆེ་ཁོག་ཡངས། wise and broad-minded རྒྱལ་ཁབ་ཀྱི་དབུ་ཁྲིད་ནི་ཤེས་ཆེ་ ལ་ཁོག་ཡངས་པ་ཨིན། The head of a nation should be wise and broad-minded.

ཤེས་མདོག་བདེན་མདོག pretending to be knowledgeable and honest མི་ཛྭ་ གཡོ་དེ་ཚོས་ཤེས་མདོག་བདེན་མདོག་བྱེད་ཀྱི་རེད། The hypocrites will pretend to be knowledgeable and honest.

ཤེས་ལྡན་ཡ་རབས། educated and decent སློབ་གྲྭ་ཡག་པོའི་སློབ་ཕྲུག་རྣམས་ཤེས་ ལྡན་ཡ་རབས་ཤེ་གཅིག་ཨོང་། The students from good schools are well educated and well behaved.

ཤེས་ནུས་སྤྱོགས་ཚོད། to the extent of one's knowledge and ability ངས་རང་གི་ཤེས་ནུས་སྤྱོགས་ཚོད་ཁྱེད་རང་ལ་རོགས་པ་བྱེད་ཀྱི་ཨིན། I will extend my help to you according to my knowledge and ability.

ཤེས་འབྲོན་གཉིས་དམན། Lit.: One who is low in educational standard and efficiency/ Sense implied: Used for an expression of one's humbleness concealing one's knowledge and experience.

ཤེས་མེད་གླུད་རྒུང་། stupid and dull ཤེས་མེད་གླུད་རྒུང་དེ་ཚོས་ལག་རྩོལ་མ་ གཏོགས་བྱེད་མི་ཐུབ། Stupid and dull people cannot do anything except manual work.

ཤེས་བཞིན་དུག་འཐུང་། Lit.: to take poison knowingly/ Sense implied: to risk danger knowingly/ སེམས་སྐྱོ་པོ་མེད་དུས་ཤེས་

236

བཞིན་དུ་དུག་འབྱུང་ཉེན་ཡོད། There is a danger of taking poison knowingly when one is not happy.

ཤེས་ཡོན་བེད་སྤྱོད། use of education and learning ཀུན་སློང་བཟང་པོ་ ཡོད་ན་ཤེས་ཡོན་བེད་སྤྱོད་ཡག་པོ་ཐུབ་ཀྱི་རེད། One can utilize well one's knowledge and learning if one has a good motivation.

ཤེས་ཡོན་བསམ་བློ། intellectual thinking/ love for education/ interest in learning ཤེས་ཡོན་བསམ་བློ་ཡོད་པའི་མི་ལ་གྲོས་རིས། Discuss and get suggestions from intellectual persons.

ཤེས་ཡོན་སློབ་སྦྱོང་། knowledge and learning བོད་ཕྲུག་རྣམས་ཀྱི་ཤེས་ཡོན་ སློབ་སྦྱོང་ཆེད་བོད་པའི་སློབ་གྲྭ་ལོགས་སུ་བཙུགས་པ་རེད། Separate Tibetan schools were opened for educating the Tibetan Children.

ཤོག་བུ་སྣུམ་ཟན། Lit.: paper absorbing oil/ Sense implied: permanent mark གྲོགས་པོ་སྡུག་ཅག་མཉམ་དུ་ཕྱིན་ན་སྤྱོད་ངན་ཤོག་བུ་སྣུམ་ ཟན་བཞིན་དུ་འགོས་ཀྱི་རེད། If one accompanies a bad friend, one will catch bad habits, as permanent a mark as a paper absorbing oil.

ཤོག་བུ་རླུང་འཁྱེར། Lit.: A paper being carried away by wind./ Sense implied: easily carried away by rumours གནས་ཚུལ་ གོ་མ་ཐག་ཤོག་བུ་རླུང་ཁྱེར་ནང་བཞིན་གནང་མི་དུང་། One should not be like a paper carried away by wind as soon as news is heard.

ཤོག་བུར་རས་རྫས། Lit.: taking a paper for a cloth/ Sense implied: Pretending to be what you are not.

ཤོག་སྒུག་རླུང་འཚངས། Lit.: to inflate a paper bag/ Sense implied: To provoke someone against others.

གཤེ་གཤེ་རོ་འདྲ་གཅིག བཀའ་བཀྱོན་རོ་འདྲ་གཅིག Lit.: scolding to death/ Sense implied: to rebuke or scold terribly. ཁ་སང་དགེ་ ལགས་ཀྱིས་ང་ལ་བཀའ་བཀྱོན་རོ་འདྲ་གཅིག་གནང་བྱུང་། Yesterday the teacher rebuked him and me like anything.

བདད་གྲུ་སྨྲས་དག A good centre of metaphysics བདད་གྲུ་དང་སྒྲུབ་གྲུ་ གཉིས་གལ་ཆེ་ཆུང་གཅིག་པ་རེད། A centre of metaphysics and meditation are equally important.

བདད་བདེ་མཇལ་བདེ། easy to talk to and meet/ accessible ང་ཚོའི་ ཇེས་སྟོན་པ་ལ་སྐད་ཆ་བདད་བདེ་པོ་དང་མཇལ་བདེ་པོ་ཡོད་རེད། Our Director is very easy to meet and talk to.

བདད་རོགས་གཏམ་རོགས། A person with whom one gossips/ companion/ friend ཁོང་ང་འི་བདད་རོགས་གཏམ་རོགས་ཡག་པོ་གཅིག་ཡིན། He is a very good friend with whom I can discuss things.

བདད་ས་བུ་མོ་ཕོག་ས་མནའ་མ། Lit.: Scolding one's daughter is a subliminal remark on the bride./ Sense implied: An indirect hint.

བདལ་བདལ་བཏང་བ། to rinse/ to gurgle (e.g. mouth) ཨོ་མའི་སྟོང་ཏེ་ བདལ་བདལ་བཏང་རོགས། Please rinse the milk pot.

238

ས་སྐྱེས་རྡོ་སྐྱེས། Lit.: ..where soils and stones have come about/ Sense implied: A place where one is born.

ས་འཁོད་སྐྱོམ་ལ་རྡོ་འབུར་འདོན། Lit.: Pebbles popping-up on a levelled ground./ Sense implied: A miscreant among peaceful people.

ས་འཁྱག་གདན་དང་རྡོ་འཁྱག་སྔས། Lit.: damp ground as a mattress and a cold rock as a pillow/ Sense implied: To have endured hardship. མི་ལ་རང་དབང་མེད་དུས་ས་འཁྱག་གདན་དང་རྡོ་འཁྱག་སྔས་སུ་བྱེད་དགོས་པ་ཡིན། When one does not have freedom, one has to endure many hardships.

ས་དགེ་བཀའ་རྙིང་། The four different Buddhist lineages in Tibet, viz., Sakya, Gelug, Kagyue and Nyingma.

ས་མཆོངས་རྡོ་མཆོངས། Lit.: To jump over land and rocks./ Sense implied: excitement བོད་མི་ཚོས་གློག་བརྙན་ནང་པ་རྒྱལ་བ་རིན་པོ་ཆེ་མཇལ་དུས་ས་མཆོངས་རྡོ་མཆོངས་བྱས་སོང་། The Tibetans jumped with joy at the sight of His Holiness the Dalai Lama in the film.

ས་མཆོངས་གནམ་མཆོངས། Lit.: To jump over land and in space./ Sense implied: overjoyed.

ས་རྡུལ་བསགས་ནས་རི་རབ། A collection of soils forms Mt. Meru./ Sense implied: Small things make great things.

ས་གནས་ས་ཐོག local ས་གནས་ས་ཐོག་གི་དཀའ་ངལ་སེལ་རྒྱུ་དེ་ས་གནས་ས་ཐོག་གི་ དཔོན་པོའི་ལས་འགན་རེད། It is the duty of the local officer to solve the local problem.

ས་མ་རིབ་ཙམ། just before dusk ཁ་སང་ང་ས་མ་རིབ་ཙམ་ལ་བསླེབས་པ་ཡིན། Yesterday I reached home just before dusk.

ས་མ་རུབ་གོང་ནས་བཞུ་མར། Lit.: To use a lamp before dusk./ Sense implied: Too early to do something.

ས་གཙང་རྡོ་གཙང་། Lit.: Clean earth and clean rock./ Sense implied: Clean areas. སངས་རྒྱས་ཀྱི་སྐུ་བརྙན་དེ་གནས་ཆེན་ཁག་གི་ས་གཙང་ རྡོ་གཙང་ལས་གྲུབ་པ་རེད། The Buddha statue is made of clean soils and rocks from the great holy places.

ས་གཞིའི་འབུ་ལ་འབུ་རོགས་དང་ནམ་མཁའི་བྱ་ལ་བྱ་རོགས། Lit.: Insects on earth have their company and birds in the sky have their company./ Sense implied: Everyone must have one's company

ས་འོག་དར་ཐག Lit.: To weave silk underground./ Sense implied: To plot a conspiracy, to instigate. ཟིང་འཁྲུག་དེ་ས་འོག་ དར་ཐག་ཚོ་ལས་བྱུང་བ་རེད། The riot was caused by underground instigators.

སུ་ཡིན་ན་ཡང་། whosoever སུ་ཡིན་ན་ཡང་ང་ས་ཁ་གཏད་བཅག་གི་ཡིན། I will challenge whosoever it might be.

240

ས་རིབ་མ་རིབ། semi-dusk time, at about dusk ངའི་པ་ལགས་ཁ་སང་ས་

མ་རིབ་ཚམ་ལ་ནང་དུ་ཕེབས་བྱུང་། My father came home yesterday at
about dusk.

ས་རི་ཐང་གསལ། Lit.: The linings of earth are clear on the
ground./ Sense implied: No matter what one says, one's
deeds are obvious through one's actions./ Very clear..

ས་རོ་དོ་རོ། Lit.: ·The remains of earth and stones./ Sense
implied: ruins གནས་ཆེན་ཁག་གི་ས་རོ་དོ་རོ་དེ་ཚོ་དེང་སང་རྒྱ་གར་གཞུང་གི་

བདག་པོ་བརྒྱོན་གྱི་ཡོད་རེད། Today government of India takes care of
the ruins of the great holy places.

ས་ལས་རྡོ་ལས་། Lit.: Soil and stone work./ Sense implied:
Manual work such as working in a construction of a
house. དྲུག་ཅུ་རེ་གྲངས་སྐབས་བོད་མི་ཚོས་ས་ལས་རྡོ་ལས་རྐྱང་རྐྱང་བྱས་པ་རེད།
In 1960's Tibetans worked only as manual workers.

ས་བཤད་རྡོ་བཤད། senseless talk དུས་ཚོད་བཟང་པོ་དེ་ས་བཤད་རྡོ་བཤད་དང་
བསྐྱལ་ན་སྐྱུགས་པ་རེད། It is foolish to spend one's good time in
senseless talk.

ས་གསང་རྡོ་གསང་། Lit.: Secret soil and stone./ Sense implied:
extremely secret སོ་པ་འཛིན་བཟུང་ཐུབ་ན་ས་གསང་རྡོ་གསང་ཤོར་གྱི་རེད། If
spies are arrested matters of utmost secrecy would be
disclosed.

སང་འགྱངས་གནངས་འགྱངས། Lit.: delaying for tomorrow and the
day after tomorrow./ Sense implied: Procrastination ལས་

241

ཀ་སང་འགྱངས་གནང་འགྱངས་བྱེད་ན་ཆར་རྒྱ་ཁག་པོ་རེད། It is difficult to finish a task if one procastinates.

སང་ཉི་གནངས་ཤི། Lit.: Dying tomorrow or the day after tomorrow./ Sense implied: The uncertainty of death.. མི་ལ་མངོན་ཤེས་མེད་ཅང་སང་ཉི་གནངས་ཤི་སུས་བཤད་ཐུབ་ཀྱི་རེད། Who can tell when one will die, tomorrow or the day after tomorrow, as humans are not clairvoyant.

སང་སང་གནངས་གནངས། Lit.: Tomorrow and the day after tomorrow./ Sense implied: Procrastination སངས་རྒྱས་ལ་ཀ་ཁ་ Lit.: to teach Buddha the alphabets/ Sense implied: Unnecessary and improper efforts

སངས་རྒྱས་ལ་དམྱལ་བ་དྲིན་ཅན། དམྱལ་བ་ལ་སངས་རྒྱས་དྲིན་ཅན། Lit.: Hell is grateful to Buddha and Buddha is grateful to hell./ Sense implied: Everything is interdependent or mutually beneficial.

སུ་བཟང་སུ་སྐྱིད། Who is better and happier.. མི་ཚེའི་ནང་སུ་བཟང་སུ་སྐྱིད་ངས་ཤུ་ཐུབ་ཀྱི་མ་རེད། I cannot say who is better and happier in their life.

སེམས་ཆུང་ཆུང་། ཕྱགས་སེམས་ཆུང་ཆུང་། meek, piously humble ངའི་གྲོགས་པོ་ཕྱགས་སེམས་ཆུང་ཆུང་རེད། My friend is meek and simple.

སེམས་ཆུང་བག་ལྷུན། unassuming and modest སཁས་པ་སེམས་ཆུང་བག་

242

སྤྲ་དཀོན་པོ་རེད། Unassuming and modest scholars are very rare.

སེམས་ཐག་གཅོང་བཅད། fully determined བོད་མི་ཆིག་སྟོང་ཐམ་པ་ཨ་རེར་འགྲོ་རྒྱར་སེམས་ཐག་གཅོང་བཅད་རེད། One thousand Tibetans were fully determined to go to the United States.

སེམས་སྡུག་སྐྱ་ངན། sad and mournful མི་ཤི་བའི་རྗེས་སུ་སེམས་སྡུག་སྐྱ་ངན་ཞེ་དྲག་བྱས་ཀྱང་ཕན་ཐོགས་གང་ཡང་མེད། It is of no use to be sad and mournful over the death of a person.

སེམས་ཐམ་ཡིད་ཆད། sad and distressed ང་ཚོས་རང་གི་ཕ་མ་ནམ་ཡང་སེམས་ཐམ་ཡིད་ཆད་བཅུག་རྒྱུ་མེད། We should never let our parents feel sad and distressed.

སེམས་བག་ཡངས་པོ། easy going or broad-minded སེམས་བག་ཡངས་པོ་མེད་ན་ལས་ཀ་ཆེན་པོ་བྱེད་ཐུབ་ཀྱི་མ་རེད། One cannot perform a great job if one is not broad-minded.

སེམས་འཚབ། ཕྱགས་འཚབ། worry/ hesitation/ to be agitated ལས་ཀ་འདིའི་ཐོག་ལ་སེམས་འཚབ་གནང་མི་དགོས། You need not worry about this task.

སེམས་འཚབ་སློ་ཕམ། nervous and hesitant མི་བྱབ་ཆུང་ཁ་ཤས་ཀྱིས་སེམས་འཚབ་དང་སློ་ཕམ་དང་མི་ཚེ་བསྐྱལ་བ་རེད། Some silly people spend their lives in hesitation and nervousness.

སེམས་ཤུགས་སྤར་བ། To boost someone's spirits./ to encourage སློབ་སྟོང་ལ་སེམས་ཤུགས་སྤར་བ་ནི་ཐབས་ལ་མཁས་པའི་བྱ་བ་རེད། It is wise act to encourage someone in/for studies.

སེམས་འཕྲོར་བ། ཕྱུགས་སེམས་འཕྲོར་བ། to admire/ to fall in love བུ་མོ་ མཛེས་མ་ལ་སྐྱེས་པ་ཚོ་སེམས་འཕྲོར་བ་རེད། A man falls in love with beautiful woman.

སེམས་ལྷོད་བག་ཡངས། relaxed and easy going གྲོང་གསེབ་པ་མང་ཆེ་བ་ སེམས་ལྷོད་བག་ཡངས་ཡོད་པ་རེད། Most of the villagers are relaxed and easy going.

སེར་སྐྱ་རྒན་གཞོན། Lit.: Monks and laity; old and young/ Sense implied: All people.. སེར་སྐྱ་རྒན་གཞོན་ཆང་མ་ལ་བཀྲ་ཤིས་བདེ་ལེགས་ཞུ། I wish Tashi Delek to all, monks and laity, and young and old.

སོ་ནམ་མཁོ་ཆས། agricultural implements རྒྱ་གར་དུ་སོ་ནམ་མཁོ་ཆས་ཆང་ མ་བཟོ་གྲྭ་ནས་ཐོན་པ་རེད། All the agricultural implements in India are produced from industries.

སོ་ཟད་རྐན་ཕྱུག Lit.: It touches the palate when the teeth is exhausted./ Sense implied: Becoming older..

སོ་སོ་གཅིག་པུ། alone/ one-self ཁང་པ་འདི་སོ་སོ་གཅིག་པུ་ལ་བདག་ན་ཡག་པོ་ ཡོད་རེད། It would be nice if the house is owned by you.

སོ་སོ་སོ་སོ། each and every/ one's/ individually མི་ཚང་མ་སོ་སོ་སོ་ སོའི་ལས་ཀ་ཧུར་ཐག་བྱེད་ཀྱི་རེད། Everyone will strive hard to do his/her work.

སོམ་ཉི་ཟེ་ཙོམ། doubt/ qualm/ suspicion གཞུང་དོན་ལ་སོམ་ཉི་ཟེ་ཙོམ་བྱུང་ན་ བཀའ་འདྲི་ཞུ་དགོས། When one feels doubt over the meaning of a text, one should ask.

སོར་མོ་བཅུ་ནས་གང་བཅད་ཚ། Cutting any of the ten fingers would be painful.

སྲ་བརྟན་ཕྱུགས་འཕེར། reliable and durable རྡོ་ཡི་ཁང་པ་རྣམས་སྲ་བརྟན་ ཕྱུགས་ཕེར་ཡོད་རེད། Stone buildings are durable and reliable.

སྲ་བརྟན་འགྱུར་མེད། immutably firm སྐྱེས་བུ་དམ་པའི་དམ་བཅའ་རྣམས་སྲ་བརྟན་ འགྱུར་མེད་ཡིན། The pledges of great beings are immutably firm.

སྙིན་པོ་མིར་བཙུས། Lit.: A cannibalist disguised as a human../ Sense implied: The wicked pretending to be good.. བོད་ ཀྱི་ཐོག་རྒྱ་ནག་གིས་སྙིན་པོ་མིར་བཙུས་ཀྱི་སྲིད་བྱུས་ལག་བསྟར་བྱས་ཡོད། The Chinese implemented the policy of a cannibalist disguised as human on Tibet.

སློབ་ལོ་སོན་པ། School-going age ཁོང་ལ་སློབ་ལོ་སོན་པའི་ཕྲུ་གུ་གཉིས་ཡོད་རེད། He has two children of school-going age.

སློབ་གསོ་སྐུལ་སླུག to advise and guide ཕ་མས་རྟག་ཏུ་རང་གི་ཕྲུ་གུ་ལ་སློབ་ གསོ་སྐུལ་སླུག་གནང་བ་རེད། Parents always advise and guide their children.

གསང་རྒྱ་ཁྲིམ་བསྒྲགས། To hawk or disclose secrets everywhere..

སོ་པའི་ལས་འགན་གཅིག་ནི་གསང་རྒྱ་ཁྲོམ་བསྒྲགས་སུ་མི་གཏོང་བ་དེ་ཡིན། One of the duties of spies is not to disclose secrets in the market place.

གསང་སྔགས་ཁྲོམ་བསྒྲགས། To teach Tantra in a market place (sarcastic remark) གསང་སྔགས་ཁྲོམ་བསྒྲགས་བྱེད་ན་སྡིག་པ་ཉེན་ཏུ་ཆེ། It is a great non-virtuous act to teach Tantra in a market place.

གསང་བ་ཕྱི་གྱུར། disclosing a secret ཚོགས་མི་ཚང་མ་མཐུན་པོ་མེད་ན་གསང་བ་ཕྱི་གྱུར་ཡོང་མདོག་མེད། There is no doubt that secrets will be disclosed outside if the members of the club are not friendly.

གསང་རང་མཁས་ཀྱང་ཕྱེད་མི་མཁས། One may be wise in keeping the secret but others are wiser in disclosing them.

གསང་བ་བསམ་གྱིས་མི་ཁྱབ་པ། inconceivable secret སངས་རྒྱས་ཀྱི་ཡོན་ཏན་ཐམས་ཅད་གསང་བ་བསམ་གྱིས་མི་ཁྱབ་པ་ཤ་སྟག་རེད། All qualities of Buddha are secret as well as inconceivable.

གསར་པ་གསར་རྒྱང་། brand new/ fresh ང་ཚོའི་ལས་ཁུངས་ལ་ཀམ་པུ་ཊར་ གསར་པ་གསར་རྒྱང་གཅིག་བསྐྱལ་བས་འདུག A brand new computer has been brought to our office.

གསར་མིན་རྙིང་མིན། neither new nor old.. མི་ཁ་ཤས་དུག་ལོག་གསར་མིན་ རྙིང་མིན་ལ་དགའ་པོ་བྱེད་པ་རེད། Some people like clothes which are neither new nor old.

གསལ་ལ་མ་གསལ། Lit.: neither clear nor ambiguous/ Sense

implied: dim དེབ་འདིའི་ནང་ལ་དོན་དག་ཁ་ཤས་གསལ་ལ་མ་གསལ་འདུག Some of the meanings in this book are neither clear nor ambiguous.

གསུང་བཟོ་དོད་པོ། One who is skillful in the art of speaking. ལྷ་ས་བ་ཚོ་གསུང་བཟོ་དོད་པོ་ཞེ་དྲག་ཡོད་རེད། The people from Lhasa are very skillful in the art of conversation.

གསེར་བྱེ་མཉམ་འདྲེས། Lit.: To mix gold with sand./ Sense implied: To have both good and bad together..

གསེར་ས་འོག་ལ་ཡོད་ཀྱང་འོད་ནམ་མཁའ་ལ་ཕྱུབ། Lit.: Even though gold is beneath the earth, it shines in the sky.

གསོད་བརྡུང་མནར་གཙོད། Lit.: To kill, beat and torture./ Sense implied; exploitation and murder རྒྱ་མིས་བོད་མི་ཚོར་དུས་རྟག་ཏུ་གསོད་བརྡུང་མནར་གཙོད་བྱང་བ་རེད། The Chinese always exploited and killed Tibetans.

གསོལ་ཇ་བཞེས་ཏོག Lit.: tea and biscuits/ Sense implied: refreshment མཛད་སྒོ་གྲུབ་པའི་རྗེས་སུ་གསོལ་ཇ་བཞེས་ཏོག་བྲ་སྒྲིག་ཞུས་ཡོད། Refreshments are arranged after the function.

གསོལ་རས་གནང་སྟོན། gift/ reward/ prize དེ་རིང་ནི་སློབ་གྲྭའི་གསོལ་རས་གནང་སྟོན་གྱི་ཉིན་མོ་དེ་རེད། Today is the Prize Distribution Day of the school.

བསགས་སྤྱངས་ཉམས་ལེན། Practice of the accumulation of merits

and purification of non-virtues དགེ་རྩ་མ་བསགས་སྡིག་རྣམ་ལེན་ ཡག་པོ་ཡོད་རེད། My teacher is good in the practice of the accumulation of merits and purification of non-virtues.

བསད་ན་ཆེ་ བརྡུང་ན་ཆུང་། Lit.: Too big to be killed and too small to be beaten./ Sense implied: To be in dilemma with respect to punishing someone རྐུན་མ་འཛིན་ཐུབ་ན། ཉེས་པ་བསད་ན་ཆེ་ བརྡུང་ན་ཆུང་བའི་དཔེ་བཞིན། ད་ཉེས་པ་ག་རེ་གཏོང་དགོས་རེད། Even if one could catch the thief what sort of punishment could be given to him since he is a case of too big to be killed and too small to be beaten.

བསམ་རྒྱུ་དྲན་རྒྱུ་མེད་པ། Lit.: unable to think and remember/ Sense implied: One who has no feelings/indifferent བསམ་རྒྱུ་དྲན་རྒྱུ་མེད་པའི་མི་ལ་སྐྱིན་པ་ཟེར། One who is unable to think or remember anything, is called a stupid person.

བསམ་ངན་གདུག་རྩུབ། Lit.: an evil and cruel thought/ Sense implied: wicked people སྤྱི་ཚོགས་ནང་ལ་བསམ་ངན་གདུག་རྩུབ་བྱེད་ན་ གཞན་དང་མཐུན་གྱི་མ་རེད། One cannot live harmoniously in a society with evil and cruel thoughts.

བསམ་ངན་སྤྱོད་ངན། Lit.: evil thought and deed/ Sense implied: wicked people སློབ་ཕྲུག་འགའ་ཤས་བསམ་ངན་སྤྱོད་ངན་ཤ་སྟག་བྱེད་ཀྱི་འདུག Some students are always engaged in bad thoughts and deeds.

བསམ་ངན་ཕུང་སློར། evil thought of destruction རྒྱ་མིས་བསམ་ངན་ཕུང་

སྐྱོར་ལ་བརྟེན་ནས་ང་ཚོས་རང་གི་ལུང་པ་ནས་བྲོས་དགོས་བྱུང་། Due to the evil thought of destruction of the Chinese we had to fled our country.

བསམ་ཐོག་དོན་འཁེལ། Lit.: putting the ideas into practice/ Sense implied: to fulfil one's wish.. དཀའ་ངལ་མ་རྒྱབ་ན་བསམ་ཐོག་དོན་ འཁེལ་ཡོང་རྒྱུ་ཁག་པོ་རེད། If one does not work hard it is difficult to fulfil one's wish.

བསམ་ངན་ཆེ་པོ། A very evil thinking person../ ཆོས་པ་རྣམ་དག་ཆོ་ བསམ་ངན་ཆེ་པོ་ཁྲིན་ནས་ཡོད་མ་རེད། A good practioner is never an evil minded person.

བསམ་པ་ངན་པ་མི་ལ་བྱེད་ན་སྐྱོར་བ་ཚུབ་པ་རང་ལ་འཁོར། Evil designs cast upon another will rebound oneself./ Do unto others as you would be done by.

བསམ་པ་རྣམ་དག pure intention བསམ་པ་རྣམ་དག་གི་ཐོག་ནས་ལས་ཀ་བྱེད་ན་ དོན་དག་འགྲུབ་ཀྱི་རེད། One shall fullfil one's purpose if one works with a pure intention.

བསམ་བློ་འཁྱེར་སྟངས། the way of thinking/ attitude བསམ་བློ་འཁྱེར་ སྟངས་ཡག་པོ་ཚོར་བའི་སྐྱིད་ཆེ་བ་ཡོད། People with good attitudes are happier.

བསམ་ཚུལ་འཛོལ་མེད། unmistaken thought/ without minunderstanding ཁོང་གིས་འདི་སྐྱོར་བསམ་ཚུལ་འཛོལ་མེད་མཁྱེན་གྱི་ འདུག He knows about this without misunderstanding.

བསིལ་དྲོད་སྙོམ་པོ། moderate climate/ good climate འབེང་ལོར་གྱི་གནམ་
གཤིས་ལོ་འཁོར་མར་བསིལ་དྲོད་སྙོམ་པོ་འདུག Bangalore has a moderate
climate throughtout the year.

བསྲི་ཚགས་གྲོན་ཆུང་། Lit.: to curtail one's budget/ Sense implied:
economical བསྲི་ཚགས་གྲོན་ཆུང་གནང་ན་ཟླ་བ་གཅིག་ལ་སྒོར་མོ་ལྔ་བརྒྱས་ལྕང་
གི་རེད། If one is economical, Rs. 500/- will be enough for one
month.

བསྲེགས་བཅད་བདར་གསུམ། Lit.: The three-fold way of burning,
cutting and rubbing (for experimenting with gold)./
Sense implied: the correct way of experimenting གསེར་ལ་
ལྕད་ཡོད་མེད་བསྲེགས་བཅད་བདར་གསུམ་བྱེད་ན་ཤེས་ཀྱི་རེད། Whether there is
a mix-up with gold or not can be ascertained through the
three-fold way of burning, cutting and rubbing.

བསླབ་པ་སློབ་གཉེར། study and training (generally in
monasteries).དགོན་པའི་ནང་ལ་བསླབ་པ་སློབ་གཉེར་ཚུལ་བཞིན་གནང་ན་མཁས་
པ་ཆགས་ཀྱི་རེད། If one studies well and get trained properly in
a monastery, one will become a good scholar.

བསླབ་བྱ་བརྒྱ་ལས་སྦྱ་བསྱན་གཅིག་དགའ། A lesson learned is better
than a hundred pieces of advice.

250

༼ད༽

ཏུ་རེ་ཏུ་རེ། ཏུ་རེ་ཏུ་རེ་ཚ་པོ། ཏུ་རེ་ཏུ་རེ་བྱེད་པ། careless and restless

ལྷ་འབོད་ཀླུ་འབོད་བྱེད་པ། Lit.: To provoke gods and water-sprite./
Sense implied: To plea desperately to someone for help.

༼ཨ༽

ཨ་རོགས། This word is used when you call your
friend./Hallo!

ཨ་ལ་ལ། Of course/ by all means/ no doubt

ཨ་ལེ་པེ་ཀོ། doll Children like
dolls.

Notes

1. Edited by Barbara Nimri Aziz and Matthew Kapstein, *Soundings in Tibetan Civilization; Proceedings of the 1982 Seminar of the International Association for Tibetan Studies,* Manohar Publishing, India 1985, pp.20-34.
2. Stephan V. Beger, *The Classical Tibetan Language,* State University Press of New York, 1992, pp.191-251.
3. Losang Thonden, *Modern Tibetan Language Vol.I & II,* Library of Tibetan Works and Archives, Dharamsala, 1993.
4. Tashi, *A Basic Grammar of Modern Spoken Tibetan,* Library of Tibetan Works and Archives, Dharamsala, 1990.
5. Melvyn Goldstein With Gelek Rinpoche and Lobsang Phuntshog, *Essentials of Modern Literary Tibetan,* Munshiram Manoharlal Publishers Pvt Ltd.,India, 1993.
6. Melvyn C. Glodstein and Nornang; Modern Spoken Tibetan: Lhasa Dialect; University of Washington Press; Seattle and London.
7. Lobsang Phuntsok Lhaphungpa: *Textbook of Colloquial Tibetan, Revised edition,* Manjusri Publishing House, New Delhi, 1972.
8. Pema Chhinjor, New Plan Tibetan Grammar and Translation, 1993.